ARDOR IN THE COURT!

SEX AND THE LAW

JEFFREY MILLER

ECW PRESS

Copyright © Burden of Proof Research Inc./Jeffrey Miller, 2002

Published by ECW PRESS
2120 Queen Street East, Suite 200, Toronto, Ontario, Canada M4E 1E2

All rights reserved. No part of this publication may be reproduced, stored in a retrieval system, or transmitted in any form by any process — electronic, mechanical, photocopying, recording, or otherwise — without the prior written permission of the copyright owners and ECW PRESS.

NATIONAL LIBRARY OF CANADA CATALOGUING IN PUBLICATION DATA

Miller, Jeffrey, 1950 –
Ardor in the court!: sex and the law / Jeffrey Miller
ISBN 1-55022-528-6

1. Sex and law — History. I. Title
K183.M53 2002   345´.027   C2002-902168-5

Cover and Text Design: Tania Craan
Production: Mary Bowness
Typesetting: Gail Nina
Printing: Transcontinental

This book is set in Bembo and Trajan

The publication of *Ardor in the Court!* has been generously supported by the Canada Council, the Ontario Arts Council, and the Government of Canada through the Book Publishing Industry Development Program. Canada

DISTRIBUTION
CANADA: Jaguar Book Group, 100 Armstrong Avenue, Georgetown, ON, L7G 5S4

UNITED STATES: Independent Publishers Group, 814 North Franklin Street, Chicago, Illinois 60610

EUROPE: Turnaround Publisher Services, Unit 3, Olympia Trading Estate, Coburg Road, Wood Green, London N2Z 6T2

AUSTRALIA AND NEW ZEALAND: Wakefield Press, 1 The Parade West (Box 2066), Kent Town, South Australia 5071

PRINTED AND BOUND IN CANADA

ECW PRESS
ecwpress.com

TABLE OF CONTENTS

INTRODUCTION
SOMEWHAT EMETIC, NOWHERE APHRODISIAC ix

CHAPTER ONE
CONSENTING ADULTS, MORE OR LESS 1

CHAPTER TWO
ALL IN AND BEYOND THE FAMILY
Adultery, Criminal Conversation, and Other Complications of Family Law 19

CHAPTER THREE
BEYOND MARRIAGE AND THE MISSIONARY POSITION 65

CHAPTER FOUR
PERSONS PUBLIC, PERSONS PRIVATE
The Law of Indecency 89

CHAPTER FIVE
I KNOW IT WHEN I SEE IT
Pornography and Free Expression   127

CHAPTER SIX
THE WAGES OF SIN
Prostitution and the Sex Trade   157

CHAPTER SEVEN
CRIME AND CONTROVERSY   183

CHAPTER EIGHT
YOU SAY "COCOTTE," I SAY "HARLOT"
Imputations of Unchastity   231

NOTES   255

INDEX   273

Th'expense of spirit in a waste of shame
Is lust in action, and till action, lust
Is perjured, murd'rous, bloody, full of blame . . .
All this the world well knows yet none knows well,
To shun the heaven that leads men to this hell.

WILLIAM SHAKESPEARE, SONNET 129

INTRODUCTION

SOMEWHAT EMETIC, NOWHERE APHRODISIAC

When publisher Jack David asked me if there might be a book in "sex and laws," I replied that there could be a life's work. Ninety-nine per cent of law is about testosterone, or thinking with one's willy. The marketing department was thrilled. I had just handed in a more general work subtitled "Not Completely Serious Ruminations on Law and Life," and the bottom-line guys were circulating my brief asides on bestiality and breast implants in a stripper's buttocks. Thus was *Ardor in the Court!* born, along with my panic about my "literary reputation" — if any, as lawyers like to say.

The book struck both Jack and me as something that would have a ready market, of course. He is not in business to go bankrupt, and I do not spend years writing books so that they will go unread. However, we have tried hard to approach the subject intelligently, without leering, coyness, or what our law calls "undue exploitation."

As U.S. Supreme Court Justice Benjamin Cardozo pointed out in his *Law and Literature*, the law reports can be a mine of instruction. They are pre-eminently instructive on human nature, and of course there is nothing so human, or natural, as sex.[1] What's more, they report the human tragicomedy fully, and mostly objectively. While one admires that 1983 headline from the *New York Post*, "Headless body found in topless bar," the giddy approach is generally not the most productive.

In fact, a writer could spend a lifetime studying sex and the law yet cover only the margins of the subject. Most of what I consider here I have come across in my daily work as a writer on legal subjects, but also as an ordinary reader of newspapers and magazines who is surprised, if not unnerved, every time he notices a rectangle of cardboard on his office wall certifying that the local law society has admitted him "to practice at the Bar of Her Majesty's Courts in Ontario." As we always suspected, Her Majesty knows not what she wreaks.

For primary sources I have relied mostly on the law reports and texts. In a field rife with innuendo and rumor, they are the most trustworthy, at least concerning the facts in any particular case. When cases are unreported, as with jury trials, I have relied on press reports, mostly from major dailies such as the *New York Times*, the *Times* and *Independent* of London, and the like. In one case, in the interests of local color, my primary source was the aforementioned *New York Post* — reporting on that aforementioned top- and briefly bottom-heavy woman who worked in a topless and virtually bottomless, I suppose, bar (see Chapter One, number 9). For ease of reference, the cases are numbered in the text, with sources listed under the matching numbers in the notes.

---

[1] Mind you, Justice Cardozo's precise words were, "For quotable good things, for pregnant aphorisms, for touchstones of ready application, the opinions of the English judges are a mine of instruction and a treasury of joy." The same is not generally true of human sexual relations, let alone law reports generally.

It probably sounds odd to say that cases about sex were in part selected for their "intellectual interest." It might seem, rather, that preparing a book like this provides the author month after month of titillation and hormonal overdrive. But as George Steiner once noted of pornography, "One can whip or be whipped; one can eat excrement or quaff urine; mouth and private part can meet in this or that commerce. After which there is the gray of morning and the sour knowledge that things have remained fairly generally the same since man first met goat and woman." This applies equally to reading court judgments in which accused pornographers raise freedom of expression as shield and sword. The fifth or sixth time that our judges toy with the definition of obscenity, the flesh and even intellect are willing, but the eyes glaze. As District Judge John Woolsey wrote in 1933 of James Joyce's *Ulysses*, in concluding that the book was not obscene, "The effect ... on the reader undoubtedly is somewhat emetic, but nowhere does it tend to be an aphrodisiac."

What of intellectual and sociological interest remains? Consider that during the months I was finishing this book, the U.S. Democratic Party lost an election after its leader, the country's president, enjoyed oral sex with a young intern "not his wife" (as the law puts it), and pleasured her with a cigar, in the White House, then lied about it under oath — causing him to be cited for contempt of court and lose his right to practice law. Shortly thereafter, another young intern disappeared after a Democratic congressman admitted to sharing a "close relationship" with her. The story itself disappeared from the headlines only after terrorists flew airplanes into the World Trade Center and Pentagon, some of them believing, apparently, that Islamic law granted "martyrs" sexual congress with 70 virgins in the afterlife.

Not long before all this, under the delusion that he was impressing love interest Jodie Foster, the film star, a young man shot President Ronald Reagan and his press secretary. Congress held hearings in which a bright young lawyer accused a nominee for the U.S. Supreme Court of sexually harassing her by discussing pornographic movies and complaining of pubic hairs on his can of cola. Comedian Bill Cosby was compelled to prove publicly that he had not fathered a child in an adulterous relationship, and pop culture magnate Michael Jackson was accused of sexually abusing young boys. Self-professed "feminists" across the world cheered when Lorena Bobbitt castrated her abusive husband and threw the offending member across a highway — only to see it reattached and star in pornographic movies. An obscure psychiatric disorder became a household word after erotomaniacs persecuted David Letterman, Anne Murray, Steven Spielberg, and many other celebrities — and, again during the actual writing of this book, one of them murdered British television newscaster Jill Dando. Only relatively recently have western governments decriminalized homosexuality, and just as our governments live off tobacco taxes while telling us not to smoke, prostitution remains legal, and taxable, while making arrangements to transact it can land you in chokey. And never mind the headlines, consider the Bible and the Koran, the sacred law that provides the foundation for much of our secular law, particularly law governing human sexuality, as well as marriage and divorce: prescriptions in the Ten Commandments against adultery and sexual covetousness; Onan and the evils of masturbation; Sodom and Gomorrah; Susannah falsely accused of fornication by the elders; Matthew's warning that "whoever looketh on a woman to lust after her hath committed adultery with her already in his heart" — a warning that exposed poor Jimmy Carter to so much ridicule, from the religious and irreligious alike, when he simply admitted to having given in to such secret (and most would say harmlessly human) longings. Clergymen, and ecclesiastical courts, have regularly insisted that sexual frigidity between marital partners is a crime against what God has joined. And so on. The point here is that like law in general, the legal and moral complexities of sex pervade every culture.

Constantly in the background, of course, is that what we consider socially and politically "correct" is a matter of the sensitivities of the age. Colonial Massachusetts hanged men convicted of buggery, but also adulterers. In post-colonial America, adultery and fornication (sex outside marriage) remained crimes, and countries with strict Islamic regimes still occasionally punish such offenses with hanging or beheadings. Under the unusually squeamish Anthony Comstock, who served as special agent at the U.S. post office from 1873 to 1915, it was illegal to send contraceptive devices or even information about birth control or abortion through the mail. And where the age of consent was once as low as ten, Groucho Marx would later remark that he was waiting six years to read *Lolita*, by which time she would be 18.[2] In Spain, the age of consent remains at 13, the putative age of Shakespeare's Juliet.

In Montreal, in 1900, a cabaret singer was fined $50 for just mentioning the "breasts of the young girls of Lezignan and of the women of St. Nazaire" while making "gestures towards his chest" (number 56). In 1910, the New York courts held that a newspaper libeled socialite Emilie Snyder simply by alleging that her "Irish maid" allowed a process server to enter Snyder's bathroom, surprising her as she bathed (number 151).

News services reported in 1939 that "Mrs. J. L. Allen" and her daughter, Betty, tarred and feathered a student nurse because she was friendly with Mrs. Allen's husband, a Calgary anesthetist. Mrs. Allen and Betty said that Nurse Alice Knowles had promised to stay away from their *paterfamilias* but the accused women discovered that Dr. Allen telephoned Knowles "when he had said he was phoning his bookie." A local magistrate sentenced wife and daughter to jail, rejecting their plea that they felt provoked beyond self-control.

---

[2] Nabokov's novel explores, of course, a middle-aged man's sexual obsession with a pre-pubescent girl.

Sixty-three years ago, Maurice Healy wrote a whole book on the quaintness of practicing at the Irish bar. His anecdotes include an account of a rape trial in Listowel, during which the complainant "gave her evidence with a complete absence of embarrassment, and with such readiness to go into detail" that the judge warned the jury that they "daren't hang a dog on it." According to Healy, at the end of the proceedings the foreman advised the judge that the jury had found the accused man not guilty "but should your honor be wishful to hear any more evidence, we wouldn't be stopping you." That story is not in the main part of this book, because in these purportedly more open-minded times the foreman's remark would be considered indelicate at best.[3]

In Quebec as late as 1959, *Lady Chatterley's Lover* was criminally obscene. And while you can no longer sue someone in Britain or Canada for criminal conversation — for, that is, alienating your spouse's affections through an adulterous relationship — some U.S. courts still hear such actions.

Again, during the preparation of this book, executives at the British supermarket chain Tesco's talked of renaming packaged versions of spotted dick (the traditional suet pudding whose raisins provide the "spots") spotted Richard. Because of the unintended sexual pun, shoppers, they claimed, were embarrassed to buy it. In an age when leering, salivating sex, itself, is used to sell everything from beer and symphony subscriptions to automobiles and laundry soap, an age when we regularly hear the "f word" and see nearly naked people on television and in the street, an era when "virtually" blowing other humans to smithereens is entertainment for children, the fact that someone might free-associate the name of a fatty dessert

---

[3] In these assertively earnest days, we are more likely to be reminded that the "complainant's demeanor" is only one element of the evidence before the trier of the case: see, for example, number 119 in Chapter Seven.

with the slang term for the male member . . . is offensive. Not long before, during the Bobbitt trial, I hadn't heard the word "penis" so often in so short a period since the day I attended a baseball game where the nut vendor had a speech impediment.

While solemnly advising us that we are beyond irony, the news media attempted to outdo each other in hilarity over *State v. Bobbitt*, fully conscious that they would not joke around if the victim of the mutilation were a woman. In the lifestyle or books sections, after all, our newspapers advise us that "herstory," to the extent that it is distinct from "history," is superior largely because it eschews *lex talionis*, the law of an eye for an eye — fists and knives and throwing someone's body parts out of cars. But in the press circus around the Bobbitt case, men nervously found new truth in Freud, while women felt gleeful with their new sense of power. Lawyers, supposedly civilization's bad guys, worried about the rule of law, at least insofar as they realized that adopting biblical rules of vengeance and sexual regulation — the stoning of adulterers, the immolation of homosexuals — is devolution, decivilization, a throwback which much of the world purports to scorn as religious extremism. The case became a totem for our ambivalence and downright hypocrisy about sex, making the "battle of the sexes" into another commercialized entertainment, another World Wrestling Entertainment media extravaganza. John Wayne Bobbitt apparently was an abusive husband. But if we are to begin taking the law (literally) into our own hands, if the battle of the sexes is to become an arms race, what, and whose, will be cut off next? Who wins, by what measure?

My wife, Phyllis Miller, proved her usual patient and supportive self during the research and writing of this book, and I don't mean that, either, in any lurid sense. (What does one make, though, of her failure to imitate Sir Richard Burton's spouse who, four centuries ago, burned Sir Richard's translation of the *Kama Sutra*, fearing it would ruin *his* literary reputation?) In addition to Geoffrey Burn, who first asked me nearly 20 years ago to write "something allegedly amusing" for what became *The Lawyers Weekly*, I want to acknowledge my similarly indulgent, if sometimes lurid, editors there during the past 19 years: Michael Fitz-James, Donald Brillinger, Beverley Spencer, Jordan Furlong, and Thomas Claridge — as well as interim editors Norm MacInnes, Jim Middlemiss, and Richard Furness. Don Brillinger in particular brought many innovations to the newspaper which permitted me the wide berth my journalistic idiosyncracies seem to demand. Thanks are due assistant editor Ann Macaulay, as well.

Sir Robert Megarry's *Miscellany-at-Law* and *Second Miscellany-at-Law* have become sacred texts, along with that awesome, unacknowledged masterpiece, *The English Reports*. The entire staff at the magnificent Great Library of Osgoode Hall (the historic site of the law society of which I am a proud member) has been similarly indispensable. I owe special appreciation to librarians Jeanette Bosschart, Riitta Nummela-Recouso, Margaret Revell, Theresa Roth, Karen Teasdale, Florence Hacker, and their assistant, the late Charlie Mackie. Charlie, may he rest in peace, always performed his job with a dignity and kindness that perfectly complemented the grand surroundings, and he always made the work lighter.

Some of the material in this book had an airing in a different form on "Basic Black," the Saturday variety show on CBC radio. Producer David Malahoff, another rare gentleman, brought Arthur Black and me together, and in the early years of my legal journalism career, Joe Coté and Mareka Mayer at CBC Toronto's "Metro Morning" were similarly supportive, as were Phil Jackman and the op-ed staff at the *Globe and Mail* in Toronto.

Tracey Millen, Jen Hale, and Amy Logan have been unstintingly helpful, and their boss, Jack David, is a godsend, or at least a miracle worker, having restored my faith in publishing as a profession for decent people who actually like books for their own sake. It was my friend Derek Lundy who first told me so, while propping me up at the Pilot Tavern and nodding gamely with his mouth full of chicken satay as I raged on yet again about the writer's so-called life. As copy editor, Nadia Halim answered a battle-scarred writer's prayers, tackling the manuscript with intelligence, a deft and sparing hand, and perhaps most importantly, good humor.

As to help with specific material covered in these pages, Brian Burns, Chief Deputy Clerk of the Rhode Island Supreme Court, assisted me with real aplomb on the Goldshine naughty novelties case. And Ishmael Reed gave me some awesome leads, and quotable remarks, on reckless eyeballing.

D.H. Lawrence remarked that sex proved God had a sense of humor. But it was my parents, Obbish and Naomi Miller, who taught me that, while sex was often ridiculous, there was nothing dirty about it. And my grandmother, Gertie Smookler, along with her hilariously ribald sisters — my great aunts (in all the senses of the phrase) Bette Rosenbloom, Ethel Levin, and Blanche Turner — proved it.

CHAPTER ONE

CONSENTING ADULTS, MORE OR LESS

"There's no place for the state in the bedrooms of the nation."

PIERRE ELLIOTT TRUDEAU

1   Some f—k etymology

The law has called fornication different things at different times. Generally, it means sex outside marriage, even if one or both of the participants are married. Fornication was once a felony in Britain, although an old folk etymology has it that sex-starved sailors were allowed a holiday from the law on the sovereign's birthday. The exemption supposedly spawned the word *fuck*, by way of the abbreviation "Fornication Under Consent of the King."

The 18th-century legal historian William Blackstone speculates that ecclesiastical law was soft on "open and notorious lewdness . . . owing perhaps to the celibacy of its first compilers." It seems just as likely that frustration would have made them bitter and harsh.

The American colonies punished fornication by flogging the convict in public. In 1664, for example, the county court in Charles County, Maryland, ordered that Agnes Taylor endure 20 lashes "at the whipping Post in the Publicke View of the People for having Played the whore." In both the motherland and the colonies, historically there has been debate about the evidence needed to prove the offense: some judgments say that if no pregnancy resulted, there was no fornication. This suggests that the real worry was that children growing up in straitened circumstances would have burdened the community and become anti-social as they matured. In his section on fornication, Blackstone speaks of separate prosecutions for failing to support bastard children, but none for simply *having* an illegitimate child, "for otherwise the very maintenance of the child is considered as a degree of punishment." However, in early America, bearing an illegitimate child was sometimes a separate crime, and of course the poor and dispossessed suffered the most. The Charles County court of 1664 also ordered 12 lashes for Ann Cooper for "having had A Bastard," and 38 years later a Delaware court sentenced Hannah Dickens to 21 lashes in public for having borne "one bastard male child of her body."

Under a New York law of 1848, a man who seduced a woman, or who had "illicit connexion with any unmarried female of previous chaste character," could end up in jail for five years. A similar Georgia law passed in 1882 expressed what law professor Lawrence Friedman characterizes as "almost poetic wrath." It punished men who "by persuasion and promises of marriage, or other false and fraudulent means" managed to "seduce a virtuous unmarried female, and induce her to yield to his lustful embraces, and allow him to have carnal knowledge of her." An 1886 Ohio law singled out male teachers, giving special attention to teachers of "mu roller skating, athletic exercise" — presumably because of the one-to-one professional relationship typifying such instruction. Even consensual sex with pupils, no matter what their age, was illegal.

Psychiatrists sometimes dignify or even defend sexual relationships with their patients as "erotic transference," and until recently the law was cowed, doing little to stop them taking advantage of vulnerable patients. Whether this is "classist" — favoring "omniscient" physicians over their susceptible charges — or a function of the more private and complex doctor-patient relationship is a question for sociologists.

Although rarely prosecuted today, fornication appears on modern statute books in the United States. In recent years, Texas imposed a fine of $500 for such conduct. In Arizona, fornicators could go to jail for as many as three years for living together — living, in the statute's terms, "in a state of open and notorious cohabitation."

In some countries which base their law on *sharia* or Islamic jurisprudence, whipping is still the preferred punishment, and when fornication can be characterized as flagrant adultery, the offender might be stoned to death. It has become notorious that the recent Taliban regime in Afghanistan took this to extremes. Women convicted of fornication could face whipping and prison terms of four to ten years in jail. Hypocritically, their prosecutors also sometimes forced them into sexual slavery. If caught in the act, fornicators could face execution. Marriage without the consent of one's family was considered a form of fornication, punishable by two years' imprisonment. Nasira Gulam Dasteghir, caught hugging her boyfriend, endured 31 strokes of the lash.

In 2000, under stern application of *sharia*, a Nigerian court sentenced a 17-year-old girl to 180 lashes of a cane, which sentence an appeal court reduced to a mere 100 strokes, administered after the girl gave birth to an "illegitimate" child. The next year, another Nigerian woman, 35-year-old Safiya Husseini, faced stoning for "adulterous fornication." As practiced in Iran and Nigeria, stoning has been carried out by wrapping the condemned prisoners in sheets and burying them up to their waists. If they are able to escape while the stoning is underway, they are pardoned. There is no record of anyone's escaping.

After she divorced her husband, Husseini became pregnant and her ex-husband died. The Nigerian courts consider this not just fornication, but the more serious offense of adultery (more serious because it disrupts family life), even though Husseini has sworn that her second cousin raped her several times, and that she never consented to sexual relations with him. On the day slated for Husseini's execution, a Nigerian court allowed her appeal. The appeal court's reasons remain obscure at this writing, but the local governor has denied that international pressure played any part. In the result Husseini has just escaped with her life, while her lawyer is spared the metaphysical feat of proving that her youngest daughter was fathered by her dead husband and not her cousin. Under Islamic law, the lawyer has said, children can gestate for seven years. He intended to argue, apparently, that under *sharia*, the ex-husband could have impregnated Husseini before he divorced her.

2 Hide your daughters; here comes the landlord

Possibly because it is graphic about class oppression, the idea of a legal "right of the first night" — the *jus primae noctis* or *droit du seigneur* — has a persistent hold on the popular imagination. Most scholars now agree, however, that no such right ever existed in post-Biblical times, certainly not in western law.

As usually stated, the "right" was that of the sovereign, the lord of the manor, a cleric, or a shaman to have sexual intercourse with a new bride, before her husband, on her wedding night. The recent movie *Braveheart* had the British King Edward I enshrining the right in a statute to oppress the Scots. There is no record of such a law.

No one doubts that the powerful demanded sexual favors of the lower orders, just as they do today, and it is generally accepted that vassals were sometimes required to pay their lords "pre-coital" fees — they were expected, that is, to buy a form of license to have sex with their new wives, or to pay the lord a sort of dowry. In some places, the church also demanded such fees, as our modern registry offices do by secular law, for marriage licenses. Apparently in some cases the church required that newlyweds abstain from sex for several days after the marriage, but permitted them to buy their way out of the torturous rule by paying a license fee. Modern historians believe that the fee requirements merged in the popular imagination with feudal customs and with myths about the *droit*, which date back to the Gilgamesh epic of about 1900 B.C. There, the ruler of Uruk, the capital of Babylonia, was allowed first access to brides, in honor of his status.

A *droit de cuissage* — from the French *cuisse*, meaning thigh — apparently existed in late medieval France. As a reminder that the vassal maintained rights and property, including his family, by his suzerain's grace, the lord placed his naked leg into the marital bed. German scholar Jörg Wettlaufer gives an interesting related example from 15th-century Catalonia, concerning a peasant's revolt that prefigures *Braveheart*. The ruling classes in the Catalonian Pyrenees subjected the peasants to "certain humiliating taxes." The peasants felt particularly aggrieved by the lord's *cuissage*-like wedding-night practice of getting into bed with the bride, then climbing over her. By 1784, Beaumarchais used a full-blown *droit du seigneur* as a plot device in *The Marriage of Figaro*.

Wettlaufer writes that ritual defloration practiced in some non-European cultures, sometimes by a serf (in the belief that there was danger in the blood spilled on intercourse with a virgin), has been confused with the supposed *droit*.

While there is no proven first night law or right, the Anglo-American legal system has permitted sexualized favors taken in lieu of rent. To catalogue, secure, and of course tax his newly-acquired real estate in Britain, William the Conqueror created a land tenure system in 1085. It worked like our registry systems today. William divided England into seven circuits, which were personally assessed by a group of commissioners and registered in *The Domesday Book*. To continue using the registered land, the tenants had to perform tasks incidental to their tenancies. These tenures — contracts for services in exchange for land — ranged from the practical to the picayune and whimsical. Four "Bond-men," for example, held a messuage (a house with the surrounding buildings and land) "by the service of making the Gallowes and hanging the Theeves," as well as plowing, reaping, making "the Lords malt," and other menial jobs.

Tenures called "serjeanty" involved direct service to the king, "keeping the Gaol of the County of Exeter," "weighing the Money coming from the Exchequer," "finding footmen with bows and arrows." And because rest and recreation were important to the armed forces then as now, "John Warbleton holds the manor of Shirefield, in the County of Southampton, of the King in Capite [as tenant-in-chief], by the Grand Serjeanty, viz., by the Service of being Marshall of the Whores" — an arrangement known, according to one commentator, as "Pimp Tenure." (Beyond providing sexual catharsis to the armed forces, the serjeanty also subjected Warbleton to "dismembering Condemned Malefactors, and measuring the Gallons and Bushels in the King's Household.") Similarly, William Hoppeshort held "Half a Yard-Land" in Bockhampton "by the Service of keeping for the King six Damsels, to wit, Whores at the Cost of the King."

Of course, the sexual double standard had the force of law at the time. Where pimp tenure aided fornication among certain men, other tenures were specifically aimed at deterring fornication among women by using public humiliation as punishment. In Somersetshire, one widow held land on a manor only until she married or was "found incontinent," but she could pay penance for any incontinency and repossess her property "if she come into the next Court, riding astride upon a Ram, and in open Court do say to the Lord, if he be present, or to his Steward, these words:

> "'For mine Arse's Fault take I this Pain,
> Therefore, my Lord, give me my Land again.'"

Another widow held lands in Berkshire and Devonshire on the condition that she remain chaste. If she gave into temptation, she could still save her interest if "she comes into the next Court held for the Manor, riding backwards upon a Black Ram, with his Tail in her Hand, and says the Words following . . . :

> *Here I am*
> *Riding upon a Black Ram,*
> *Like a Whore as I am;*
> *And for my Crincum Crancum*[1]
> *Have lost my Bincum Bancum;*
> *And for my Tail's Game*
> *Am brought to this Worldly Shame,*
> *Therefore good Mr. Steward let me have my Lands again."*

3   Don't give me that bull

Still, in his *Fragmenta Antiquitatis, Or, Antient Tenures of Land, and Jocular Customs of Some Manors* (1784), Josiah Beckwith suggested

---

[1] "A word applied playfully to anything full of twists and turns, or intricately or fancifully elaborated": *Oxford English Dictionary* (1971). "Bincum bancum" is more mysterious, but perhaps it derives from "bink," a bench, seat, or shelf?

that customary law could occasionally manage compassion for the young woman who had been seduced and abandoned, even in medieval times. The manorial court in Worthynbury, Flintshire, Beckwith says, could "recompence" such an ill-used maiden if she completed an ordeal. Town authorities shaved and greased a three-year-old bull, and the jilted woman was to grab its tail. Two men goaded the bull and if the woman could hold on when it reacted, "she was to have it by Way of Satisfaction; if not, she got nothing but the Grease that remained in her Hands."

Given the times and attendant difficulties of women, perhaps the better view remains that the bull ordeal was "more likely a punishment for unchastity" — yet another public humiliation, rather than recompense for love's labor lost.

4   Unquiet enjoyment

"Your freedom to swing your fist ends where my nose begins." So goes the old saw about constitutional democracy. Ears seem to be protected, too, judging by a Canadian landlord and tenant decision of the spring of 1990, evicting a young woman from her apartment for moaning during sexual intercourse. A former neighbor testified that her family had moved after being awakened by the woman's enthusiasm several nights a week, as often as two or three times a night, for periods of 30 to 60 minutes. The building superintendent said that he had heard the moaning while in the street outside the building, and the vocal tenant put the problem down to poor insulation, not undue enthusiasm. A district court judge ruled that the landlord was entitled to evict the woman insofar as she "substantially interfered with the reasonable enjoyment of the premises [by the other tenants] for the usual purposes."

Nine years later, the highest courts in Britain decided that tenants' "right to quiet enjoyment" of their rented homes did not include adequate sound-proofing from such exertions. The housing in question was public ("council") housing built during Victorian times and just after the First World War. One tenant complained that the walls were so thin, she could hear her neighbors' "private and most intimate moments" — everything from lights being switched on, pots and pans being placed on the stove, "conversations, what TV station they are viewing, when they go to the toilet, when they make love." Another tenant added singing, walking, and arguments to the list, as well as "bringing up phlegm, sneezing, [and] bedsprings." While the leases guaranteed tenants quiet enjoyment, the courts held that this did not require the councils to bring the sound-proofing up to modern standards. "Read literally," Lord Hoffman wrote in his House of Lords ruling, the covenants for quiet enjoyment "would seem very apt. The flat is not quiet and the tenant is not enjoying it. But the words cannot be read literally." The words "quiet enjoyment" had a technical legal meaning "different from what they would today signify to a non-lawyer who was unacquainted with their history." Quiet enjoyment did not connote a right to be "undisturbed" by the everyday activities of one's neighbors. Rather, Lord Hoffman wrote, the rule was "caveat lessee." What the tenant received under the lease depended on the state of the home when she agreed to rent it. Here, on signing the leases the tenants were aware that the buildings were old and in spotty repair. They had "an inherent structural defect for which the landlord assumed no responsibility." Of course, this reasoning ignores the fact that people who live in public housing generally are poor and have little power to bargain with landlords over the terms of their accommodation.[2]

---

[2] In an attempt to address this latter point, Lord Millett noted: "No one, least of all the two councils concerned, would wish anyone to live in the conditions to which the tenants in these appeals are exposed. For the future, building regulations will ensure that new constructions and conversions have adequate

5   Roving farm hands

There is a general sense that the workplace used to be a more sexually-charged environment, and that it was not uncommon for men to chase their secretaries around the desks. In fact, though, employees were sometimes fired for simply boasting about their sexual exploits, even if the supposed conquests were ancient history. A Canadian case from the early 20th century provides a ready example. Patrick, a sheep-rancher in Middlesex County, Ontario, had grown to trust his hand Denham to the point that he left Denham in charge when he was out of town, a frequent occurrence, permitting Denham free access to Patrick's house. As part of their employment agreement, Patrick also provided Denham and his family a house nearby, and one cow.

In June, 1908, rancher Patrick remarked that he thought highly of a young woman, identified in the *Ontario Law Reports* as "Miss A." Denham, who had worked with Patrick for seven years, replied that she was "not so fine and straight" as Patrick thought, "for he had had his hand up her clothes and on her private parts." A few days later, evidently feeling a new familiarity with his boss, Denham also bragged that he had slept with a "Miss X" before she was married.

Patrick discussed these conversations with a friend, saying he was thinking of firing Denham because of them. Patrick's friend said that Denham had told him about the Miss A incident during a trip to the

---

sound insulation. But the huge stock of pre-war residential properties presents an intractable problem. Local authorities have limited resources, and have to decide on their priorities. Many of their older properties admit damp and are barely fit for human habitation. . . .

"These cases raise issues of priority in the allocation of resources. Such issues must be resolved by the democratic process, national and local. The judges are not equipped to resolve them. All that we can do is to say that there is nothing in the relevant tenancy agreements or current legislation, or in the common law, which would enable the tenants to obtain redress through the courts."

Chicago stock yards two years earlier; it had happened, Denham had told him, in Patrick's barn. This information made up Patrick's mind.

Denham denied fornication with Miss X, and when he sued Patrick for unjustly firing him and breaking his employment contract, none was proved in court. Contesting the allegation that Miss A had been only 13 or 14 at the time of the fondling (Denham said she was 22), he admitted fondling her, but called it "accidental." In any event, it had occurred *eight years in the past*, during the first year of his service with Patrick.

Miss A was not called as a witness. Although Denham had proved himself a reliable employee and law-abiding person ever after the incident, whatever it may have been, three judges of the Ontario Divisional Court found that he had been lawfully fired. What was decisive for Sir John Boyd, the chancellor of the province, was Denham's braggadocio — the fact that his mind "appeared to dwell with satisfaction" on the Miss A encounter, whether or not it had really happened. It was "alike discreditable to boast of the act and disparage the woman." With a wife, three young children, and a serving-maid in his house, Patrick had good reason to worry whether Denham was "of lewd mind and habit." Patrick had reasonable grounds, that is, to feel that Denham's personal life could interfere with his professional one.

6   Whipping up some evidence

The age of consent in the United States was once as low as ten years old. These days, it is most often between 16 and 18 years old in North America, although it might be lower if all those involved are under the age of majority. But even while purporting to protect those of tender years, the law can seem more vengeful moralist than Christian guardian.

The sad case in point of Nannie Marler, of Dunkin County, Missouri, became widely public in 1923. A group of young men stood charged of statutory rape — of "having carnal knowledge" of Marler, "a female child under the age of 15 years." But Marler had been a prostitute from the age of 13, and at the time of the men's trials, she was in the reformatory for that reason. Given those circumstances, she was in no mood to cooperate with the prosecution of her young customers and lovers. (She did not always charge for her favors.)

The trial of one of the young men, a Mr. Snow, included a remarkable series of exchanges between the trial judge, W.S.C. Walker, and others in the court, about how to "encourage" Marler to testify. Because Marler was already in custody, it would have been fruitless, Judge Walker remarked, to send her to jail for contempt. He preferred, as he put it, to "instruct the sheriff or her mother to give her a good licking" during the lunch break. Snow's lawyer, W.R. Hall, suggested "that she be sent to jail and not given anything to eat but water and bread." When Judge Walker asked Marler whether she would prefer to answer the questions or "be whipped by the sheriff," she replied, "It don't make any difference to me."

The sheriff then offered "to take her back to jail and put her in the dungeon," but the judge continued to plump for whipping, never mind that it had "gone out of fashion, even in our schools" and "this generation is being raised to think they are too good to be whipped." The ensuing discussion about the legalities (Did the court have the jurisdiction to order whipping? Could Marler's mother legally consent to having the sheriff whip the girl in her stead?) suggest, perhaps, that the officials were not just play-acting to scare Marler into testifying. Then again, Judge Walker rejected Hall's suggestion that Marler be tied up by the thumbs. "No, the warden of the penitentiary got into trouble for tying them up by the thumbs." The sheriff had yet another idea: "Nannie knows we have a crazy man down there, and I'll put her in with that crazy man unless she will talk. . . . I'll put her up there and let her wait on that crazy man; he is sick."

Marler finally testified, and the court convicted Snow, sentencing him to two years in prison. But Marler's ultimate cooperation won her no compassion when Snow appealed to the Supreme Court of Missouri. No one there questioned the value of testimony virtually beaten out of a reluctant, wretched witness. Justice Higbee of the higher court cast the girl as the whore of Babylon in a contemporary *Paradise Lost*. Her "seductive influence" made the "boys . . . more sinned against than sinning. They did not defile the [already fallen] girl. She was a mere 'cistern for foul toads to knot and gender in.'" "A lecherous woman," Justice Higbee fulminated, "is a social menace; she is more dangerous that T.N.T., more deadly than the 'pestilence that walketh in darkness or the destruction that wasteth at noonday.'" Justice Higbee went on to quote the biblical proverb about the "strange" (promiscuous) woman whose lips drip honey but whose end is hell, yet in all his exegesis conspicuously left out Jesus's famous dare that the first stone should be cast by him "who is without sin." "This wretched girl," he concluded, the adjective being as close to sympathy as he came, "was young in years but old in sin and shame."

Of course, self-righteous indignation was no basis on which to overturn Snow's conviction of having sex with an underage girl. Along with his irrelevant attack on Marler's character, Justice Higbee held that the trial judge erred in allowing the prosecution to show that Snow's witnesses were facing the same charge as Snow — and that they therefore had reason to make Snow look more sinned against than sinning. The witnesses (the other young fornicators) had testified that Snow believed that Marler was 16, and that he later offered to marry her in front of her mother. Justice Higbee also said that the trial judge erred in allowing the prosecutor to make inflammatory remarks in his closing address: the marriage offer was a loveless sham, the prosecutor had charged, and all Snow "cares for is to satisfy his lustful desires and his fiendish disposition towards women."

7   The living started before the cohabiting, see?

As noted in Chapter Six, the courts sometimes refuse to enforce contracts which assist those involved in illicit sexual relationships. Where prostitution or "living off the avails" is illegal, the courts will not hold a working girl to her promise of sex, even if she got paid for it without "performing." Of course, this cuts both ways. In a 1984 Wyoming case, a justice of the peace found it irrelevant that a female buyer had already partly paid for a 1970 Pontiac with $100 cash and 50 sex acts.

What if a man and woman agree to "live in sin" as a trial run to see what it would be like if they married? This was the background of the 1982 Australian case, *Seidler v. Schallhofer*. The couple agreed that Schallhofer would return girlfriend Seidler's contribution to house payments if the trial cohabitation did not lead to marriage. It did not. Schallhofer argued that, because the contract facilitated fornication, it was against public policy, and therefore the court could not hold him to his contract with Seidler. The court ordered him to pay up, retorting that the hanky-panky existed before the contract.

8   Paying the price

What, again, about a man who leases an apartment for his mistress, and "constantly" visits her there for "immoral purposes" while the rent goes unpaid? In 1910, Justice Charles Darling said that, because the landlord knew what was going on at the Southampton Row address in London, he couldn't sue for the rent owing — a little over £72. The landlord was aware, Justice Darling found, that the mistress got the rent from her lover as "the price of her immorality." Therefore, the lease amounted to a contract for an illegal and immoral purpose. It was irrelevant that the tenant was "merely the mistress of one man" rather than "a common prostitute. . . . That fornication is sinful and immoral is clear. The Litany speaks of 'fornication and all other deadly sin,' and the Litany is contained in the *Book of Common Prayer* which is in use in the Church of England under the authority of an Act of Parliament."

Of course, this might be fine Christian morality, but it is the sort of legal non-argument that makes most judges shake their heads. True to his moralist agenda, Justice Darling compounded the illogic: because fornication was illegal in the ecclesiastical courts, he wrote (illegal, that is, if the fornicators were prosecuted within eight months of their criminal act, so as not to create bastards), and because a statute from 1284 (!) called on the king not to punish the bishops for taking jurisdiction over such offenses where the king did not, "fornication is therefore illegal in the sense that it is contrary to the law as recognized in various statutes, and it is immoral." To begin with, while Parliament might have given the Protestant church its blessing, so to speak, no lawyer since Thomas More would argue that religious law trumps secular law in democracies and constitutional monarchies: the contrary is precisely the legacy of Henry VIII and his decision to change religions, and the law, so that he could marry his dead wife's sister. And nowhere does the law accept such a fragile daisy-chain of relationships among various laws and authorities.

9   A happy, if flat, ending

"DANCER GETS 30G IN THE END," the *New York Post* headline put it. "BETTER THAN A KICK IN THE BUTT."

Mary Gale was working as an exotic dancer in Hackensack, New Jersey, when she decided that plastic surgery would improve her career prospects. She had a local surgeon round out her breasts from an A to a C cup. He also pumped artificial substances into her lips. Then, Gale bought a new chin and forehead, and in 1990, when she was 33, she decided that her rear end was too flat. To obtain a fuller, rounder behind (something which, her lawyer admits, most women in our society would prefer to avoid), she went to Park Avenue in Manhattan, and the offices of Dr. Elliot Jacobs.

A jury seems to have believed, or wanted to believe, that Jacobs did not forewarn Gale that, for her $6,500 (U.S.), he was going to stitch silicone breast implants into her buttocks. Not altogether surprisingly, the result, according to Gale, was that "it looked like I had two tits on my butt."

Reporters who saw the photographs agreed ("Her claims were buttressed by photos taken shortly after the operation that showed what looked like two small breasts protruding from about halfway up her rear end"), but Jacobs testified that Gale gave fully-informed consent for the procedure. He told the jury that if she'd been patient for six months to a year, the implants would have "contoured." Gale countered that she couldn't even sit down right, let alone wave her bathykulpic bottom around in a bar. She looked like a "freak show," she said. So, after just three weeks, she had Jacobs remove the implants.

She returned to bumping and grinding within two months. And although Gale displayed her allegedly scarred behind in public for years and years to follow — during four more years of dirty dancing and subsequent visits to the beach in a thong bikini — she hired New York lawyer Cynthia Matheke to sue over residual scarring, lost wages, and mental anguish. After deliberating for four hours, the jury found that Jacobs breached his duty to explain to Gale the full nature and risks of the surgery.

Apparently the jurors believed Matheke's story that the deep tan on Gale's "glutes," in a photo from 1996, was in aid of hiding the scars. They seem to have rejected lawyer Paul Paley's closing argument for Jacobs that Gale's persistent fondness for letting it all hang out was the equivalent of a "smoking gun" or "bloody glove," showing that there was no residual damage from the surgery.

Apparently not content with a legal miracle, Gale complained that the $30,000 in damages did not even cover her expenses. But it could be that the jury gave her exactly what it felt justice demanded. Its reasoning might have gone like this: sanction physician Jacobs for not explaining medical procedures properly, and possibly for exploiting Gale's desperate vanity. At the same time, deny Gale her big tort payday, given that the reasonable litigant would have learned something about the risks as she subjected herself to more plastic surgeries than Frankenstein's monster.

CHAPTER TWO

ALL IN AND BEYOND THE FAMILY

Adultery, Criminal Conversation, and Other Complications of Family Law

"On a scale of adulterousness, a snog is 1, and having lunch, stone cold sober, and laughing at the jokes of another man is a 9."

BRITISH COMEDIAN JENNY ECLAIR

10 Impossible consideration — and not very considerate, either

Everyone knows that marriage is a form of contract, but promises to marry can carry the same weight. "Engagements" sometimes amount to a contract that a court will enforce by awarding the disappointed party money, or something else of value. In 1979, for example, a young American man, Tim Kowalke, won a settlement of 4,380 chocolate chip cookies after his fiancée broke her promise to marry him.

The courts face a dilemma, however, when an already-married person promises to marry a third person. Generally, if Smith promises to marry Jones and Jones is unaware that Smith is already married to Mrs. Smith, the law has said that Smith owes Jones something at least for falsely claiming that he was in a position to marry her. In England during the 1950s, Perry Shaw's estate suffered a type of double jeopardy for such double dealing. Shaw married a "Miss Jones" while he was still married to Cecelia Shaw. That made him liable to the second Mrs. Shaw (the Miss Jones that was) for purporting to be a bachelor, and it invalidated his marriage to her as bigamous. Then, Cecelia died, making Shaw genuinely single and "available." Because he did not then go through a valid wedding ceremony with Miss Jones, his estate was additionally liable to her for breach of his long-past original promise to make her Mrs. Shaw number two.

Older U.S. law said the same thing about seductions under promise to marry. In both instances, judges found that, in trusting cads to act in good faith, the women had given up something — a "consideration" — that contract law recognized as compensable. The cads were held to their promises at least to the extent of paying money damages. In this way the judges circumvented the rule in contract law that "impossible consideration [marriage by an already-married person] is no consideration."

11 On further consideration

Another contract rule says that "*past* consideration is no consideration," which again can apply to absconding cads. In order to win compensation, the plaintiff must have given or given up something other than sexual favors shared before any proposal of marriage. When in the 1940s Gloria Schumm threw over the famous actor Wallace Beery for another man, Beery felt his legal obligations to her were mostly past, even though she had given birth to his child.

Schumm was, after all, soon to marry her new companion. In return for her promise not to sue Beery for paternity, and not to use the name "Wallace" or "Wally" in the baby's name, the star of *Treasure Island*, *Grand Hotel*, and *The Mighty McGurk* admitted that Schumm needed financial help. He had told her, she claimed, that he would support and educate the child as if they were all living as a family, pay the child $25,000 when he turned 21 "to give him a fair start" in adulthood, take out life insurance policies to secure those payments, and pay Schumm anything else necessary to raise the child in a way befitting the son "of a prominent public man of wealth." For each of nine weeks after his son's birth, Beery paid Schumm $25. He then repudiated all her claims against him.

At the California District Court of Appeals, Judge Minor Moore could not see how Schumm's promise not to bring a paternity suit, or restraining herself from naming the baby Wallace, amounted to sufficient consideration to create a binding contract. Beery would have been obliged to support his son, paternity suit or not. And, even if the court believed that Beery would pay $134,000 merely to protect the name Wallace, people of that name were "as numerous as the leaves of Valambrosa." There was no benefit to Beery, or detriment to his former lover.

But on further appeal, Justice Jesse Carter held that it was "commonly considered a privilege and honor" for a child to bear his father's name. Because of Beery's wealth and fame, "the use of his name and forbearance to bring an action may have great intrinsic value." Schumm's threat to launch a paternity suit did not subject Beery to duress that voided the contract; it merely advised Berry that she would exercise a legal right if he didn't agree to her terms. The contract was good: Beery had to pay what he promised to pay.

A few years later, a Maryland court held that Hilda Boehm's promise not to prosecute Louis Fiege in "bastardy proceedings" was a fair trade-off for Fiege's promise to support Boehm's child — even though blood tests later proved that Fiege was not the father.

Fiege denied even having sex with Boehm, who claimed that the child was a product of fumblings with Fiege in his car. Fiege said that, by threatening to have him prosecuted in "bastardy proceedings," Boehm terrorized him into an agreement to pay childcare expenses. After the child's birth in 1951, Fiege paid a total of $480 toward Boehm's medical expenses, salary loss, and childcare. Then he took the paternity test and stopped paying. Boehm brought a bastardy charge against him, and when that failed she sued him for her childcare costs until the day in 1954 when she gave the child up for adoption. At this point, she was single, 35, and working as a typist. The Maryland Court of Appeals accepted her claim that she made the bastardy allegations in good faith, never mind the blood tests. In other words, it apparently believed that she and Fiege had sexual intercourse. But it also seemed to ignore the fact that, even acting in good faith, Boehm was dead wrong about the paternity. "The fact that a man accused of bastardy is forced to enter into a contract," it ruled, "to pay for the support of his [sic] bastard child for fear of exposure and the shame that might be cast upon him as a result, as well as a sense of justice to render some compensation for the injury he inflicted upon the mother, does not lessen the merit of the contract, but greatly increases it." Fiege had a moral obligation to Boehm and the child, the court held, without remarking on the obligations of the actual father, and while translating Fiege's moral duty into a legal one. The logic, if any, seems to be that, as Blackstone implied a century earlier, the childcare expenses were a sort of fine for fornication.

12   "This contract is so one-sided, I am astonished to find it written on both sides of the paper."

Marriage contracts or "domestic agreements" usually assume equality of bargaining power, a supposed requirement of legitimate contracts. But in history, their purpose was often quite the contrary: the idea was to maintain patriarchal disequilibrium.

When, for instance, William Dagg discovered in 1867 that his girlfriend Catherine Jeffries was pregnant by him, he agreed to marry her. The couple had met, apparently, at a "hydropathic hospital" (a clinic offering fashionable "water cures") where Dagg worked as a porter and Jeffries as a cook. Dagg the porter seems to have viewed poor Jeffries as significantly below his station: she was, after all, a girl who *would*. Before solemnizing their marriage, he drafted an agreement for both of them to sign. Its purpose, apparently, was to remind Jeffries that the marriage was for appearances only — and, presumably, to "legitimize" the child — unless she made herself otherwise respectable and deserving of the porter with pretensions:

> *This is to certify that whereas the undersigned parties do agree that they will marry, and that only to save the female of us from shaming her friends or telling a lie, and that the said marriage shall be no more thought of, except to tell her friends that she is married (unless she should arrive at the following accomplishments — viz., piano, singing, reading, writing, speaking, and deportment); and whereas these said accomplishments have in no way been sought after, much less mastered, therefore the aforesaid marriage shall be and is null and void; and whereas we agree that the male of us shall keep his harmonium in the aforesaid female's sitting room, we agree that it shall be there no more than four months, and that from that time the aforesaid and undersigned shall be free in every respect whatsoever of the aforesaid and undersigned female, as witness our hands this 1st of ____, 1867.*

A month following the marriage, the child was born, after which William paid Catherine two shillings and sixpence per week but otherwise had nothing to do with her or the baby. He stopped the payments when he discovered Catherine was living with another man, and eventually, in 1882 (15 years after the "wedding"), petitioned the English Court of Probate, Divorce, and Admiralty for a dissolution of the marriage.

Despite the "certification" that the marriage was a sham, the court refused to let William off the hook. It found that, in fact, there *was* no marriage contract, because Catherine had been in no position to haggle. And her subsequent degradation, the court added, was a direct result of William's failure to provide for and protect her as a husband should: because of *his* behavior, she lacked the resources to improve and support herself as the contract demanded. Surprisingly, the court did not consider the question of whether Catherine really ever understood the terms of the ambiguous "agreement," which itself alleged that she was illiterate.

Fifty-six years later, a similarly heavy-handed "agreement" was drafted for the opposite end, of securing a wife's absolute fidelity. Under threat of death, 18-year-old Estella Blitz had written as dictated to her,

> *I undersigned Estella agree to marry Mohamed on the following conditions: (1) I know well that he is an old-fashioned Egyptian and I know all about the Egyptian habits and character and I promise to follow all these habits and character without any exceptions; (2) I promise not to go out anywhere without my husband; (3) I will never have men or boy friends of me nor ask any man or boy to visit me at home nor see any man or boy outside or have any appointments; (4) I promise not to write to anybody friend of mine in Egypt or anywhere else abroad, man, boy, girl or lady; (5) I promise not to dance with any man or boy at home or at any other home or at any dancing hall in any feast or in any other circumstance; (6) I know well that Mohamed is not rich at all and he can't promise anything*

except just keeping me comfortably; (7) I confess that I write these conditions with my own wish and without any obligation from any side, and that I am conscious and responsible, and if I break any of these conditions I have to separate, and have no right to claim any penny from Mohamed at any Court, whether Egyptian or English.

The couple had been married in a registry office in England, but Mohamed then returned to his railway job in Egypt. They had never lived together or consummated the marriage.

When Estella applied to dissolve the relationship, the judge, Sir S.O. Henn Collins, did not go into the legal dubiety of the terms of the "agreement" — that, for example, much of it seemed contrary to public policy, at the very least on the ground that it interfered with the administration of justice — and he remarked that "in 99 cases out of 100" Estella's story about the threats and coerced marriage agreement would be incredible. But he believed that she had written the document under fear and duress. This time, that was enough to invalidate it.

13   The thin blue line between Daddy and Sugar Daddy

Women have always held their own in the battle of the sexes, of course, including on the front of sexual scheming. A notable 1992 case features an 83-year-old man adopting his 31-year-old mistress, even though she maintained an affectionate relationship with her biological parents.

Johannes Saarnok grew up in Estonia. When he arrived in Sherbrooke, Quebec, in 1944, he had $600 to his name. He moved to British Columbia where he made his fortune in logging. He was married for 48 years, and when his wife died in 1985, he felt desperately lonely. At a funeral just before his wife's death, he had met

Eva McNeil, who also had grown up in Estonia, where her parents still lived. McNeil lodged with Saarnok's business partner, and in 1988 Saarnok invited her to a party at his apartment. After the other guests had gone to bed or home, McNeil offered herself sexually to Saarnok. Then, she promised to render him similar favors up to three times a week if he would change his will to make her sole executrix and beneficiary. He was 79, she 27.

In the ensuing months, as part of the connubial arrangement, Saarnok bought McNeil an apartment worth $83,500, furniture worth $6,357, and a Corvette for $48,732. He transferred half his interest in his own apartment to her, changed his will as she had asked, issued checks to her totaling $13,000, and paid her $45,000 in purported wages for her efforts as his personal secretary. In April, 1988, without advising authorities that McNeil had living biological parents, Saarnok formally adopted her as his daughter. Soon thereafter, McNeil introduced him to her mother in the hope that she would take on the mistress role. That was when Saarnok came to his senses. He sued McNeil, alleging that she had defrauded him through undue influence.

In her defense, McNeil took a two-pronged approach. On the one hand, she denied any sexual goings-on, and insisted that her newfound prosperity arose from the everyday beneficence of a father toward his doting daughter — plus a salary for secretarial services rendered. "In the alternative," she made the argument familiar in cases where prostitutes try to evade debts (see Chapter Six): if there was sex involved, any agreement between her and Saarnok offended the general public welfare (it was "void as against public policy"), and the courts could not assist Saarnok in obtaining restitution.

Not surprisingly, the Supreme Court of British Columbia swept all of this aside as codswallop. Justice Leggatt noted, among other things, that McNeil prevailed on Saarnok to adopt her as a sort of insurance policy against her claim on everything he owned: "The defendant must have been aware that by becoming a legally adopted daughter she would always have a claim on the plaintiff's estate regardless of any change in the will. . . . This court has no difficulty in coming to the conclusion that this was a scheme or plan cleverly designed by the defendant to take advantage of an elderly, lonely, and vulnerable person. . . . The offer of sexual favors was but one part of an elaborate scheme devised by the defendant to deprive the plaintiff of large portions of his property." Justice Leggatt revoked the adoption and ordered McNeil to return all the money and property to Saarnok except a fur coat Saarnok had given her.

14 Soft, short, and shrivelled, but only sometimes, naturally

The old law of annulment or "nullity of marriage" strikes the modern reader as harsh. But in some cases it ensured the wife several years of financial support when she might otherwise have lived in straitened circumstances. It was based on church law, and even where the marriage was absolutely sexless, it denied either spouse an annulment unless the couple had cohabited (albeit without sexual relations) for three years. If the couple said they could not consummate because of "incapacity" — because, that is, there was some physical obstruction to sexual intercourse — they anyway were condemned to remain husband and wife until three years of continuous cohabitation had passed. A 1730 case from England demonstrates how strict this was in application. In 1727, a man named Welde married Lord Aston's young daughter. It turned out that he had a shortened ligament which prevented penile erection. Surgeons corrected the problem, but in mid-1729 Welde told his father-in-law that "what the physicians and surgeons applied to him signified nothing; for that, whenever he attempted to consummate, something came across him that shrivelled up his privy parts to nothing." By

1730 Mrs. Welde was still a virgin and, when she complained, Welde mildly replied, "My dear, if it appears after three years that I have not consummated, we cannot in conscience live together."

When the couple sought an annulment in court, Welde's lawyer pointed out that his client was not merely "bewitched," but still suffered from a physical incapacity. Nonetheless, the court denied the wife an annulment. Noting that the strained atmosphere had caused the wife to live most of the time at her father's even after Welde became technically "functional," the court said that there was no legal incapacity and the marriage had to continue.

Forty-eight years later, a Mrs. Anderson was similarly frustrated, never mind that she was still a virgin after two years of marriage. The report of her appeal to the consistory court — where deputies of the local bishop sat to determine questions of canon law — gives little more than the judge's coy note. The medical inspectors "could only say it appeared soft and short which does not always continue. Therefore, three years' cohabitation necessary."

15   But isn't that incest?

These "incapacity" strictures persisted into the next century. If anything, by 1828 the courts were even less sympathetic. A 60-year-old man named Brown took a 52-year-old as his wife, only to discover that she had some sort of vaginal obstruction. The couple cohabited unhappily for nearly a year, and still the court was not content just to note that the obstruction was "curable." "Mrs. Brown was past the age of child-bearing at the time of the marriage," it editorialized, and "therefore the primary and most legitimate object of wedlock, the procreation of issue could not operate." Anyway, "a man of sixty who marries a woman of fifty-two should be contended to take her '*tanquam soror*'" — as if she were his sister. Adding insult (upon insult) to injury remains a judicial prerogative.

16 The curse of Onan, again (and again)

Another 35 years later, little had changed. In 1863, a 27-year-old wife left her husband, albeit after only two months of cohabitation, seeking an annulment "by reason of the impotency of the man." The medical inspectors reported: "We, the undersigned medical inspectors appointed to examine and report upon the condition of the generative organs of Henry E, do hereby declare that we have made a careful examination, and find that the external organ, *viz.* the penis and the two testicles, of the said Henry E, are perfectly natural and well formed, and, as far as we are able to judge, fully competent to perform their functions. However, it appears that Henry E, who is 29 years of age, has been the subject of [epileptic] fits since he was five years old, and that he has practised excessive self-abuse, masturbation, and has continued to do so since his marriage in 1861. Considering the foregoing facts, we cannot but believe that there is a want of proper virile power."

The report ingenuously comments that, as epilepsy "is not a sufficient cause of impotence ... the more probable cause is one of a mental or moral character, *viz.* self-abuse; this we know, if carried to any great extent, induces an aversion to the female sex. This cause is remediable, and remains entirely at the option of the person concerned. Self-control may restore the natural feeling towards the wife." Henry agreed with an inspector that he was "addicted to an unnatural practice," and admitted that he masturbated as many as five times a day. Another physician remarked that "it is prejudicial to a woman's health to sleep with a man without consummation," but the court ruled: "Even assuming her to be a virgin intact, . . . the medical men negative [i.e., rule out] malformation; they negative impotency from disease or natural infirmity; but they ascribe the non-consummation of the marriage to temporary incapacity, occasioned by the indulgence of a disgusting and degrading habit, and believe that such incapacity will continue until that habit is corrected." The marriage remained legal.

17 Impossible justice?

Occasionally, however, the courts took pity on the sexually functional spouse, albeit seemingly heedless of the dysfunctional partner's feelings and future. Around the time of the Henry E litigation, another court granted the husband an annulment upon finding that the wife's constricted vagina was capable of enlargement, but she had not expressed any interest in the surgery and it was dangerous.

Some 20 years earlier — in February, 1842 — a man identified by *Robert's Ecclesiastical Reports* only as D.E. had married A.G. He was 25, she 26. They slept in the same bed for nearly three years, but achieved only minimal "penetration." It turned out that the unfortunate A.G. had a cul de sac in her vagina and no uterus. Not realizing the extent of the problem, D.E. recommended "simple remedies aided by horse exercise." A.G. dutifully followed her husband's advice but medical examination revealed that her vagina was only two inches long.

Dr. Lushington decided for the ecclesiastical court that "unnatural" or "imperfect coitus" was no coitus, or at least not legal consummation. An annulment on such grounds was preferable, he reasoned, to subjecting D.E. "to the misfortune of a barren wife." What was more, "there is not a natural indulgence of natural desire; almost of necessity disgust is generated, and the probable consequences of other connections with men of ordinary self control become almost certain. I am of the opinion that no man ought to be reduced to this state of quasi-unnatural connection and consequent temptation, and, therefore, I should hold the marriage void. The condition of the lady is greatly to be pitied, but on no principle of justice can her calamity be thrown upon another."

18 New frontiers in metaphysics

Of course, there is dysfunctional, and then there is dysfunctional. In 1995, Nedjelko Juretic, a 66-year-old Vancouverite, advertized in a Honduran newspaper for a wife. Twenty-three-year-old Brenda Ruiz answered, from Honduras, and apparently it was opportunism at first sight. Ruiz agreed to move into Juretic's apartment in a Vancouver building he owned and, barring unforeseen obstacles, to marry him. Nuptials transpired about two months after Ruiz reached Vancouver, whereupon Ruiz informed the not surprisingly vexed Juretic that they could consummate only if he did not touch her.

Juretic never managed this feat, although he seems to have thought it possible, if unpalatable as a form of "rape." The trial judge went along with these metaphysics, noting that Juretic and Ruiz lived otherwise as man and wife for five months, until Ruiz moved out and became involved with another man. And in 1999 the British Columbia Court of Appeal affirmed the trial judge's refusal to annul the marriage insofar as Juretic's inability "to obtain an erection does not reach the standard of invincible aversion." The court seems to have regressed three centuries to the old canon law view that, never mind Ruiz's own aversion to mutual arousal, sexual congress was not medically (or at least psychosexually) impossible. Thus did Canadian law give new meaning to the biblical adjuration, *"Noli me tangere."* Touch me not — but here's your Viagra.

The appeal court did not interfere with the trial judge's division of property, according Ruiz ten per cent of Juretic's property (Ruiz had nothing and contributed nothing), exclusive of the apartment building, which was worth $947,000. The judge threw in $60,000 worth of Juretic's Canada Savings Bonds, but did not mention the $87,000 Juretic held in mutual funds.

19 Impossible, doubly extraordinary, and maybe cruel

In 1821, Delaware passed a statute which awarded an automatic divorce to anyone whose spouse became a Shaker or joined some other "sect or society" which swore off sexual intercourse. The law assumed that a religious belief that "relations between husband and wife [were] void and unlawful" amounted to a form of cruelty or irreconcilable difference. However, in 1980, the English Court of Appeal held that denying one's husband sexual intercourse of more than once per week was not a form of cruelty entitling him to a divorce. Mr. and Mrs. Mason (the report does not provide first names) were married ten years when Mrs. Mason began withholding sexual congress because Mr. Mason refused to use birth control, she said. Then he had a vasectomy, and his physician advised him that weekly intercourse would verify whether or not the operation had worked. Although Mr. Mason was sleeping with another woman at the same time, and eventually left Mrs. Mason for that woman, he still contended that his wife unreasonably denied him "access" of more than once a week during the three months before he absconded. "It seems to me quite impossible," Justice Ormrod held, "for any court to find that the refusal by a wife to have sexual intercourse more often than once a week is unreasonable. It seems to me an extraordinary proposition. It is still more extraordinary in the context of this case."

20 Ripeness is all, times four

The law also has involved itself where matters threaten to become overbearing, pun intended. Most notable is a dispute over a clause in the will of wealthy Toronto lawyer and horse-racing enthusiast, Charles Millar, who died in 1926 on Halloween — aptly, some have said, given his penchant for practical jokes. In the will he left shares in the local jockey club to vociferous opponents of gambling; stock in the O'Keefe brewery, founded by Irish Catholics, to each Protestant minister in Toronto and all the Orange order lodges of the county; and a Jamaican vacation property to three men who couldn't stand each other. But the clause that brought him immortality worldwide is clause nine. In short, it gave all the residue of Millar's estate, about half a million dollars — a great fortune at the time — to the Toronto woman who had the most babies in the ten years following Millar's death.

Specifically, the clause read:

> *All the rest and residue of my property wheresoever situate, I give, devise and bequeath unto my Executors and trustees . . . to convert into money as they deem advisable and invest all the money until the expiration of nine years from my death and then call in and convert it all into money and at the expiration of ten years from my death to give it and its accumulation to the mother who has since my death given birth in Toronto to the greatest number of children as shown by the registrations under the Vital Statistics Act. If one or more mothers have equal highest number of registrations under the said act to divide the said moneys and accumulations equally between them.*

The press enthusiastically followed the competition, dubbing it the Great Toronto Stork Derby, and as late as 2002, the case still had media legs, inspiring a television movie. Millar described the will, in its own opening paragraphs, as "necessarily uncommon and capricious because I have no dependents or near relations and no duty rests upon me to leave any property at my death and what I do leave is proof of my folly in gathering and retaining more than I required in my lifetime." Nonetheless, when the ten years passed, his distant relatives objected to clause nine, and the ensuing dispute took a two-year journey all the way to Canada's highest court.

The relatives attempted to present evidence by clergy, physicians, psychologists, social workers, and sociologists that clause nine was "against public policy." In this way, they proposed to prove that it promoted illegitimacy and early death among children and their mothers, as well as moral and physical decay, and that it was "disgusting and revolting." More graphically, the relatives "suggested that in cases in which the husband ceased to be fecund in course of the race, the contestants might be tempted to resort to other males to do his office" — to, in other words, adultery or fornication.

In fact, the eventual competitors were all "from exceedingly humble circumstances," and four married mothers (the "winners") each gave birth to nine children during the ten-year period. Another woman, Lillian Kenny, claimed to have had 11 children, but the registrar of births refused to register two of them: Kenny had a stillborn daughter which she tried to register fraudulently as twins. Three more of her children were stillborn and did not qualify under the will's terms.[1]

By the time the dispute reached the Supreme Court of Canada in 1938, even mothers claiming through "illegitimate children" had lawyers. The judges refused to consider any expert evidence on clause nine's effect on public policy, ruling that this was a question of law for them to decide without assistance from laypeople. Still, the

---

[1] The *Vital Statistics Act* allowed the registration of live births only. In deciding that a stillborn child was not covered by the word "children" in Millar's will, the trial judge, Justice Middleton, quoted the Victorian English judge, Lord Ellenborough: "Lord Ellenborough with a brevity and directness, now unhappily rare, said . . . , 'In order to come under the denomination of a bastard, must not the child be born alive? All the provisions in the several statutes assume the birth of a child, which of course must be born alive.'" Lord Ellenborough was plain-speaking, all right, and very conservative. He once described transportation of convicts to Australia, including the poor who stole to eat, as "a summer airing by an easy migration to a milder climate."

relatives thought that they had solid precedent from England on their side, a wills case from 1853 called *Egerton v. Brownlow*. The Earl of Bridgewater had left a large amount of land to Lord Alford for 99 years, but added that "if Lord Alford shall die without having acquired the title of Duke or Marquis of Bridgewater," he could not pass his interest in the land to his heirs. (That is, the gift was good for his lifetime only, no matter how long or short that was.) Lord Alford died without acquiring either title, and his heir went to court, complaining that the condition that Lord Alford win the titles was void because it offended public policy. The Judicial Committee of the House of Lords agreed, saying that such conditions could encourage beneficiaries like Lord Alford to bribe high officials or take other desperate and unworthy measures to secure the gift in the will; if it permitted such conditions, the court suggested, the titled classes would soon be filled with liars and cheats. But even with this case in their back pockets, at every level Millar's relatives struck out. The Supreme Court of Canada affirmed the trial judge, Justice William Middleton, in his ruling that:

"I know no ground of public policy which recognizes the undesirability of having children at too frequent intervals. It may well be that there are many distinguished physicians and others who believe this to be the case, but public policy as such lags far behind the opinions of scientists and sociologists. . . . No judge has a right to declare that which he does not himself believe in to be against public policy simply because it is against his opinion and his idea of that which is for the welfare of the community."

Chief Justice Lyman Duff multiplied such examples, including the one first proposed in England: it was common for people to leave property to A for his life, then to B forever after. This might create a remote danger that B would kill A (to get the property for himself as soon as possible), but no one said this made the gift void as against public policy.

More unhappily, the unwed mothers also lost out — which was generally viewed as a victory at the time, given that the will would not encourage "bastardy." One of them, Pauline Mae Clarke, really had borne ten children during the period in issue, but Justice Middleton ruled that one child was delivered outside the Toronto city limits and the other five were "illegitimate" as "born in open adultery" — after Clarke had put up three of her others for adoption! Clarke admitted that the last five children were not her husband's but those of her lover, David Madill, and, while there was no proof that Mr. Clarke lacked "access" to Pauline during the relevant time, she had registered Madill as the birth father, with his consent. Still, Justice Middleton doubted that she "became so utterly depraved as to be living with two men at the same time. I think, in effect, that disregarding all laws concerning marriage and divorce, she put off the old man and all his works before she took the new." Clarke's real problem was that the word "children" in the will could not include the last five: firmly established law said that, unless the will specifically specified otherwise, a gift there to "children" meant "legitimate children" only.

Justice Middleton admitted that it was clever of the relatives to argue that, because Millar's gift was to the mothers and not the children, the legitimacy rule did not apply. And he noted that clause nine probably was "prompted rather by sympathy for the mothers of large families, who are often extremely poor people, not unmingled with a grim sense of humor." But none of this changed the so-called presumption of legitimacy.

Justice Middleton concluded his judgment with strong words for Millar — assuring him notoriety over fame — summing up the pathetic Depression-era spectacle: "As to the effect of such a gift, the testator's [Millar's] attitude seems to me rather like the throwing of a handful of coins for the pleasure of seeing children scramble for it." Although Millar could not have foreseen the economic collapse of the 1930s, the joke ended up expensive and rather cruel.

As for the relatives, whatever their motives, and whatever they were entitled to put forward as evidence, the cases of Kenny and Clarke showed that they clearly had some valid sociological arguments. But viewing all of the circumstances, Justice Middleton remained unimpressed: "The argument by the next-of-kin purports to be based on high motives of public policy and not upon mere greed, but the next-of-kin have waited until all the harm possible has been done, instead of prosecuting their claim immediately after Mr. Millar's death, when the evils, which it is said result from the tendency detrimental to public policy set forth, might have been prevented."

On the Sunday before he died, Millar himself had characterized his last testament as a "fool will."

21 The law is open to all, just like the Ritz Hotel

Henry VIII excommunicated the Catholic Church so that he could marry his sister-in-law, Katherine of Aragon, but divorce usually remained beyond the reach even of the gentry for 150 years, never mind the steady decline of church law. As late as 1856, it required an act of Parliament. In sentencing a prisoner for bigamy, the English judge Sir William Maule is said to have provided some version of this sarcastic commentary on the predicament of "holy deadlock":

> *Prisoner, you have been convicted of the grave crime of bigamy. The evidence is clear that your wife left you and your children to live in adultery with another man, and that you then intermarried with another woman, your wife being still alive. You say that this prosecution is an instrument of extortion on the part of the adulterer. Be it so, yet you had no right to take the law into your own hands. I will tell you what you ought to have done, and, if you say you did*

not know, I must tell you that the law conclusively presumes that you did [because "ignorance of the law is no excuse"]. You ought to have instructed your lawyer to bring an action against the seducer of your wife for criminal conversation. That would have cost you about a hundred pounds. When you had recovered (though not necessarily actually obtained) substantial damages against him, you should have instructed your proctor to sue in the Ecclesiastical Courts for a divorce a mensa et thoro *[separation under religious law, which maintained some jurisdiction over marriage]. That would have cost you two hundred or three hundred pounds more. When you had obtained a divorce* a mensa et thoro, *you should have appeared by counsel before the House of Lords in order to obtain a private Act of Parliament for a* divorce a vinculo matrimonii *which would have rendered you free and legally competent to marry the person whom you have taken on yourself to marry with no such sanction. The bill might possibly have been opposed in all its stages in both Houses of Parliament, and altogether you would have had to spend about a thousand or twelve hundred pounds. You will probably tell me that you never had a thousand farthings of your own in the world; but, prisoner, that makes no difference. Sitting here as an English judge, it is my duty to tell you that this is not a country in which there is one law for the rich, and another for the poor. You will be imprisoned for one day, which period has already been exceeded as you have been in custody since the commencement of the assizes.*

22   By an act of faith, two wrongs can make a right

To circumvent the legal prejudice against divorce, some spouses attempted to fudge incapacity. *Bury's Case*, from the age of Henry and his six wives, shows how the unhappy couple might still be unable to get on with their lives. The archbishop of Canterbury dissolved the Burys' marriage, accepting Mrs. Bury's complaint — confirmed by doctors — "of the unfitness and impotence of procreation in her husband." Mrs. Bury then purported to marry and had a child by Cary, perhaps not counting on the fact that Mr. Bury would also remarry and impregnate his new wife. The secular courts decided that the Burys had never legally divorced and "should be compelled to commune and cohabit as man and wife, because the holy church was deceived in its former judgment." Presumably this made them and their second spouses fornicators, and, worse, rendered their children "bastards," prejudicing their right to inherit property.

23 Stitched up for serial monogamy

In the earliest days of Anglo-American common law, you could be a bigamist even if your spouse was dead. Marriage to or by a widow constituted bigamy. Following the colonial period, American leaders considered polygamy a foreign perversion. In 1862, Congress passed the *Morrill Act* to outlaw the practice on pain of a fine of as much as $500 and imprisonment for up to five years. When Utah Mormons objected that this violated their freedom of religion and conscience, the U.S. Supreme Court upheld the act's constitutionality, even though the reasons given by the trial judge when he leaned heavily on the jury to decide against the defendant, George Reynolds, had nothing to do with the law: consider, the trial judge said, "the consequences to the innocent victims of this delusion. As this contest goes on, they multiply, and there are pure-minded women and there are innocent children, innocent in a sense even beyond the degree of the innocence of childhood itself. These are to be the sufferers; and as jurors fail to do their duty, and as these cases come up in the territory of Utah, just so do these victims multiply and spread themselves over the land."

Reynolds' lawyers argued that "the offense prohibited ... is not a *malum in se* [evil or illegal in itself]; it is not prohibited by the Decalogue [the Ten Commandments]; and, if it be said that its prohibition is to be found in the teachings of the New Testament, we know that a majority of the people of this territory deny that the Christian law contains any such prohibition." As Reynolds felt that polygamy was his religious duty, he denied that he had any criminal intent.

Chief Justice Waite, writing for the Supreme Court, ruled that polygamy was always "odious among the northern and western nations of Europe, and, until the establishment of the Mormon Church, was almost exclusively a feature of the life of Asiatic and of African people. . . . By the statute of 1 James 1. (c. 11), the offense, if committed in England or Wales, was made punishable in the civil courts, and the penalty was death." In 1788, the state of Virginia adapted the English statute, the court noted, including the death penalty as a punishment, after freedom of religion was enshrined in the U.S. constitution.

> *From that day to this we think it may safely be said there never has been a time in any state of the union when polygamy has not been an offense against society. . . . Marriage, while from its very nature a sacred obligation, is nevertheless, in most civilized nations, a civil contract, and usually regulated by law. Upon it society may be said to be built, and out of its fruits spring social relations and social obligations and duties, with which government is necessarily required to deal. In fact, according as monogamous or polygamous marriages are allowed, do we find the principles on which the government of the people, to a greater or less extent, rests. Professor Lieber says polygamy leads to the patriarchal principle [under which a group of families is subject to the despotic rule of the eldest male among them], and which, when applied to large communities, fetters the people in stationary despotism, while that principle cannot long exist*

> *in connection with monogamy. . . . An exceptional colony of polygamists under an exceptional leadership may sometimes exist for a time without appearing to disturb the social condition of the people who surround it; but there cannot be a doubt that, unless restricted by some form of constitution, it is within the legitimate scope of the power of every civil government to determine whether polygamy or monogamy shall be the law of social life under its dominion.*

To excuse some from the *Morrill Act's* operation because of their religious belief, Chief Justice Waite added, would introduce

> *a new element into criminal law. Laws are made for the government of actions, and while they cannot interfere with mere religious belief and opinions, they may with practices. Suppose one believed that human sacrifices were a necessary part of religious worship, would it be seriously contended that the civil government under which he lived could not interfere to prevent a sacrifice? Or if a wife religiously believed it was her duty to burn herself upon the funeral pile of her dead husband [as women sometimes have done in India], would it be beyond the power of the civil government to prevent her carrying her belief into practice?*

Religious belief was not "superior to the law of the land." Otherwise "every citizen [would] become a law unto himself. Government could exist only in name under such circumstances. A criminal intent is generally an element of crime, but every man is presumed to intend the necessary and legitimate consequences of what he knowingly does. Here the accused knew he had been once married, and that his first wife was living. He also knew that his second marriage was forbidden by law. When, therefore, he married the second time, he is presumed to have intended to break the law."

Chief Justice Waite also summarily dismissed Reynolds' complaint that the trial judge's exhortations about "innocents" unfairly appealed to jurors' passions or prejudices. "All the court did," the court held, "was to call the attention of the jury to the peculiar character of the crime for which the accused was on trial, and to remind them of the duty they had to perform."

Later, of course, some scoundrels made a career of bigamy. Professor Friedman cites the 1888 *New York Times* story of Aldrich Brown, who married 17 times, absconding each time after no more than ten days' cohabitation. At the time, Brown was a tall and handsome 45-year-old. He favored "sewing girls in wealthy families," appropriating "their little savings, their valuables and wearing apparel."

24   The Belly-Inspection Writ or, the spirit is willing — but to whom?

Sir Francis Willoughby dies in 1597, leaving five daughters as his heirs. A few weeks later, his widow, Dorothy, announces that she is pregnant. Will it be a male who will trump his sisters and become the sole heir? Or, is Dorothy faking it, to divert the estate to her own family's blood-line?

Blackstone tells us that the Goths used to kill a woman "suspected to feign herself with child, in order to produce a suppositious heir." They regarded her as committing "the most atrocious theft." The slightly more civilized British law developed the writ *de ventre inscipiendo*. The "heirs presumptive," as Blackstone calls them — the daughters in our example — could ask a court to order the local sheriff to shut the widow up in her "castle" and have 12 knights attend upon her with 12 midwives. The midwives inspected her and, if they reported that she was in fact pregnant, the court might order that she be kept under a sort of house arrest, and subjected to daily belly inspections, until she delivered under the watchful eyes of several of the midwives. If the midwives found that the woman was not pregnant, "any issue she may afterwards produce, though within nine months," Blackstone explains matter-of-factly, "will be bastard."

On the other hand, if Dorothy had remarried soon after Sir Francis's death and had a child who, in this time before paternity blood tests, could have been the child of either husband, the child was "said to be more than ordinarily legitimate; for he may, when he arrives to years of discretion, choose which of the fathers he pleases." If you can be more than ordinarily legitimate, who says you can't be a little bit pregnant?

The "suppositious birth" business is not as unlikely as it sounds. Two centuries later, in 1903, an enterprising seductress in New York "borrowed a child" to convince former lovers — serial victims, it turned out — that they owed her support payments. Still, the writ *de ventre* could be monstrously invasive, and in practice the courts grew more sensitive to its effect on the poor widow. Generally, if the woman consented to a simple examination by a couple of midwives, and to their presence at the birth, that sufficed. In the especially sad case of *Aiscough*, in 1730, the Lord Chancellor himself heard that 19-year-old Sir John Chaplun died two months after his marriage to the 16-year-old daughter of Morris, a bailiff. Sir John's three sisters were most unhappy to learn, it seems, that, short though the marriage was, Morris had persuaded Sir John to make a will leaving everything to his daughter. When the daughter claimed that she was pregnant after only the two months of marriage, the sisters petitioned for a belly-inspection writ. They asked that the court shut the widow up in her matrimonial home, which she said was drafty, out of repair, and — in remotest Lincolnshire — far from her family and friends in London. On also hearing that, given the other stresses in the young widow's life, the folderol with two dozen examiners could induce a miscarriage or some other horrible mishap, Lord Chancellor King took pity on the girl. She apparently wasn't going to deliver until around Christmas, he found, when she would be at her father's, in any event. Until then, the sisters were permitted to send a couple of midwives around now and again, with adequate notice to the girl. The writ would issue "at Michaelmas."

Then again, even where the writ was employed, the courts turned a blind eye to illicit sex — probably, again, to avoid situations which made children "illegitimate" and their mothers notoriously "lewd." Six years after the death of Shakespeare, one court ignored evidence that William Theaker had never cohabited with his wife Mary before he died, and that Mary was "suspected of incontinency with Duncomb," whom she married a week after William's death. Theaker (or Thecar, as Lord Coke spells it) was the father, the court ruled. After judgment, and 40 weeks and 11 days after William's death, Mary had a daughter.

25   Tea for three

When divorce finally became more widely available, the law still would not grant it without "fault" — usually adultery, cruelty, abandonment, criminal activity, or an unconventional (criminal) sexual demand such as buggery. Adultery became the ground of preference, of course, even if spouses had to go to extra trouble to prove it. In his early days as a stand-up comedian, Woody Allen joked that his lawyer advised him the only way he could get a divorce was through an extra-marital affair. Allen volunteered. His wife, however, beat him to it, he said, although she claimed later that she had been "violated." She sued for slander, Allen added, when he remarked that it could not have been a moving violation.

The more general adultery "routine" became something of a joke among lawyers, as well, who soon discovered that the fastest way to a divorce decree was presenting the evidence according to a formula.

Bored with it all, the formidable English justice, Sir Frank Douglas MacKinnon, once threw a spanner into the well-oiled works. During a typical divorce trial, the petitioner's lawyer would ask a hotel chambermaid to recall a particular couple she encountered during her work a year or two in the past, using what Justice MacKinnon called her "superhuman powers of observation and memory." The lawyer then would show "a blurred snapshot to the witness," who would affirm that it showed the adulterous spouse but that "the petitioner-wife who just left the [witness] box was not the woman." On one occasion, after the presentation of the usual evidence, Justice MacKinnon said to the wife's lawyer, "I am not sure if I can give you a decree [of divorce]. You have called the chambermaid to say her usual piece. She has said she saw them in bed. But she has not said she took them early morning tea. I thought that was a necessary incident in the depravity of adultery."

26 I'll see your virgin, and raise you one house-maid

Particularly cagey lawyers could turn the routine nature of the set-piece to their ultimate advantage. In 1866, Lord Campbell petitioned for a divorce on the ground that his wife had committed adultery with much of the society page — the Duke of Marlborough, the head of the London fire brigade, a general, a physician to the aristocracy. The wife fired a squib when she replied that Lord Campbell himself had slept with a housemaid. Lord Campbell's evidence showed that the housemaid was still a virgin. Then, however, Lady Campbell's lawyer, Sir Charles Russell, cross-examined her former personal maid, Rose Baer, a chief witness for Lord Campbell. Baer had testified in chief that when the wife and the Duke stayed overnight at a country house, in the morning Lady Campbell's double bed showed signs that two people had occupied it. Lord Russell got Baer to admit that Lady Campbell had fired her some four years before the divorce trial, and two years before Lord Campbell supposedly approached her to be a witness. Her evidence fell completely apart when she asked the court to believe that she had no idea how Lord Campbell knew where to find her, and that she agreed to testify without discussing with Lord Campbell why he was asking her to go to court as a witness. "So you agreed to give evidence," Lord Russell asked Baer, "without knowing what it was all about?" Without saying the words "revenge" or "collusion," Lord Russell had put them firmly in the court's mind.

27 And she was proceeding in a nor-r-rtherly die-rection

The related legalese was also formulaic, of course, to the point of parody. The English barrister and legal historian R.G. Hamilton offers two examples. In one case, the husband alleged that his wife abandoned him, which by the formula became "absconded from matrimonial cohabitation, and has never returned thereto." The wife's lawyer sent a "request for further and better particulars" specifying precisely "the manner of said absconsion." First she was a pedestrian, the husband's reply came, then she took the bus.

Hamilton's colleague Glyn Burrell formulaically claimed for a client that a certain couple "lived and cohabited and frequently committed adultery together." The opposing lawyer tendered a request for particulars, demanding to know whether the "period was continuous or intermittent." Burrell responded that cohabitation was continuous, but presumably the adultery was intermittent.

28 Modesty forbids fuller description

Predictably, the trumped-up divorce routine became a business when it migrated across the Atlantic. New York authorities prosecuted Henry Zeimer and W. Waldo Mason in 1900 for perverting the course of justice by paying young women to falsely claim adultery in court. Professor Friedman writes that the women would testify that they knew the plaintiff's husband, then blush, weep briefly, and "leave the rest to the judge."

29   These boots were made for judgin'

Typically, perhaps, F.E. Smith serves as the extreme case of lawyers in adulterous situations — extreme both because Smith was literally involved as home-wrecker, and was so notoriously cagey that he went on to become lord chancellor (the highest non-political justice official in Great Britain) despite the fact that he brained the enraged husband and supposedly murdered another man for accidentally insulting a lady. Assuming that the sundry canards about Smith — Lord Birkenhead — are even remotely credible, he made a habit of sailing close to gale-force winds. Tales of his courtroom daring as a barrister — at great risk to his clients one would have thought — have become legendary among lawyers. There was the day, for example, that a judge informed Smith that he had read Smith's materials and was "no wiser now than I was when I started." "Possibly not, m'lord," Smith is said to have replied, "but far better informed." According to William Camp, when Smith was a young circuit judge and was riding a Liverpool tram one day, he saw a man jostle a disembarking woman. He punched the man, who fell and hit his head on the pavement. The man soon died. Smith fled the country and while in Malta was caught *in flagrante delicto* by a paramour's husband. The enraged husband entered the bedroom brandishing a handgun and a knife. While the woman desperately pled not guilty, Smith retrieved a chamberpot from under the bed (the story goes) and slammed the pot over the husband's head. He then ran in his stocking-feet ("over cobblestones") to a ship, and arrived back in

England to discover that he was not to be prosecuted for the tramcar manslaughter. The moral of the story, Smith cavalierly said, was "never take your boots off when you're having fun with a woman."

30 Ignorance of the facts of life is no excuse

Since Adam ate the forbidden fruit, human ambivalence about the facts of life has led some people to commit unintentional adultery, in broad daylight and fully aware that they were having sexual intercourse with someone, as the law books put it, "not their spouse." In 1948, for instance, a Mrs. Barnacle alleged adultery against her husband and obtained a divorce decree. Then, the king's proctor (a Crown lawyer) discovered that Mrs. Barnacle herself had been living with a lover. Justice Wallington, the trial judge, berated her lawyer for being overly delicate with her and allowing her to persist in the delusion that she wasn't committing adultery unless she got pregnant in the process.

Justice Wallington fumed that it was high time that solicitors laid it on the line to their conveniently deluded clients. He was weary, himself, he complained, of hearing "well-educated and well-informed businessmen of forty and upwards" who thought it was adultery only if the woman was under 50. The proctor had informed him that past litigants also swore that adultery was "getting a girl in trouble," "drinking with men in public houses," and possible only after sunset.

A jury in an 1836 lawsuit for criminal conversation — in which the wronged spouse sues his partner's lover for ruining the marriage — refused to believe that adultery could take place on a public pathway during daylight, not to mention in a library under circumstances carefully sidestepped in the case report. But when the case was appealed, the reviewing court could not restrain itself from ordering a new trial, considering that the defendant lover, a lawyer, had been found hiding in a closet in the plaintiff husband's house, coming and going at odd hours (sometimes with his boots off), and spending half an hour in a stable with the plaintiff's wife.

Four years before *Barnacle*, Justice Wallington himself refused to believe that adultery was possible in the cab of a truck. He denied the husband a divorce based on the wife's adultery in such circumstances. When the husband appealed, Lord Greene took exception to Justice Wallington's deduction that because the alleged adulterers disappeared from view they had ended up on the cab floor. Lord Greene agreed that anything approaching genuine adultery would have been impossible down there, but added that Justice Wallington perhaps should have resisted falling back "on his own knowledge of the layout and dimensions of the cabs of lorries." "Their disappearance from view," Lord Greene wrote of the alleged adulterers, "was clearly consistent with their bodies being supported in a semi-recumbent position by parts of the seat next to the driver's seat." Considering the couple's "long history of passionate intimacy, . . . there was no element of unfamiliarity or reluctance to contend with. . . . They could have overcome such inconveniences as existed." Therefore, Lord Greene could not, himself, believe that the wife had gone to the truck merely to ask the defendant to stop spreading rumors about them, and then passed the time of day discussing chickens and tomatoes with him.

In another English case six years after *Barnacle*, Justice Karminski played it even safer. "Nobody yet attempted to define adultery," he observed, "and I do not propose to rush in where wiser men have not." All the same, "manual satisfaction" — masturbation — was not adultery, his lordship held, no matter how offended a wife might feel about what her husband and mistress were doing.

These two lines of judicial embarrassment merged, as it were, as late as 1984, when a woman in Toronto was charged with performing an indecent act by masturbating a man with her breasts in the front seat of a truck. But the prosecution was forced to withdraw the charge when the judge found that even this was impossible. "The only way she could perform an act of masturbation," he told a skeptical assistant crown attorney, "is to use her hand."

"Well, your honor," the prosecutor replied, "in my respectful submission, the hand and the breast are just two different parts of the body and the act of masturbation could take place using either."

The judge admitted that there was some sense to this, but then considered the evidence that the woman had draped herself over the man, who had lain on the seat and rubbed himself against her. "There is nothing in the information read to me that indicates that she performed any act," the judge decided, "except being there."

31 The affair that launched a thousand quips

The dangers of this sort of presumption — a species of what lawyers call judicial notice, an exemption from the usual rules of evidence which permits the judge to rely on his own knowledge (without expert assistance) about something that is widely recognized — are more soberly demonstrated by the spat between British justices McCardie, a trial judge, and Lord Scrutton of the English Court of Appeal. In 1932, Justice McCardie held that 67-year-old Charles Searle, a Cambridge physician, was liable to John Place, a 33-year-old grocer's assistant, for stealing — the legal phrase was "enticing and persuading away" — the affections of Place's wife, Gwendoline. Searle accomplished this, Place said, during four to five years' worth of intimate weekly dinners. This ended in fisticuffs between the men, upon which Gwendoline drove off with Searle, never to return.

On appeal, Lord Scrutton overruled Justice McCardie, holding that, to succeed in his lawsuit for enticement and persuading away, Place was not obliged "to show that the will of his wife" was "overborne by the stronger will" of Searle. It was sufficient that Searle persuaded Gwendoline away without undue influence or coercion. Lord Scrutton represented the whole dispute as a ridiculous attempt to refight the Trojan War, but over an unworthy Helen — a sordid little time-waster for the courts. His fulminations extended to Justice McCardie for relying on extra-legal "sociological knowledge" in reaching his decision in Searle's favor. In lines deleted from the published reports of Lord Scrutton's ruling, he remarked: "If there is to be a discussion of the relationship of husbands and wives, I think it would come better from judges who have more than theoretical knowledge of husbands and wives. I am [a] little surprised that a gentleman who has never been married should, as he has done in another case, proceed to explain the proper underclothing that ladies should wear."

McCardie was unmarried, all right, but it became clear after he shot himself dead the next year that he had large gambling debts, kept a mistress in the country, and a London aristocrat — "a titled lady" — claimed she carried his child. In short, he was a man of the world. For a brief time between the appeal in *Place* and Justice McCardie's death, he refused to supply his files to any panel of the Court of Appeal on which Lord Scrutton sat.

32 The best-laid schemes of Scottish divorce lawyers

Neither does adultery connote that only adults can do it: the term referred, originally, to adulteration of the cuckold's bloodline. In a groundbreaking 1958 case, the Scottish Court of Sessions noted this while still refusing to believe that adultery could include artificial insemination — procreation without sex. The presiding judge, Lord Wheatley, thought that to hold otherwise would father horror and loathing. Ronald George Maclennan had not had "access," as Lord Wheatley put it, to his wife Margaret Euphemia from May 31, 1954 on. All the same, she had a child 14 months later, on July 10, 1955. But when Ronald sued, Margaret denied adultery outright. She had been inseminated artificially, she said, with the seed of someone she didn't even know, and that was not adultery at law. Undeterred, Ronald replied, "Adultery is adultery, including with a syringe."

Reviewing the authorities from Moses to the *All England Law Reports*, Lord Wheatley disagreed. "The idea of *conjunctio corporum* [bodily intercourse] seems to be an inherent concomitant" of adultery, he ruled. "The idea that adultery might be committed by a woman alone in the privacy of her bedroom, aided and abetted only by a syringe containing semen, was one with which the earlier jurists had no occasion to wrestle." Precedent showed that a woman could be impregnated by "alien" seed without committing adultery. There were, for example, two English cases where the courts annulled marriages for non-consummation, despite the fact that children were born of the relationships. In the first case, the wife had become pregnant by artificial insemination with her husband's semen. In the second, penetration had been frustrated, but not fertilization.

Still, while "unilateral adultery is possible," Lord Wheatley decided, "as in the case of a married man who ravishes a woman not his wife, . . . self-adultery is a conception unknown to the law" — even with a consenting syringe. Otherwise, Lord Wheatley wondered, where a physician assisted the artificial insemination, was he to be a co-respondent in an adultery action (and therefore subject to an action for criminal conversation)? Was the donor an adulterer? What if the donor died? Then, Lord Wheatley said, the woman would not only be an adulteress, but a necrophiliac. No, the judge said, adultery was not simply adulteration of the genetic line, but "the physical contact with an alien and unlawful sexual organ." A fine romance.

33   When he was bad, he was really bad

Other attempts at innovative "family" litigation have spurred similar fears about expanding liability for sperm donors and non-relatives generally, concerns that the term "extended family" could be stretched beyond sense. In early 2001, residents of Toronto, Canada, awoke to learn that their mayor, Mel Lastman, had participated in a 14-year secret affair with his former office assistant. Lastman is a Canadian version of New York's Ed Koch — an uncomplicated man previously notorious for his hair-weave and as the Bad Boy, after the chain of discount furniture stores that made his fortune. (As one of the first self-made entrepreneurs to feature himself in advertising for his own business, Lastman built his political career partly by shouting "No-o-o-body" in television commercials which asked "Who's better than Bad Boy?") The affair with Grace Louie lasted from 1957 to 1971, while both Louie and Lastman were married. Until 1974, Louie contended that Lastman had fathered two of her sons, now 42 and 39. Then, in exchange for $27,500 ($25,000 as a one-time payment, and $2,500 for Louie's legal fees), she signed a release agreeing not to sue Lastman or claim any blood relationship between him and the boys. Although Louie raised the boys to believe that her husband was their father (Lastman being styled as an avuncular family friend who paid the rent for a while and brought them gifts), in 2001, 30 years after the affair ended, she decided to go public by suing Lastman for his purported failure to provide support for her and the boys while he and his family lived extravagantly. The sons brought a similar lawsuit, but both were dismissed before Lastman even filed a defense.

By the time she sued, Toronto, already Canada's largest city, had doubled in size and Lastman had become the new megacity's first mayor. Grace Louie repudiated the release, saying that she signed it in desperation, coerced by Lastman, while she was disabled from working and after a five-year separation from her husband. She argued that, in the circumstances, the release was invalid as "unconscionable."

When the case was in its earliest stages, the court accepted Louie's assertions that she and her sons lived in poverty — that, in fact, the boys had to leave school to help support her — while the entire city marveled at the Lastman family's conspicuous consumption, having seen home videos on news shows of son Dale's bar mitzvah, which looked less like a religious confirmation than the coronation of an African potentate. But Mary Jane Benotto, the judge hearing the motion to strike out the Louies' lawsuits, rejected all of their claims as having "no hope of success" at trial. The Louies were attempting to claim "retroactive child support," Justice Benotto ruled — they were trying to convert a legal scheme meant to provide for dependant children into "a weapon" to collect unrelated damages decades after the fact, when Grace was 68 and the "boys" were middle-aged men. Justice Benotto pointed out that the lawsuits bizarrely implied that Lastman had "a *duty* to contradict" Grace Louie's choices not to tell her sons about the mayor 20 or 30 years earlier. The judge specifically rejected the sons' claim that "the very fact that Mr. Lastman 'participated in the act of procreation' creates a fiduciary relationship" — a close connection with them in which Lastman had a parental-like duty to protect their interests. To accept such a claim would mean that "every parent who placed a child for adoption would be in an ongoing fiduciary relationship with the child and liable in damages for breach of fiduciary duties. So too would a sperm donor, an egg donor and others who participate in procreation." Of course, this has turned out to be no idle anxiety: several suits have been launched in the U.S. where grown children claim damages against their parents for raising them improperly and causing them to fail as adults — for breaching a fiduciary obligation of parenthood.

34   The scarlet letter wasn't that bad, after all

As noted elsewhere in this volume, some Islamist states still punish adultery with Biblical or Koranic severity, sanctioning death (by stoning or beheading), at least if the adulterers are caught in the act. Less bloody-minded interpretations of Islamic law provide that adultery is proved only if four men witness it and the accused person confesses of her own will. Stricter interpretations hold that any pregnancy outside marriage is proof of the offense.

The Puritan pilgrims to America sometimes regarded adultery as a capital crime. In 1644, for example, the Massachusetts Bay Colony hanged adulterers Mary Latham and James Britton after Mary boasted of playing away on her elderly husband. But even in such a censorious time and place, compassion occasionally insinuated itself, compelling juries to acquit the clearly guilty, and firmly establishing the "jury nullification" that is now so popular on American television shows when the writers can't think how else to get sympathetic defendants out of jail. Perhaps sensing the popular reluctance, the colonies often sentenced adulterers to be "sett upon the gallows ... with a Rope about their necks," the rope's far end being tied to the gallows. Following this public display for an hour or so, the convicts were "severely whipt" and, in New Hampshire, they were obliged "for ever after [to] weare a Capitall Letter A of two inches long and proportionable in Bignesse, cutt out in Cloath of a contrary Colour to their Cloaths and Sewed upon their Upper Garments, on the out Side of their Arme or on their Back in open View."

Despite the so-called sexual revolution and a sex-based economy — sex is big business, itself, as well as the basis on which most products, from cola to couches to Cadillacs, are marketed — some American states remain harshly punitive, if not actually homicidal, about adultery. As recently as 2000, the North Carolina Court of Appeals upheld actions brought by jilted wives for criminal conversation. In a notorious case a year earlier, Dorothy Hutelmyer claimed that she had a "fairytale marriage" until Margie Cox left her own husband and went for Dorothy's spouse Joseph. Dorothy presented evidence that Joseph had written her love poems, went to church with her, and coached children's soccer during their 18-year marriage. Then Cox's marriage broke up and, where once Cox had dressed in a "matronly" way around the office, she became "openly flirtatious" with co-worker Joseph and "spent increasingly more time alone" with him. "Defendant's [Cox's] co-workers testified that she changed her appearance. She cut and dyed her hair and wore short skirts, low-cut blouses, and tight clothing to the office," displaying her legs over the arm of a chair in Joseph's office. Hutelmyer left Dorothy and eventually married Cox. The appeal court upheld a jury award to Dorothy of $500,000 compensatory damages plus another $500,000 in punitive damages against Cox, for alienation of affection and criminal conversation.

In other jurisdictions, Dorothy might have received something like these compensatory damages through division of family property when her marriage collapsed. But punitive damages arising from adulterous relationships are unusual, and probably hypocritical given the time and place. The appeals court justified them on the ground that "the evidence tended to show that defendant publicly displayed the intimate nature of her relationship" with Hutelmyer by holding hands with him at work. As well, she "frequently straightened Mr. Hutelmyer's ties and brushed lint from his suits at business functions. Another co-worker testified that in 1994, during a work outing at a Putt-Putt [miniature golf] facility, defendant stood very close to plaintiff's husband and ate ice out of his drinking cup." Worse, Cox's neighbors snitched that she "welcomed plaintiff's husband into her home at all hours of the day and night, despite her knowledge of the harm that their relationship would cause his wife and three young children" and she traveled with Hutelmyer on the business trips he once shared with Dorothy.

35 Too many hotheads

More notoriously, the law has been merciful to men who kill their wives and lovers during "in-the-act" adultery. In 1716, William Hawkins stated the law as it still exists in many jurisdictions: if a spouse discovers *in flagrante* adultery and gets the irresistible urge to attack, he (and now she) will be guilty of manslaughter and not murder. However, according to Blackstone in 1769,

> *if there be a sufficient cooling-time for passion to subside and reason to interpose, and the person so provoked afterwards kills the other, this is deliberate revenge and not heat of blood, and accordingly amounts to murder. So, if a man takes another in the act of adultery with his wife, and kills him directly upon the spot, though this was allowed by the law of Solon as likewise by the Roman civil law (if the adulterer was found in the husband's own house) and also among the ancient Goths, yet in England it is not absolutely ranked in the class of justifiable homicide, as in the case of a forcible rape, but it is manslaughter. It is however the lowest degree of it: and therefore in such a case the court directed the burning in the hand to be gently inflicted, because there could not be a greater provocation.*

The 1683 prosecution of John Maddy led Blackstone to this deduction that dispatching your wife's fancy man is not a serious homicide. Upon surprising Frank Mavers in bed with Mrs. Maddy, Maddy brained him with a stool. The British Court of King's Bench accepted Maddy's plea of provocation and convicted him of manslaughter instead of murder. Then, accepting Maddy's plea of clergy (a plea for mercy, originally available only to clerics, but eventually extended to anyone who was literate), the judges released him after directing "the executioner to burn [his thumb] gently, because there could be no greater provocation than this." As you could "plead your clergy" only once in a lifetime, authorities branded Maddy to mark the fact that he now had a criminal record but was "in mercy." But they did it "gently," on the presumption that he already had suffered enough.

In most places where Anglo-American law applies, Blackstone's proviso to the provocation defense, that the aggrieved spouse kills "on the sudden and before his passion had time to cool," is essential. Section 232(2) of the current Canadian *Criminal Code*, for example, says that "a wrongful act or insult that is of such a nature as to be sufficient to deprive an ordinary person of the power of self-control is provocation enough ... if the accused acted on it on the sudden and before there was time for his passion to cool." Otherwise, any such defense could *encourage* adultery, as where a latter-day Maddy suspects adultery but says nothing or even facilitates a tryst so that he can do away with the illicit lovers. (See, for example, the *Burger* case below.) Some statutes, however, have proved even more "compassionate," at least to cuckolds. Until quite recently, legislation in Utah, New Mexico, and Texas said that it was justifiable homicide — completely excusable, in other words — to kill at least the interloper when you came upon him in the act with your spouse.

Article 1102 of The Texas *Penal Code*, repealed in 1973, stated that "a homicide is justifiable when committed by the husband upon the person of any one taken in the act of adultery with the wife; provided the killing take place before the parties to the act of adultery have separated." The result of such state-sanctioned self-help was that a Texas husband (not a wife) could get away with murder on discovering *in flagrante* adultery, but not with "mere" mayhem. In 1922, a Texan named Sensobaugh caught his wife and her lover in compromising circumstances. He "pulled a gun" on the man and tied him up, specifically telling him that he didn't want to kill him. Instead, he cut off the man's penis with a razor, for which mercy the Dallas County Court convicted him of criminal assault.

Sensobaugh appealed, claiming that article 1102 provided him a defense. If you could kill someone for having sex with your wife, why couldn't you simply make a gelding of the same rogue stallion? The Court of Criminal Appeals admitted that if only Sensobaugh had ended the lover's life, or at least cut off his genitals with the intent to make him bleed to death, the law would probably have held him blameless. But this was a case of cold-blooded forbearance, a fate for Sensobaugh, if not the lover, worse than death. The appeals court affirmed his fine of $300 and jail sentence of 60 days.

In jurisdictions where statutes do not condone homicide during adulterous provocation, juries have occasionally moved beyond *Maddy's Case*, finding an avenging cuckold not guilty even of manslaughter. For a time, even Georgia's judges interpreted statutory criminal law so as to make adulterous provocation a complete defense (i.e., a defense leading to an acquittal), in the mould of self-defence: "A killing to prevent the beginning or the completion of an adulterous act," one court ruled in 1948, "is justifiable homicide under the law." The Georgia statute did not provide the defense explicitly, and even the judicial or "unwritten" law did not permit the killing of the wife: "Killing the lover to prevent adultery could be justifiable homicide to protect the marriage," another Georgia court reasoned as late as 1977, "though killing the spouse could not be justifiable because it would terminate the marriage."

In the 1977 case, *Burger*, the cuckolded husband had spied on his wife and her paramour for some time. Waiting one day until they were engaged in flagrantly compromising behavior, he shot both of them. The court called his plea of justifiable homicide an "absurd and dangerous" judicial creation, and concluded: "In this day of no-fault, on-demand divorce when adultery is merely a misdemeanor, and when there is a debate raging in the country about whether capital punishment even for the most heinous crimes is proper, any idea that a spouse is ever justified in taking the life of another — adulterous spouse or illicit lover — to prevent adultery is uncivilized. This is murder; and henceforth, nothing more appearing, an instruction of justifiable homicide may not be given."

36   Imagine what happens if you play a Mormon

In 2001, Egypt passed a law requiring actors to divorce their "real-life spouses" in order to play a married person in films. The law also stipulates that, following production of the film, the actor must divorce the screen spouse and remarry the former real-life spouse.

37   'Til death or a buyer with the asking price do us part

From the Middle Ages to the 19th century, there was something of a master-servant view of the relationship between husband and wife. It was not much of a leap to the popular belief that married women themselves could be subjects of a contract — that they could be treated, as the modern phrase goes, "as objects," chattel and cattle.

In an infamous case from 1302, Sir William Paynel produced a contract for the purchase of his "wife," in an attempt to claim the dower due her — the one-third share of property that became payable to her on her original or "true" husband's death. ("Community property" of roughly 50 percent per spouse is an idea whose time only recently has come.) Paynel had bought Margaret Commoys from her husband John some time before. The bill of sale read:

> *To all the faithful and Christ &c., John Commoys sendeth greeting: Know that I have delivered and committed of my free-will to the Lord William Paynel, Knt., Margaret of Commoys my wife, and*

have also given and granted, and to the said William released and quit-claimed, all the goods and chattels which the said Margaret has, or hereafter, may have: and also whatever belongs to me of the goods and chattels of the said Margaret with their appurtenances, so that neither I, or any other person in my name, can or ought to exact or claim the goods or chattels of the said Margaret with their appurtenances forever: I will and grant, and by these presents confirm, that the said Margaret shall be and remain with the said Lord William, according to the will of the said William.

In language and effect, the document was a deed, just like one for the sale of a house or barn. Sir William and Margaret seem also to have presented the king's court with certificates from the Archbishop of Canterbury and the Bishop of Chichester attesting that they had defeated charges of adultery (that is, allegations that Margaret was already married while having relations with Sir William) in ecclesiastical court by calling compurgators, witnesses that vouched for the truth of the couple's claim that they lived innocently as man and wife. The judges nonetheless found the two to be adulterers, and declared that "William and Margaret do take nothing by their petition but be in mercy [in danger of criminal prosecution or execution] for their false claims."

In 1768, the "consideration" in another such transaction, a woman named Ann Parsons, produced the contract for the sale of her own person, asking the court to stop her husband John from harassing her and her "buyer." "For the support of his extravagancy," she petitioned, John Parsons, clothmaker, had sold her "with all right, property, claim, services, and demands whatsoever" to John Tooker, gentleman. The contract price was £6.6s., something like $11 U.S. reckoned at today's exchange rate. But the modest price and rise in social stature were apparently not the only considerations in Ann's firm transfer of loyalty. Within three months of the sale, John

Parsons had turned up at John Tooker's door, demanding more money and threatening Tooker and Ann with death.

In other words, there was long, sad legal precedent for the fateful wife-auction in the opening pages of Thomas Hardy's *The Mayor of Casterbridge*, when Michael Henchard, drunk on spiked mead and in a reckless fit of youthful macho, sells his wife Susan at a country fair for five guineas — £5.5s (about $9). Hardy based the sale on two reports he had found in the *Dorset County Chronicle*, Casterbridge being his pseudonym for the English town of Dorchester:

> *25 May 1826:* SALE OF WIFE: *Man in Brighton led a tidy looking woman up to one of the stalls in the market, with a halter round her neck, and offered her for sale. The woman has two children by her husband — one of whom he consents to keep. The other he throws in as a makeweight to the bargain.*

> *6 December 1827: At Buckland near Frome, a labouring man named Charles Pearce sold his wife to shoemaker Elton for £5 and delivered her in a halter in the public street. She seemed very willing. Bells rang.*

The price for a wife could be nominal, sometimes as little as a pint of local ale. Stranger still, the "delivery up" of the woman in a halter was conventional, the parties evidently believing that this lent some formal validity to the transaction — the way in medieval times a conveyance of land was sealed by the exchange of a clod or twig from the land sold. Susan Henchard's belief in the legal propriety of wife-selling was established folk wisdom, so widespread that the parties not only frequently made such sales at market stalls, in the same way they dealt with cows and pigs, but even paid tax on them to government regulators. By the time Hardy wrote of the practice, it had become almost banal. A "shipping news" item in the edition of the *Times* for March 30, 1796 reads,

> *On Saturday evening last, John Lees, steel-burner, sold his wife for the small sum of sixpence to Samuel Hall, fellmonger [a seller of hides], both of Sheffield. Lees gave Hall one guinea immediately to have her taken off to Manchester the day following by the coach: She was delivered up with an halter round her neck, and the clerk of the market received fourpence for toll. It would be well if some law was inforced to put a stop to such degrading traffic!!*

Judging by a similar report a year later, little heed was paid the concluding editorial remark:

> *On Friday a butcher exposed his wife to sale in Smithfield market, near the Ram Inn, with a halter about her neck and one about her waist, which tied her to a railing, when a hog-driver was the happy purchaser, who gave the husband three guineas and a crown for his departed rib. Pity it is there is no stop to such depraved conduct in the lower order of people.*

There is no record of the *Times* ever calling the same sort of flesh-trading among high society and royalty "depraved conduct." According to an *Observer* report for July 23, 1797, a blacksmith from a village near Leeds had sold his *pregnant* wife for two guineas to a man he claimed was the child's "real father." This was done, "agreeably to an engagement drawn up by an attorney for that purpose."

38 The undivided ancient estate known as Mary Howard

Not altogether surprisingly, the Wild West yields its own example of such a transaction, or a proposed one, although it seems more a deed of gift (not a contract, because one party gets something for nothing) than an offer to sell. It includes the word "bargain," but perhaps only in a reckless sense, on the cruel premise that there would be no takers for anything but an outright give-away. The document, which a British law journal has called "A Precedent from America," was originally published in June, 1861 in Colorado, having been witnessed by the Clerk of the District Court there:

> *Know all men (and women) by these presents that I, John Howard of Canon City of the first part, do hereby give, grant, bargain, convey, and quit claim all my right title, and interest in and to the following (un)real estate, to wit: The undivided ancient estate known as Mary Howard, the title of which I acquired by discovery, occupation, possession, and use, situate at present in the town of Denver, Jefferson Territory, together with all the improvements, made and erected by me thereon, with all rents, profits, easements, enjoyments, long suffering, and appurtenances thereto in any wise appertaining, unto _____, of the second part; to have and to hold unto the _____, so long as he can keep her without recourse upon the grantee [sic?], as endorser.*

The offer was probably drawn in the spirit of Mark Twain rather than earnest. The "grantor," John Howard (evidently misnamed as "grantee" in the deed), had reason to know that it was not legally binding. He was a judge.

CHAPTER THREE

BEYOND MARRIAGE AND THE MISSIONARY POSITION

"If it weren't for pickpockets I'd have no sex life at all."

RODNEY DANGERFIELD

39 Tragic by any name

Whether there is a distinction between sodomy and buggery has been a vexed, and sometimes tragic, question for judges. In 1718, one Wiseman, the master of the Kent workhouse (a debtor's prison), had anal intercourse with one of his 11-year-old charges. He was charged with buggery, but several of the judges thought that buggery was possible only between males, at least under the English criminal statute of the day. One of the judges, Fortescue Aland, whose own report documents the case, disagreed and felt "exceeding sorry that such a gross offence should escape without any punishment in England when it is a crime punishable with death and burning at a stake, all over the world besides."

Justice Fortescue Aland wrote to the Lord Chancellor, the Earl of Macclesfield, who replied "that he wondered at the variety of opinions; that he had not the least hesitation in agreeing it to be plain sodomy" the same as if the poor child had been a male. "The difference of the subject only makes it more inexcusable."

"The word buggery made use of, is not a term of art appropriated to the common law," Justice Fortescue Aland concludes, "but the punishment is provided, because of its being a vice so detestable and abominable, and against nature. Buggery with the most filthy, or the most dreadful creature, is buggery, tho' never so unlikely to be committed, and though the lawgivers had thought it impossible it ever should be committed. Besides the unnatural abuse of a woman seems worse than either that of a man or a beast; for it seems a more direct affront to the Author of Nature, and a more insolent expression of contempt of His wisdom, condemning the provision made by Him, and defying both it and Him."

"Buggery is an Italian word," Fortescue Aland continues, "and comes from *bugeriare,* to commit unnatural sin." The modern view is that it derives from *Bulgarus,* meaning Bulgarian, by way of a Bulgarian sect of Albigenses. Western Europeans apparently regarded the sect as heretics who practiced sodomy. In any event, Justice Fortescue Aland notes that both the Greeks and Romans "made use of girls" in this way, and that the Latin phrase *venus postica* — "love from the rear" — "hints at this very case." In the result, the court found that buggery was just a "species" of sodomy, that Wiseman was guilty of the crime charged, and that the appropriate penalty was death.

40   Not in the dictionary

In the late 1800s, Ohio law defined sodomy as "carnal copulation in any opening of the body, except sexual parts, with another human being, or with a beast," and stipulated a maximum penitentiary term of 20 years in the breach. But what of cunnilingus? That was the question before the Indiana Supreme Court on Halloween, 1923. The prosecution charged Benny Young with conspiracy to breach a state law against "the abominable and detestable crime against nature with mankind or beast." The statute defined such behavior, along with enticing minors to masturbate, as sodomy.

The state might have argued that cunnilingus was a form of masturbation, and therefore amounted to sodomy under the Indiana law, but the court ruled that it was sodomy under the statute no matter what the dictionary or the common (judge-made) law said. The statute's purpose, the court ruled, "was to strengthen the law prohibiting unnatural sexual practices. . . . To that end the words 'masturbation or self-pollution' were chosen by the legislature to define the evil intended to be corrected."

Young attempted to point out that the female involved was willing and that the act in question was consummated, such that there was no "conspiracy." This has the rather bizarre air of asking to be tried for a more serious offense — doing it instead of planning it — on the desperate off-chance, perhaps, that the court will say you can't be tried twice on the same facts, even for different crimes. In any event, the court said that it was up to the state, not Young, to select the charge.

The issue remains a live one in Utah, apparently, but framed in an ultramodern fashion: at this writing, Derrick Sundquist, of American Fork, is arguing that a state sodomy law forbidding him from having oral sex with his 16-year-old girlfriend violates his constitutional right to free expression. Sundquist was 19 when authorities charged him with misdemeanor sodomy, which in Utah carries a maximum penalty of a $1,000 fine and six months in jail. Utah permits 16-year-olds to have consensual sex with a person who is no more than four years older, but outlaws sodomy altogether among the unmarried.

41   The more things change . . .

In *Wiseman* (number 39), Justice Fortescue Aland notes that if the Saxons convicted a man of buggery, they buried him alive. As late as 1929 the word *buggerall*, meaning "nothing," was just as rude among Saxon descendants as *fuck all* (meaning the same thing) remains today in polite company. Dylan Thomas managed to get it past BBC censors that year, however, disguised as the Welsh village of Llareggub in his *Under Milk Wood*. Today Britons affectionately call their own children "the little buggers," and *buggerall* has become everyday language on television. But *plus ça change*: recently the Taliban government in Afghanistan adopted the Saxon approach, which they contended was the proper penalty for sodomy under Islamic law (*sharia*). For months, religious authorities debated the appropriate punishment of homosexuals. Did the *Koran* require that sodomites be thrown from cliffs, or was it from buildings? The mullahs decided that *sharia* required collapsing a wall on the convicts as they lay in a trench. When too many convicts survived this treatment, the mullahs amended the law to permit the executioners to drive bulldozers over the collapsed wall. Nigerian authorities say that *sharia* requires stoning for such crimes.

42   The love that dare not speak its name

Oscar Wilde's 1895 prosecution for homosexuality produced a poetic and notorious euphemism for his sexual predilection. Wilde rashly sued the Marquis of Queensbury, the father of Wilde's lover, Sir Alfred Douglas, alleging that the marquis libeled him by accusing him of "posing as a somdomite" [*sic*]. As one British critic noted, this merely added injury to insult — "the man who has more brains in his little finger than all the rest of them in their whole body goes and commits worse than suicide in this way." Wilde recklessly ignored that stating a truth, no matter how damaging, is a defense to a libel allegation. In the course of proving that Wilde was a "sodomite" with a penchant for working-class boys, Queensbury provided Crown prosecutors with enough evidence to put Wilde away for two years of hard labor on the treadmill at Reading Gaol. During cross-examination in the criminal trial, Wilde asserted:

> *The 'love that dare not speak its name' in this century is such a great affection of an elder for a younger man as there was between David and Jonathan, such as Plato made the very basis of his philosophy, and such as you find in the sonnets of Michelangelo and Shakespeare. It is that deep, spiritual affection that is as pure as it is perfect. It dictates and pervades great works of art like those of Shakespeare and Michelangelo. . . . It is in this century misunderstood, so much misunderstood that it may be described as 'the love that dare not speak its name,' and on account of it I am placed where I am now. It is beautiful, it is fine, it is the noblest form of affection. There is nothing unnatural about it. It is intellectual, and it repeatedly exists between an elder and a younger man, where the elder has intellect and the younger man has all the joy, hope, and glamour of life before him. That it should be so, the world does not understand. The world mocks at it and sometimes puts one in the pillory for it.*

Homosexuality remained a crime until 1967 in Britain, and a barrier to certain high offices long after. On discovering that a male magistrate dressed as a woman in public, the lord chancellor asked for the judge's resignation. Although transvestism was not illegal, the chancellor's office reasoned that the judge's couturial predilections could weaken public confidence in the administration of justice.

43 The beast within

Prosecutions for bestiality have a long history in Anglo-American and civil law. In the 17th century, some Puritans believed that birth defects in livestock constituted evidence of the crime. Early colonists in New Haven, Connecticut, for example, accused Thomas Hogg of sexual intercourse with a sow which caused the animal to bear a "monstrous" piglet. The magistrates conducted him to the sty in question and ordered him to "scratch at" two sows there. The piglet's mother responded with what the magistrates interpreted as "lust," sealing Hogg's fate: death by hanging.

In 1642, authorities at Plymouth charged Thomas Granger, a boy of about 17, with buggery of "a mare, a cow, two goats, five sheep, two calves and a turkey." Granger was hanged and the poor animals were slaughtered, which practice itself had long, and idiotic, legal precedent. In the name of European Christianity during the Middle Ages and Renaissance, cows were racked for "confessions." If men buggered helpless mares or asses, the animal routinely suffered the same fate as the bugger, usually by being burned at the stake or buried alive. In some cases, the animal was first mutilated. In France in 1572, a legal opinion was published that, while criminals were normally to be delivered completely naked to the hangman, it was not unlawful for a criminal pig to be led to its death with a rope leash on its neck.[1] Thirty-one years later, Massachusetts sentenced Benjamin Goad to hang for the "unnatural and horrid act of Bestiallitie on a mare in the highway or field," as "instigated by the Divill" at two o'clock in the afternoon. The court also stipulated "that the mare you abused before your execution in your sight shall be knockt on the head."

During 1692 in West New Jersey, one Mary Myers and a group of children said they saw a black slave "ride upon a cow," which responded with "the usuall Motions of Cows when they had taken

---

[1] Considering what humans have done to the planet they claim God gave them to cherish for their dominion, one can't help but agree with the Brazilian lawyer appointed in the 18th century to defend some termites, "praising the industry of his clients, the white ants, and declaring them to be in this respect far superior to their prosecutors, the Grey Friars."

the Bull." A jury convicted the man of buggery and the judge sentenced both him and the cow to death.

44 Aberrant possibilities

Back in the motherland, in 1889 a man named Brown stood charged with attempting to commit unnatural offenses with "a domestic fowl," namely, a duck. Brown admitted the offense at the Essex assizes, and the Chief Justice of England, Lord Coleridge, sentenced him to 12 months at hard labor. Later, someone advised Lord Coleridge that a man in an earlier case had been acquitted of the same offense on the grounds that a duck was not an animal and therefore the offense as charged could not be proved. Lord Coleridge convened a judicial panel to consider the question, and several of the judges said they had heard of the earlier acquittal. It rested, apparently, on the conclusion that it was physically impossible for a human to "have connection" with a duck, not on the duck's legal status as an animal. If it was impossible to have sex with a duck, it was also impossible to attempt to have sex with a duck.

The evidence in Brown's case, however, was that he had regularly attempted the act, and that his yard was littered with "torn and bleeding" birds and duck corpses. In the end, at its highest (as judges like to say) *Brown* stands for nothing more definite than a duck is legally an animal, and even if "connection" with a duck is impossible, it is possible to attempt connection with a duck. In other words, Brown was guilty as charged.

45 Yet more "manual satisfaction"

The *Cooper* bestiality case is considerably less lurid, but you might say it gave new meaning to the phrase "Free Willy." In this instance, however, the mammal was a dolphin, not a whale, and his name was

Freddie. At the time of the alleged offence, in September, 1991, Freddie was lying on his back in the waters off Amble, in northern England, allegedly in a sort of trance or ecstasy.

And there were a lot of allegedlies to follow. Those making the allegations were members of a boating party. They testified in Newcastle-Upon-Tyne Crown Court that they saw Alan Cooper, a 38-year-old Manchester gardener, use his knees, swimming fins, and gloved hands to masturbate the 12-foot bottlenose for 20 minutes. The boaters cut their voyage short and went to the police . . . two days later. The police arrested Cooper . . . three months later.

Cooper, it turned out, was a long-time familiar of dolphins. He regularly swam with Freddie and had made it his "mission to see that captive dolphins are returned to their natural home in the open sea." It also turned out that one of the boating party was an arch-enemy, Peter Bloom, the manager of the Flamingoland "dolphinarium," which Cooper had been trying to close down. Bloom told the jury that people rubbing up dolphins could leave the sea creatures sexually frustrated, causing them to become aggressive against other people. Cooper told the press that Bloom had a vendetta against him.

Apparently the expert evidence created considerable doubt in the jury as to whether Cooper had, as the Crown alleged, committed "an act of a lewd, obscene and disgusting nature and outraging public decency by behaving in an indecent manner with a dolphin to the great disgust and annoyance of divers of Her Majesty's subjects within whose purview such act was committed." The presiding judge, and even the Crown, accepted defense evidence that dolphins have permanently rigid penises which they flip out of their abdomens at will "like a flick-knife." They often unsheathe themselves for perfectly non-sexual explorations of objects around them. One hears this same defense from subway *frotteurs*, of course, but in the *Cooper* case the Crown and court agreed that, as a sign of non-sexual conviviality, dolphins commonly use their penises to tow human divers by the arm or leg, for a non-sexual group swim.

Concerning such behavior in Freddie, Cooper had consulted dolphin expert Horace Dobbs. Dobbs advised, "It is extending the finger of friendship and should not be rejected." Dobbs told the court that he had seen Freddie "catch fish with his mouth, throw it in the air and catch it on his penis." This inspired defense counsel Anthony Jennings to caution the jury that it should not use human standards to determine what dolphins did with their willies: "Men do not use their penis to push the supermarket trolley," Jennings said in his closing address to the eight women and four men. "They do not use it to greet each other, apart from perhaps after a large amount of alcohol and a vindaloo on a Friday night."

Apparently counsel could track down only two other cases of outraging public decency. One case was that of a man swimming naked, without dolphins. The other was a case of wife-selling, and even then, the law reports made only very brief reference to it, an aside in a prosecution for assigning a girl into an apprenticeship for an immoral purpose. The jury acquitted Cooper, after the Crown spent nearly £34,000 to prosecute him.

46   Presumably it's short for "zoophile"

Seventy-one-year-old Frank Buble claimed that his son Philip's practice of what Philip called "zoo" finally drove him over the edge in September, 1999. The two men lived together at Frank's home in Parkman, Maine. On the morning in question, as 44-year-old Philip stepped out of the shower, Frank attacked him with a crowbar. Frank was disgusted beyond further tolerance, he said, by Philip's failure to keep up his end on the household chores, and by his sexual relationship with his dog. He admitted that he had wanted to kill Philip. Fortunately, Philip suffered only cuts and a broken arm. Frank turned himself into police and, in return for the district attorney's agreement to drop attempted murder charges, he pled guilty to aggravated assault.

Philip spoke up on his father's behalf, suggesting that he needed "serious therapy," but that a prison term would be too harsh. He added that his love for his dog was pure, and that he felt persecuted because of his defensible "sexual orientation." Unhappily, the dog was unable to give its view, assuming that anyone was interested.

47 We gotta get out of this vase

During the 1960s and '70s, young Cynthia Albritton and her "assistant" chummed around with rock stars by offering to make plaster casts of their sex organs. Manually, and sometimes orally, they would stimulate their subjects into a state of alertness and then plunge them into a flower-vase of alginate, the compound that dentists use for modeling crowns and bridges. The young artists would fill the mould with plaster and, as the plaster hardened, they paid their personal homage to its endower.

Albritton kept a log of the so-called Plaster Caster enterprise. An entry for Jimi Hendrix read:

> *We need a ratio 28:28 (a much larger than normal amount of mix) and found this just barely sufficient. He has got just about the biggest rig I've ever seen! We had to plunge him through the entire depth of the vase. . . .*
>
> *We got a beautiful mould. He even kept his hard for the entire minute. He got stuck, however, for about 15 minutes, but he was an excellent sport — didn't panic. . . . I believe the reason we couldn't get his rig out was that it wouldn't* GET SOFT*!*

Apparently Hendrix's bassist, Noel Redding, was made of less stern stuff. Although he "moulded superbly" and "only got stuck for five minutes, . . . he got panicky and began to get soft."

Sponsored by Frank Zappa, Albritton later re-cast the sculptures in bronze. Zappa planned to mount a major exhibition featuring the bronzed Hendrix, Redding, Paul Revere and all his Raiders, and Eric Burdon among others. Ensconced at his expense in Los Angeles during the early 1970s, Albritton indulged in her art with new vigor, until her apartment was burglarized in 1971 and she moved the completed bronzes to the office of Zappa's manager, Herb Cohen. After a couple of years, Cohen remarked that the casts' attraction might be wearing off in the public mind, if not in Albritton's hands. He suggested that she abstain for a while, until the market resurrected. The statues, 25 in all, stayed in Cohen's office for two decades. When Albritton attempted to reclaim them, Cohen refused to give them back, contending that he had gained ownership of the casts through some sort of legal transaction with Zappa, and that Albritton had abandoned them.

Albritton sued Cohen for $1 million, alleging (apparently) that he had stolen her work or unlawfully "converted it" to his own use. Cohen countersued for another million, claiming he had legal title to the sculptures. The trial lasted some two weeks, with the sculptures lined up on a courtroom table where the lawyers referred to them in argument as "the Hendrix," "the Redding," and so on. Geoffrey Glass, Albritton's counsel, asserted that as "Jimi Hendrix's guitar went for $500,000, his headband went for $26,000, the one-of-a-kind replica of his penis must be worth at least as much."

Superior Court Judge Lillian Stevens awarded Albritton $10,000 for her lost opportunity to display the 25 moulds. As well, she held that the statues were "the progeny of [Albritton's] original casts" and ordered Cohen to return them to their maker.

48 If the shoe fits

Fetishism is not itself illegal, but it can lead the obsessive practitioner seriously astray. Around the time that Cynthia Albritton was litigating over plaster casts of "rock star rigs," 52-year-old Charles Jones was admitting to a New York court that he had more than a passing interest in Marla Maples' shoes.

Jones had been publicity agent to Maples, the pin-up girlfriend of American billionaire Donald Trump. For three years during Jones' tenure in the job, Maples reported to police that footwear kept going missing from her apartment. Accounts vary as to the scope of the crime, but the thefts totaled between 30 and 200 pairs, and included dirty underwear. Finally, in 1992, Maples hid a video camera in her closet. It caught Jones stuffing Maples' clothing in his pockets. Apparently, he gained entry to Maples' apartment by showing the security guards at her building a forged note: "Hi, Chuck. Here's some especially great clothes and shoes, sexy and casual."

Jones admitted to taking only one pair of boots, but prosecutors alleged that he had also stolen some of Maples' soiled bras and underpants — which police found in his desk drawers and behind radiator covers in his office — as well as Maples' diary and nude photos of the pneumatic former showgirl. When officers found a duffel bag of other women's underthings in Jones' office, he told them that he couldn't remember where it all came from.

While testifying for the prosecution, Maples refused to touch her own shoes, recovered from Jones's custody, unless equipped with court-order latex gloves. It seems that for a collector such as Jones, the shoe is the actual sex object, with the owner being of secondary interest.

Jones admitted to having "a physical sexual relationship" with the shoes, and to slashing the boots so that he could experience more intimate knowledge of the footprints therein. "It's mostly the shoe," he told the jury. Some reports say that Jones' infatuation was so profound, he rejected a plea-bargain which required him to return Maples' footwear. But jurors burst out laughing when he testified that the matter was "deeper" than a fetish. It was an "irresistible impulse," he explained, yet "not the overriding force in my life." Jones claimed, as well, that, though he was an ex-Marine, Maples and her mother beat him up on discovering the thefts: "I've seen Marla Maples in action," he said. "She could take Donald Trump down."

While recognizing that Jones was suffering from mental problems, Justice Richard Andrias sentenced him to a maximum of four and a half years in prison for burglary, criminal possession of stolen property, and criminal possession of a weapon. Police found three handguns among the women's wear in his office.

49   Clotheslines make the man

The boundaries separating fetish, obsession, and even devotion to one's calling or crusade are not easily drawn, of course. In 1984, for example, police in Ste. Marie De Beauce, Quebec, arrested a man for stealing 143 bikini bathing suits from clotheslines. His motive, the police explained, was "to get back at women who didn't pay enough attention to him." He had been assembling the collection for eight years.

That same year, a butcher from Bowmanville, Ontario, attempted to market "stainless steel, chain-link underwear" to "help prevent rape." The Bouwhuis Protective Undergarment weighed about 14 ounces, with padlock, and was to sell for $179.50, mail-order. Evidently Bouwhuis got the idea from chain-mesh butchers' gloves and aprons, which are impenetrable even by sharp objects.

According to newspaper accounts, he believed that the mere sight of the garment could scare assailants away. Lawyer Jane Pepino, chair at the time of a Toronto task force on violence against women and children, was not impressed. She told the (Toronto) *Globe and Mail* that the idea "reinforced the belief that only a woman herself is responsible for her own protection."

While the BPU never seems to have caught on, it was anyway

trumped in 1999 by the Intelligent Assistance Bra, a.k.a. Techno-Bra. Kursty Groves invented the combination brassiere and personal alarm as an industrial design project for her master's degree at the Royal College of Art in London. The bra incorporates a heart monitor and a global positioning locator. When the wearer's heart rate spikes, the bra automatically signals a satellite, which pinpoints the wearer's location within five to 30 meters, the manufacturers claim. A built-in wireless phone notifies police of the woman in distress.

Finally, in 1986, the Associated Press reported that U.S. authorities seized 300 pieces of women's underwear from a thief, only to return them to him. While the 12 victims never reclaimed their "panties, bras, and body suits," the thief paid dearly for them: given that the thefts were also parole violations, he spent three years in jail.

50   Autoerotic asphyxia

The increasing influence of popular culture, and the development of technology that makes it easily accessible across the world, has precipitated lawsuits claiming that its more outrageous manifestations — vulgar lyrics, say, or behavior by rock stars that is deliberately calculated to shock (and sell recordings) — instigate antisocial conduct such as promiscuity, suicide, and violent crime. In 1987, a United States appeals court had occasion to consider whether written descriptions of trendily dangerous sexual practices amounted to inciting readers to engage in such activities.

A boy identified in the law reports as Andy found his 14-year-old friend, Troy, hanging one morning, nude, in a closet. A copy of *Hustler* magazine was at Troy's feet, opened to an article called "Orgasm of Death." The article was part of a "Sexplay" series *Hustler* was publishing "in keeping with *Hustler's* belief that the repression of natural and healthy urges is physically and emotionally damaging[.] [W]e present this series of informative articles to increase your sexual knowledge, lessen your inhibitions and — ultimately to make you a much better lover." The article described in great detail autoerotic asphyxia — creating intense physical pleasure through masturbation while hanging oneself. The idea, apparently, was to inhibit the blood supply to the brain temporarily, during orgasm.

Troy's mother and Andy sued, and a jury awarded them $182,000 — with $169,000 earmarked for Troy's mother — even though the article was not obscene and therefore attracted some protection as free expression. But the fifth circuit U.S. Court of Appeals overturned the jury's decision. It noted that the *Hustler* article warned at least ten times that autoerotic asphyxia was enormously dangerous, and that as many as 1,000 teenagers in the U.S. died while attempting it each year. What was more, the court said, even if a reader characterized the article as advocating autoerotic asphyxia, it was not inciting anything, or even giving reckless instructions. "To understand what the term means is to know roughly how to accomplish it. Furthermore, the article is laden with detail about all facets of the practice, including the physiology of how it produces a threat to life and the seriousness of the danger of harm." Besides, "incitement," the majority noted, was generally applied in a political context.

In her dissent, Judge Edith Jones remarked that it disturbed her "to the point of despair" that the courts could fashion limits on free expression to prevent libel, rioting, and various commercial misrepresentations, but they refused to "fashion a remedy to protect . . . children's lives when they are endangered by suicidal pornography[.] To deny this possibility, I believe, is to degrade the free market of ideas to a level with the black market for heroin. . . . Consumers of this material [pornography such as that in *Hustler*] so partake for its known physical effects much as they would use tobacco, alcohol or drugs for their effects. By definition, pornography's appeal is therefore non-cognitive and unrelated to, in fact exactly the opposite of, the transmission of ideas."

However, as the majority had pointed out, this was not really the issue on appeal. The issue was whether the article had incited anything as "incitement" was understood by the law.

51 Protecting what's under Monica's thong

To shield blatantly antisocial behavior, modern litigants occasionally resort to, and frequently debase, rights arguments. Sometimes they even attack the law while admitting that the behavior it forbids is inexcusable. More rarely, the court agrees, accepting the rights argument while finding the litigant's behavior "abhorrent" and without political or social value. That is the rather odd result in *State v. Scott L. Stevenson*, a recent decision of the Superior Court of Wisconsin.

Stevenson attacked section 944.205(2)(a) of the Wisconsin statutes while admitting that, statute or not, there was no redeeming value in what he did in breaking that law. After his girlfriend broke up with him, Stevenson surreptitiously climbed onto the roof of her home and videotaped her in various states of undress. The next night, he did the same thing from a tree limb, videotaping her as she used her bathroom. A neighbor called the police, who chased Stevenson down an alley and charged him with obstructing a police officer and violating section 944.205(2)(a):

> *Whoever does any of the following is guilty of a Class E felony:*
>
> *(a) Takes a photograph or makes a motion picture, videotape or other visual representation or reproduction that depicts nudity without the knowledge or consent of the person who is depicted nude, if the person knows or has reason to know that the person who is depicted nude does not know of and consent to the taking or making of the photograph, motion picture, videotape or other visual representation or reproduction.*

Writing for the majority, Justice Ann Walsh Bradley held that Stevenson's behavior did not constitute protected "expression" under the First Amendment to the U.S. constitution. Yet, the section still suffered from "facial overbreadth," Justice Bradley ruled, oblivious to the naked ironies. Its language was too broad, in other words, in that it proscribed "all visual expression of nudity, without explicit consent, including political satire and newsworthy images."

Justice Bradley apparently agreed with Stevenson that the section could outlaw "Titian's 'Venus of Urbino,' a 1528 painting of a female nude reproduced by the Yale University Press; (2) a 1927 Imogen Cunningham photograph of a nude female torso featured in *Forbes* magazine; (3) the *New York Times* publication of a Pulitzer Prize winning photograph that depicts a Vietnamese girl running nude following a napalm attack; and (4) a political cartoon appearing in *Penthouse* magazine portraying Kenneth Starr along with partially-clad Monica Lewinsky and Linda Tripp."

Yet it is questionable whether the statute covers these situations. As the state suggested, the court could read into the statute the requirement of a reasonable expectation of privacy. That is, someone violates the law only where the complainant expects privacy at the time the violator created the visual representation. And what about the socially-redeeming value of these examples versus the lurid *Stevenson* situation? The law, the old maxim goes, does not intend absurd results, such as criminalizing the publishers of Renaissance art. And, speaking of absurd and facially overbroad, does anyone honestly believe that a cartoon of Monica Lewinsky has anything to do with what was really under her notorious thong?

Dissenting Justice J. Wilcox wrote that the court would not be trespassing on the legislative turf by reading in a reasonable expectation of privacy in such cases. This itself troubled Stevenson, Justice Wilcox noted, "because the statute might still infringe on an artist's right to draw from imagination a person nude in a place where the person has a reasonable expectation of privacy" — the Lewinsky situation, perhaps. But Justice Wilcox continued: "I do not think this construction permits such an application, because an individual does not have a right to privacy or a reasonable expectation of privacy in an artist's imagination."

Certainly the Stevenson case evokes all sorts of imaginative associations. You could see his ex-girlfriend as Diana, the Roman goddess, who turned the hunter Actaeon into a hart after he spied on her while she was bathing. In his stag metamorphosis, Actaeon, a more heroic version of Stevenson, was torn to pieces by his own dogs.

Then there is the Peter DeVries novel in which a husband spices up his marriage by peeping on his wife as she gets ready for bed. He climbs onto his own roof and spies on her routine activities in his bedroom. Now, in Wisconsin, he could take Polaroids, it seems, and put them up on the Internet.

And finally there is another DeVries husband, Swallow, who feels so guilty about cheating on his wife, he makes her the hero of his daydreams, surrendering the role that he usually reserves for himself — a charitable one-upping of Justice Wilcox's remark that we don't have a right to our privacy in somebody else's imagination.

52 Peeping Tom, Dick, and Denver Bronco

Judgments against peeping Toms have always been harsh, even archetypally, as in the myth of Actaeon and Diana. The eponymous Peeping Tom was a tailor (or butcher) of Coventry, England. Legend says that he peeked through the shutters at Lady Godiva as she rode naked through town, to protest her husband Leofric's tax policies. Today, the name usually denotes a surreptitious voyeur, someone who is liable to prosecution for such crimes as "lurking by night" or "watching and besetting." In some versions of the Godiva story, poor

Tom is stricken blind — never mind that Lady Godiva's protest would not have had much force if no one hankered after an eyeful.

Now, of course, we live in an age of ubiquitous pornography and commercialization of sex — "tits and ass" everywhere. In such a culture one would think that players in the National Football League had the keys to the candy store. A lawsuit just beginning at this writing suggests that this doesn't stop them from drooling at the windows.

Forty-four NFL cheerleaders have claimed that, from 1983 to 2001, visiting players at Veteran's Stadium, home of the league's Philadelphia Eagles, spied into their locker room through peepholes, door cracks, and paint scratched off a window. As defendants, the cheerleaders name 500 John Does — NFL players to be specified after pre-trial depositions — and 29 NFL teams and their non-player employees. The cheerleaders' claim says that the "ability to peer into the cheerleaders' locker room" from the visiting team's locker facilities "and to view them in states of undress, was considered one of the special 'perks' of being a visiting team of the Eagles," a well-kept secret, they say, for nearly a decade. Some players deny it, arguing that their colleagues couldn't keep such a secret for five minutes. That sounds like "guilty with an explanation," or at least "guilty of rank stupidity." The cheerleaders, in any event, allege invasion of privacy, trespass, and emotional distress. "The actions of the defendants," the claim says, with an eye to the public or jury, "were so intentional in nature, outrageous in character and extreme in degree as to go beyond all possible bounds of decency, and are to be regarded as atrocious and utterly intolerable in a civilized community."

No doubt the cheerleaders will be called upon to explain such outrage and shame given that, like Lady Godiva, they deliberately put their bodies on display to the general public in a notoriously rowdy, puerile environment — the *Animal House* culture — for profit. Whatever the force of that argument, the legal response must remain that they have a reasonable expectation of privacy in their own locker room.

53   The cult, and disease, of celebrity

Erotomania has become so common a diagnosis that it seems to be a modern affliction: an otherwise average person develops the delusion that a celebrity — a television or movie star, a political figure, a popular singer — is infatuated with her. She obsessively tries to contact the celebrity, sometimes with hundreds of phone calls and letters, and, in some cases, by breaking into the celebrity's home. Even dozens of court restraining orders or years in jail will not overcome the delusion; often, in fact, legal sanctions add to the erotomaniac's notion that, but for the intervention of the courts or the celebrities' loved ones and associates, the love affair would blossom. Recent victims have included Meg Ryan, Steven Spielberg, David Letterman, George Harrison (who was stabbed by the stalker), Michael J. Fox, Sylvester Stallone, the singer Anne Murray, skater Katarina Witt, writer Germaine Greer, and British newscaster Jill Dando (murdered by her stalker). Some psychiatrists say that John Hinckley suffered from a form of erotomania because his motive in shooting U.S. president Ronald Reagan was to impress the movie actress, Jodie Foster. The Meg Ryan stalker is said to have driven to George W. Bush's ranch with guns in his car.

The supposed widespread nature of the phenomenon is modern, an adjunct of the modern cult of personality, but it was documented as early as 1920 by the French psychiatrist Gaëtan de Clérambault, and earlier reports exist. In his *Psychoses Passionelles*, Clérambault writes of the case of Lea-Anna, the 53-year-old mistress of a wealthy man of status. Her relationship with the man allowed her to live luxuriously for 18 years. When her lover died, Lea-Anna immediately took up with a man much younger than she. At the same time, she became convinced that George V, the king of England, was in love with her. She traveled to Buckingham Palace and parked herself at its gates, interpreting even the twitching of the window curtains as amorous messages from the sovereign.

Clérambault identified three stages of erotomania: hope, defiance, and hatred (*rancune*). The hatred is sometimes turned upon those who are close to the amorous object, those, that is, whom the erotomaniac sees as barriers to her goal — a spouse, business associates, or in one particularly shocking case from Canada, a stepfather.

R. v. Williams demonstrates that, at least in its modern form, erotomania can afflict males, and that the love object need not be a celebrity. In 1983, Peter Williams met Adele Wilson at a wedding in Edmonton, Alberta. She was 12, he 20. Two years later, Williams phoned Wilson and told her that he wanted to marry her. She replied that she was not interested, but Williams persisted, speaking to Wilson's mother about his proposal. He began stalking and persistently telephoning 14-year-old Wilson. During a single night, he phoned her house 30 times. When she was walking home from school one lunchtime, he attempted to stuff Wilson into the trunk of his car, but some eighth-grade schoolmates rescued her. For that attempted kidnapping the Alberta Court of Queen's Bench sentenced Williams to six months in prison, and probation for two years.

Williams proved true to the form identified by Clérambault. He became increasingly defiant and enraged. On his release from prison, he began stalking Wilson again, and one night broke into her mother's house, carrying an axe. He swung the axe at Wilson's brother, but fortunately another brother intervened and no blow landed. Williams went to jail for a further 90 days and the sentencing court added another two years to his probation.

Undeterred, Williams continued to stalk Wilson until he moved (for reasons not explained in the law reports) to Ontario. Williams married at 17, but still regarding her as his "prospective bride," Williams began sending Wilson money orders from Ontario, which she refused to accept. When Williams insisted that she keep the money, she applied it to legal fees incurred in dealing with his harassment. Williams returned to Edmonton and Wilson went back to court to obtain restraining orders against him. Apparently under the delusion that Wilson's 64-year-old stepfather, Norman Matheson, was sexually abusing her and frustrating his troth, Williams broke into Matheson's house. A struggle ensued, during which Williams gouged Matheson's eyes out of their sockets.

This time the court declared him a dangerous offender, meaning that he was to be imprisoned indefinitely. The Alberta Court of Appeal affirmed the sentence.

54   The exorcist visits the senate

During Senate hearings in 1991 to confirm the appointment of Clarence Thomas to the U.S. Supreme Court, Thomas' Republican supporters made abortive backroom attempts to attribute erotomania to his political arch-enemy, lawyer Anita Hill.

Hill had accused Thomas of sexually harassing her when he was her boss at the Equal Employment Opportunity Commission. The devil, Thomas supporters decided, was in the details. Hill alleged specifically that, in addition to pressing her to date him and persistently coming on to her, Thomas once called her into his office to tell her about a pornographic movie starring the freakishly-endowed actor known as Long Dong Silver. Hill added that, on another occasion, when she and Thomas were working alone in the office, Thomas picked up a can of Coca-Cola, stared at it, and asked, "Who has put pubic hair on my Coke?" The supporters set out to show that Hill was so sexually perverse herself that, when she taught at Oral

Roberts University, a profoundly conservative Christian institution, she handed back papers to her male students with her pubic hairs in the plastic covers. The attempt to gather hard evidence to support the so-called "pube affidavit," and the supposed erotomania behind it, foundered miserably. Hill showed the obverse of symptoms afflicting Clérambault sufferers: Thomas was supposedly obsessed with her, not she with him, and she had never professed to love him. But committee member Senator Orrin Hatch brandished a copy of William Blatty's *The Exorcist* during the televised hearings, alleging that Hill's pubic hair allegation was nothing more than a theft from the horror novel. Blatty had written of a pubic hair floating on a glass of gin. The committee confirmed Justice Thomas' appointment.

CHAPTER FOUR

PERSONS PUBLIC, PERSONS PRIVATE

The Law of Indecency

"I can remember when the air was clean and sex was dirty."
GEORGE BURNS

"I think on-stage nudity is disgusting, shameful, and damaging to all things American. But if I were 22 with a great body, it would be artistic, tasteful, patriotic, and a progressive religious experience."
SHELLEY WINTERS

55 Never on a Sunday

In 1656, a Boston colonial court sentenced a ship's captain to sit in the stocks for two hours because he had engaged in "lewd and unseemly behavior" on the sabbath. Upon arriving home that Sunday after three years at sea, Capt. Kemble had kissed his wife.

56   Don Giovanni's next

What is indecent, of course, is largely a matter of when and where. On May 3, 1900 in Montreal, a singer named Jourdan performed a cabaret song entitled "Les Déformées," which the law reports translate as "The Cripples," "in which the subject was the bosoms of women in St. Nazaire, Outremont, and Montreal." As Jourdan sang, "he made gestures towards his chest and his breasts" as a "kind of lascivious invitation." Only one of the verses was actually about "bosoms," it seems, but Jourdan's defense that great operas focused on sexual themes, as well as that Montreal was acting like a provincial jerkwater in prosecuting him, seems to have especially exercised Recorder A. E. Poirier, sitting in judgment. "It has been said that we are making ourselves ridiculous in Canada," Poirier fulminated,

> *by the severity of our ideas, and that we would do better in copying those which come from France. It is not correct to say that we are so severe in Montreal. The musical restaurants now exist in virtue of a municipal by-law. The accused's employers themselves are aware that this court, by a judgment of the twenty-second of January last, recognized the lawfulness of musical restaurants.*
>
> *As Commissioner of Licenses, the president of this court has contributed to the maintenance of a great number of them, too great a number, perhaps, and if the existence of some of them is now in danger, there ought to be no complaint as to excessive severity of the authorities. The abuses which occur to the great scandal of youth, abuses of the nature of that which I am at this moment called upon to reprimand, have inspired unfortunate fathers of families with fears so great that they have come to us in confidence, and it is in order to protect them and save their sons from the influences of the poison of immorality that the aid of this tribunal has been accorded to the policemen who have thought it proper to interfere.*

> *I consider it my duty to state that these constables deserve the gratitude of the public, in place of the satires of the defence, and I hope that the police will not lay down their arms after this first case.*
>
> *As to the propriety of imitating Paris and New York, there are distinctions to be made. Crime is on the increase in Montreal, there are lost children to a greater number and at ages younger than formerly; it behooves that good citizens should keep youth away from improper exhibitions, and that we should preserve them, by all possible efforts, from the danger of lascivious songs and immoral reading. The artists who come to us from France may depend upon the sympathies of our population, but for the love of art, for the glory of their country, for the honor of the institutions where they have been trained, let them avoid what may tend to corrupt the youth of our country.*
>
> *Let us borrow what is good from the cities of the old continent, but let us not pervert our noble youth with ideas of art and freedom opposed to the beautiful and the good, and productive of all sorts of evil.*

The court convicted Jourdan of giving an immoral performance and imposed a $50 fine, with six months in jail in default of payment.

57 King Solomon's a criminal in the great state of Georgia

In Georgia in 1910, a judge ruled that "the general run of citizenry of the state" would regard the copulation of cattle "as notoriously indecent" and "tending to debauch the morals." The circumstances were nothing much more than conventional farming: two men had brought a bull to a cow that was in heat and tied to a fence in a field near a public road. A woman and her children passing by had viewed nature taking its course.

In their defense, the men argued, vainly, that indecency laws applied only to humans. Judge Powell of the Georgia Court of

Appeals was not prepared to go so far as they had in Tennessee, where the public exhibition of a stud horse constituted a public nuisance. But he remarked that if someone dressed monkeys like people and allowed them to copulate on a stage, that would debauch public morals. What monkeyshines had to do with cattle in farmers' fields he did not say.

The aggravating factor was the presence of the woman and children, which led Judge Powell to refer to a 1905 Georgia case in which a young man had "emitted an indecent noise in the presence of a young woman when she was on the highway in company" with a girlfriend and after she spurned his advances. The presence of the girlfriend was significant given that in some jurisdictions you could not be convicted of public indecency unless at least two people saw or heard the offending behavior. Otherwise, it wasn't "public."

In 1848, for instance, James Orchard and James Thurtle were charged with engaging in indecent acts in a toilet at the Farringdon Market in London, England. The court described the toilet as "an inclosure formed of Portland stone, with divisions or boxes like the urinals at railway stations. . . . There was an aperture in the stone work to enable persons to look through and watch the proceedings inside." The judge held that this was not legally a public place, at least for the purposes of the offenses charged. "Every man must expose his person who goest there for a proper purpose," he ruled, never mind the most graphic indictment:

> *Fourth Count. — James Thurtle being a person of such depraved, wicked, filthy, lewd, and beastly mind and disposition as aforesaid, afterwards, to wit, on the same day and year aforesaid, with force and arms, at the parish and ward aforesaid, in London aforesaid, and within the jurisdiction of the said court, in a certain open and public place called Farringdon-market, there situate, unlawfully and wickedly, deliberately and wilfully did exhibit and expose his person*

> *and private parts to the said James Orchard, and unlawfully and wickedly, deliberately and wilfully did lay his hands on the person and private parts of the said James Orchard, with intent then and there to stir up and excite in his own mind, and in the mind of the said James Orchard, filthy, wicked, lewd, beastly, unnatural and sodomitical desires and inclinations, and to incite and move the said James Orchard to the Committing and perpetrating with him; the said James Thurtle, of divers filthy, wicked, lewd, beastly, unnatural and sodomitical acts and practices, and that the said James Orchard then and there, to wit, on the same day and year aforesaid, with force and arms, at the parish and ward aforesaid, in London aforesaid, and within the jurisdiction of the said court, in the said open and public place called Farringdon-market, there situate, unlawfully and wickedly did permit and suffer the said James Thurtle so to lay his hands on the person and private parts of him the said James Orchard, as in this count aforesaid, and was then and there consenting to, aiding and assisting the said James Thurtle in the doing and committing of the several acts and premises in this count aforesaid, in manner and form, and with the intent last aforesaid, to the great displeasure of Almighty God; to the great scandal and subversion of decency, morality, and good manners; to the evil example of all other persons, and against the peace of our said lady the Queen, her crown and dignity.*

That same year, the Crown claimed that, at a St. Margaret, Middlesex, "victualling ale-house," James Webb did

> *unlawfully, wilfully, publicly and indecently . . . expose and exhibit his private parts naked and uncovered in the presence of Mary Ann, the wife of Edward Cherrill, and of other the liege subjects of our Lady the Queen then and there being, for the space of divers, to wit, ten minutes, to the great damage and common nuisance of the said*

> *Mary Ann Cherrill and the other liege subjects of our said Lady the Queen . . . to the great encouragement of indecency and immorality. . . .*

Cherrill, who had been working the bar at the time, did not claim that anyone else had seen Webb's performance. For that reason, Baron Parke dismissed the prosecution, remarking that Cherrill perhaps "was intended not to see" the exposure. As a sort of nostalgic footnote, Chief Baron Pollock remembered "that in our older courts of justice, the judge retired to a corner of the court, for a necessary purpose, even in the presence of ladies. That, perhaps would be considered indecent now."

Lord Campell's *Lives of the Chief Justices* is more graphic about the little corner. Apparently, it was the habit of Lords Kenyon and Ellenborough, who between them acted as chief justice of Britain from 1788 to 1818, to relieve themselves in a corner of the courtroom (there being no toilets available), in a porcelain vase. They would simply turn their backs to the well of the court and find what privacy they could amid their judicial robes.

On one occasion a student had emptied into the vase some ink that had gone sludgy. "Soon after, having occasion to come to this corner," Lord Kenyon

> *was observed in the course of a few moments to become much disconcerted and distressed. In truth, discovering the liquid with which he was filling the vase to be of a jet-black colour, he thought the secretion indicated the sudden attack of some mortal disorder.*

Chief Justice Kenyon attempted to resume the trial he was hearing, but found that his hand shook so much that he couldn't write, and he adjourned the court. "As he was led to his carriage by his servants, the luckless student came up and said to him, 'My lord, I hope your lordship will excuse me, as I suspect that I am unfortunately the cause of your lordship's apprehensions.'" Apologizing profusely, the student explained what he had done. Lord Kenyon was so relieved, he invited the student to dinner.

In the Georgia cow case it was clear that the roadway was public, that an obscuring thicket was only 100 feet from where the offending act took place, and that more than one person, the mother and children, had complained of the show. If such behavior were innocent, Judge Powell wondered, what was to stop such displays in school- and churchyards? And thoughts of the church brought him to the Bible and his own relativity theory of indecency. He agreed with "distinguished counsel" for the defense that "the patriarch Jacob standing at the public watering place and holding the striped rods before Laban's bulls, rams, and he-goats, when they leaped, in order that the young might be marked with stripes, would have been guilty of public indecency" in 1910 Georgia. But the law changed with the times: "King Solomon with his thousand wives would not be tolerated in Georgia; and King David, he the man after God's own heart, could hardly justify his whole life according to the provisions of the penal code of our state." The farmers were guilty, having given deeper offense than if a lady "of refined tastes" simply had stumbled upon animals *in flagrante*. In such a case "she might be offended but not outraged."

58 Making lemonade — or maybe tomato juice — out of rotten projectiles

Even the sting of a conviction in such cases can be relative, depending not only on the community, but the accused person's state of mind. In 1727, Edmund Curll was locked in the pillory at Charing Cross for publishing *The Nun and Her Smock*. Curll's barrister had argued unsuccessfully that the book "contained several bawdy expressions but . . . no libel against any person whatsoever. . . . I thought it rather to be published on purpose to expose the Romish priests, the father confessors, and Popish religion." In other words, it was fair comment (the barrister claimed) on certain practices within the Catholic church establishment!

Still, Curll truly had the last laugh, apparently. According to *Howell's State Trials*, as he stood in the pillory he

> *was not pelted, or used ill; for being an artful, cunning (though wicked) fellow, he had contrived to have printed papers dispersed all about Charing-Cross, telling the people he stood there for vindicating the memory of Queen Anne;[1] which had such an effect on the mob that it would have been dangerous even to have spoken of him. When he was taken down out of the pillory, the mob carried him off, as it were in triumph, to a neighbouring tavern.*

59   Breaching the peace on high and down below

Beyond its amusing sidelights, Curll's conviction marked an important development in the law of obscenity and indecency: it gave the common law courts — the courts established by the crown instead of by the church — jurisdiction over alleged obscenity, and it said that obscenity could include libel (that is, matters that might abuse someone, but did not deal with sexual or related matters). Previously, only religious courts had considered purportedly obscene publications.

---

[1] Anne reigned from 1702 to 1714 and introduced parliamentary government as well as the Act of Settlement, which still governs succession to the throne in Britain.

In convicting Curll, the court expressly overruled the *Read* case, in which the Crown prosecuted the publisher of *The 15 Plagues of a Maidenhead*. The *Read* court threw the prosecution out on the basis that the ecclesiastical courts, not the Queen's courts, had jurisdiction over obscene libels. The only exception, the court said, was where someone clearly violated the sovereign's peace — acted, in the old phrase, *vi et armis*, with force and arms. And the example it gave was the notorious *Queen v. Sidley*.

In the copulating cow case, Judge Powell also refers to *Sidley*, remarking that the accused man, the actor and parliamentarian Sir Charles Sidley, had thrown bottles containing an "offensive liquor" from a balcony. In fact, in 1663 Sir Charles pled guilty to "shewing himself naked in a balkony, and throwing down bottles (pist in) *vi et armis* among the people in Convent Garden, *contra pacem*, and to the scandal of the government."

On July 1 he had got drunk with some friends, apparently, and, according to Samuel Pepys's diary, came

> *in open day into a Balcone and showed his nakedness — acting all postures of lust and buggery that could be imagined, and abusing of scripture and, as it were, from thence preaching a Mountebanke sermon from that pulpitt.*
>
> *In the middle of his discourse, he seems to have remarked that he hath to sell such a pouder as should make all the cunts in town run after him, a thousand people standing underneath to see and hear him. And that being done, he took a glass of wine and washed [his genitals] in it and then drank it off; and then took another and drank the King's health.*

Pepys reports that the Chief Justice (Lord Foster) scolded Sir Charles that "it was for him and such wicked wretches as he ... that God's anger and judgments hung over us, calling him 'Sirrah' many times." The justices then fined Sidley £2,000, committed him to prison for a week, and ordered him to be of good behavior for three years.

Where this sort of aggressively anti-social behavior was involved, the *Read* court said, the lay courts could intervene. The *Curll* court went one step further, allowing the common law courts to act even where there was no aggressive breach of the public peace.

60   Persons public, persons private

What offends about nudity is what the law blushingly calls "exposure of the person." The trouble is, the law, something like an embarrassed spinster, does not always know what it means by this.

North American and antipodean law on indecent exposure emigrated with the British colonists. The common law viewed it as mostly a nuisance, a misdemeanor. The 1824 *Vagrancy Act*, passed under George IV, deemed the first offender "a rogue and a vagabond" subject to prison for not more than three months. Repeat offenders were formally registered as "incorrigible rogues," but still faced prison sentences of no more than a year. In 1971, an English judge noted that "the word 'person' in connection with sexual matters had acquired a meaning of its own; a meaning which made it a synonym for 'penis.'" The defense lawyer in that case, I.E. Jacob, argued that this was "the forerunner of Victorian gentility which prevented people calling a penis a penis." Remaining non-committal on that etymology, Justice Ashforth nonetheless acquitted Anthony Evans of "lewdly and obscenely exposing his person with intent to insult a female, contrary to section 4 of the *Vagrancy Act*, 1824." Less than a year earlier, Evans had exposed his penis to a Ms. Ewels at the Craven Arms. But on this particular occasion, he was wearing "trousers [which] could not be fastened" so that Ewels saw a part of Evans' stomach "in a 'V' shape." Justice Ashforth ruled that, in the law on sexual offenses, "person" was used "over and over again" to mean "penis" specifically, meaning that Evans was not guilty of the offense charged.

61 You might well say "Oops"

In 1847 Queen Victoria moved indecent exposure from the *Vagrancy Act* into the *Town Police Causes Act*, which imposed a fine of not more than 40 shillings or a gaol term of not more than 14 days. The offense remained officially minor probably because, generally, it involved no physical contact, let alone violence, and the harm, at least if only adults were involved, was negligible. Then, in 1967, there came before the California courts the case of John Lynch.

Lynch was known to the police. In 1958 they had successfully prosecuted him for indecent exposure. For first offenders such as Lynch, the *California Penal Code* imposed a maximum penalty of six months in the county jail, a fine of not more than $500, or both. Lynch was sentenced to two years of probation. Then, one evening in 1967, some time after midnight, Lynch went to a drive-in restaurant. He ordered some coffee and told the carhop to bring him refills at her leisure, when she thought his current cup might be getting cold. The carhop left and Lynch began masturbating with a pornographic magazine open on the seat next to him. An emergency vehicle passed the restaurant and, because Lynch turned to look at it, he did not see the carhop return. When he discovered she was there, viewing him with his erect penis in his hand and the magazine on the seat, he said "Oops." The carhop left and observed through Lynch's rear-view mirror that, 15 minutes later, he was still "pleasuring himself."

Unfortunately for Lynch, the *California Penal Code* diverged from its English forbears. From 1872 to the 1950s, the code punished second and subsequent offenses the same way the modern statute reserved for first offenses — with a maximum of six months in jail and/or a fine of $500. But then the legislature amended the code so that repeated indecent exposure became a felony "punishable by imprisonment in state prison for not less than one year." When the state prosecuted Lynch, the trial judge sentenced him to an indeterminate term in prison — basically, a life sentence for inadvertent (albeit "wilfully blind," as the judge put it) exposure of his private parts.

Five years and an unsuccessful appeal later, and while characterized by the trial judge as a presentable fellow of "superior intellect" and "great potential," Lynch was still in custody. He had spent more than three years in the notorious Folsom maximum security penitentiary, no less. Happily (at last), on further appeal the Supreme Court of California found that the indeterminate sentence was cruel and unusual punishment, in violation of the state constitution, "so disproportionate to the crime for which it is inflicted that it shocks the conscience and offends fundamental notions of human dignity."

62 Not like Mom used to bake

Police the world over, and the more conservative members of individual communities, have continued to be nervous about public nudity, sometimes even when the nude is otherwise inanimate. Mind you, since 1981, it has at least been clear that a gingerbread cookie is probably not a legal "person." That year, a bakery in Annapolis, Maryland was selling sexually-equipped gingerbread people, well-endowed and with smiles their baker called proud, perhaps because they were fetching the comparatively up-scale price of one dollar and 50 cents per cookie. James Wright, the executive director of the Maryland Moral Majority, sent two young patrons into the bakery with that sum, to buy some of the gingerbread. With the evidence in hand, he asked the state attorney to charge the baker with selling "obscene pictures, statues or other representations" to minors.

Assistant prosecutor Frederick Paone expressed disgust with the cookies (or at least their appearance), but advised Wright that the cookies constituted "a visual representation of a gingerbread man, not a visual representation of a person." He refused to prosecute. The baker told reporters she expected sales to triple because of the free publicity.

63 Over the moon

Food, putative persons, and alleged obscenity were again conjoined in *The Queen v. Balazsy*. In mid-December, 1978, Charles Balazsy was eating at a restaurant in a small town in Ontario, Canada, when he saw some peers doing the same. He suggested to them that he could "take them." Evidently to prove this, he paid his bill, went outside, and, as Provincial Court Judge Saul Nosanchuk described it, "pulled his pants down and wiggled his naked buttocks in front of the restaurant window, with his back to the window." This attracted the attention of pretty well everyone inside the establishment. Whether it proved Balazsy could "take" anybody, the evidence did not reveal.

The police charged Balazsy "that on or about the 18th of December 1978 at the Town of Belle River, in the County of Essex, ... he did wilfully do an indecent act to wit; expose his private person in a public place in the presence of one or more persons, contrary to Section 169 Subsection (a) of the Criminal Code." In prosecuting him, Her Majesty was at pains to show that *private person* could mean "buttocks."

Judge Nosanchuk discovered in precedent that American topless dancers do not expose their persons, and so felt driven to the even more surprising conclusion that Balazsy was "'thumbing his nose' at his adversaries," not exposing his person. At law, a person was a penis or a vagina, not a breast, not a buttock, but an organ that was designed for procreation. Yet Balazsy did not escape judgment. Judge

Nosanchuk edited the charges to delete the phrase "private person" and still convicted him of committing an indecent act. While the judge agreed with Balazsy's lawyer that:

> *members of our community now have ample opportunity to view bare buttocks in any number of magazines, movies, or stage performances available for public consumption, I am nevertheless of the opinion that current standards of decency as they pertain to matters of dress in public places in Canada are such that the exposure of the bare buttocks in the manner in which it was done by the accused in this case . . . can clearly be said to be "Unbecoming; in extremely bad taste, . . . 'Offending against propriety and delicacy [and] immodest,' to use the definition earlier referred to from the* Shorter Oxford Dictionary. *Indeed the accused exhibited a part of his anatomy that, to quote from the case of the* State of Ohio v. Borchard *. . . , a decision of the Ohio Court of Appeals, 'was a part of the anatomy that instinctive modesty, human decency or self respect requires shall be customarily kept covered in the presence of other persons.'"*

But there Judge Nosanchuk's hard-nosed approach ended: he allowed Balazsy an absolute discharge on the rationale that the prosecution of the charges had been deterrent enough, and contemporary society was tolerating public displays of greater quantities of flesh.

64   A turn of the behind

In a prosecution later the same year, Chief Justice Stuart of the Yukon Territorial Court characterized *Balazsy* as "a 'mooning' performance securing the criminal law prize for an indecent act." David Hecker stood before Chief Justice Stuart on a public indecency charge after he briefly pulled down his pants in reply to friends heckling him during a curling match. The only other spectators present were the Midgetts, son and mother, sitting in the stands, and Mrs. Midgett was deeply offended. Chief Justice Stuart noted that "in days of old, masters of witty social commentary, such as Mark Twain and Ambrose Bierce, relied on a fine turn of phrase to poke humor or ridicule. Today, much lesser minds rely on a crude turn of the behind. In days of old, subtlety commonly characterized social commentary. Today, subtlety is seldom found in society obsessed with expediency. A 'moon' may be one of the expedient replacements for subtle social commentary."

But he found Hecker not guilty. Unlike Balazsy, Hecker did not give anyone "the one-finger salute" or call others "assholes" before lowering his trousers, and his behind was on display only momentarily where Balazsy stood around exposed for two or three minutes. Hecker had apologized to Mrs. Midgett, and he was only joking around with his friends. "I have the requisite reasonable doubt," Chief Justice Stuart ruled, "whether the act displayed in a base or shameful manner the degree of moral turpitude necessary to constitute an indecent act."

65 He's no angel

What, however, if the exposure is deliberately indecent, but in private? That question arose in Australia, in 1898. On October 10 of that year, Angel Gabriel Madercine arrived at the O'Donnells' front door in New South Wales. No adults were home, but six children were present, the eldest being 16. Madercine asked for water, and the children invited him to sit on the verandah. While talking with a 13-year-old girl there, he exposed himself. The girl ran to her eldest sister, who also saw Madercine expose himself, as did some of the other O'Donnell children, given that Madercine loitered at the house casually undressed for at least an hour. At his trial for indecent exposure he said that his trousers had split, but, on viewing the garment in issue, the trial judge found no sign of a rent. He held that it was irrelevant that the exposure occurred on private property. On appeal, the chief justice agreed: "I am of opinion that where an act of the kind charged in this case is committed in the presence of a number of Her Majesty's subjects, that is in itself an indictable offence." One might also say that the moment Madercine began terrorizing the household, he became a trespasser.

66 Another fiddler on the roof

What, then, of exposure on the roof on the back of a house, facing a private alleyway? At about 11 p.m. on July 31, 1863, George Thallman, a servant at No. 4 Albermarle Street in Piccadilly, London, went out on the roof of the rowhouse next door, nearly naked. He stood there for some time, facing the back windows of No. 11 Stafford Street, a club which backed onto No. 6 Albermarle. The female servants at the Stafford Street club were going to bed. They complained to their employer that Thallman was provoking them, "but were scarcely credited." Thallman pulled the same stunt the next night, for about ten minutes. This time the seven witnesses included the club's head waiter and a police constable. Thallman's lawyer artfully contended that exposure was indecent only if it were performed publicly, and that, although the houses on Albermarle fronted on a public street, "the roofs of the houses did not constitute a public place." Deputy Assistant Judge Joseph Payne told the jury that "the place and exposure were sufficiently public to bring the acts of the prisoner within the law, if they should be of opinion that he exposed himself in fact indecently, wilfully, and intentionally." The jury convicted, and the Court of Criminal Appeal later ruled that Judge Payne instructed the jury properly.

67 The Apparel-Challenged Persons?

In 1968, J. Edgar Hoover, the director of the Federal Bureau of Investigation in the U.S., cast about for ways to ban "Two Virgins," the latest recording by John Lennon and Yoko Ono. The cover featured the couple *au naturel*, frontally on the front, dorsally on the back. EMI, the recorded music multinational, refused to distribute the album. Company director Sir Joseph Lockwood asked Lennon and Ono, "Why not show Paul [McCartney] nude? He's so much better looking. Or why not use a statue from one of the parks?"

By 1991, professional prudes found the social climate more amenable. That year, the events coordinator for the city of Toronto banned the Barenaked Ladies from playing in the city hall square. Ignoring the plain fact that the cleancut band was mushier at the core than Lawrence Welk or Wayne Newton, the city's mayor of the day, June Rowlands, agreed with coordinator Dawna Proudfoot that their name "objectified women." "We do have a policy against the objectification of women or any other sector of the community," Proudfoot told the press. "If your mother or my mother saw a headline saying, 'City of Toronto presents Barenaked Ladies,' they'd be really concerned." Not long after, Rowlands appeared at a celebrity barbecue with Miss Bikini and Miss Legs, and during a subsequent election campaign, in the wake of international ridicule, the mayor called the ban a mistake. But when she attempted to present the band the keys to the city, the Ladies demurred.

68 Is a breast a person?

In general, the law has been loathe to regard breasts as sexual organs. As noted above, laws which prohibit the public exposure of "private parts" or the "private person" often do not apply to strippers in bars, for example. In New Brunswick in 1984, this led to the surprising ruling that where a man grabbed a teenaged girl's breast he was not committing a sexual assault — even though, when the teenager pulled free, the man was attempting to grope her crotch. In overturning the decision, the Supreme Court of Canada ruled that a reasonable observer would have concluded that there was a "sexual or carnal context" to the assault.[2]

Generally speaking, nudists and naturists believe that shedding clothing helps people slough off shame and prurience, allows a new sense of freedom, and promotes physical health through exposure to the elements and ease of movement. The "Topfree Ten" — a Rochester, New York, group whose aim was to make going "clothes-free" acceptable in everyday society — founded a political movement on the idea. But their first appearance in court was a mixed success. The city court acquitted them of indecent exposure at a public beach, ruling that going "topfree" was a form of expression protected by the First Amendment of the U.S. constitution. But a few of the women were dissatisfied. They wanted an acquittal based on the Fourteenth Amendment and its guarantee of equal protection under the law. They wanted the courts to say that women had as much right to walk around shirtless as men did. So they exposed themselves again.

The Ten's heightened political consciousness embraced even their organizational moniker. They had chosen "top-free" to distinguish themselves from naturists or nudists, and because "topless" had overtones of seedy bars and table-dancing. One of their leaders, representing herself in court, argued that hiding women's breasts was what made them titillating: our society was breast-obsessed because breasts were made to seem forbidden fruit. Forbidding women to

---

[2] That same year, a woman in Toronto was charged with performing an indecent act by masturbating a man with her breasts in the front seat of a truck. But the prosecution was obliged to withdraw the charge when the judge found this impossible. See number 30 above.

bare their chests discriminated against them, she added, and worked against the community interest by making people ashamed of their bodies. Women sought unnecessary cosmetic surgery, and were discouraged from natural and healthy practices such as breastfeeding.

Judge John Regan of the Rochester City Court was not persuaded. In convicting the defendants in 1989, he agreed that the prohibition against women baring their breasts was discriminatory. But, citing the Bible, he held that such discrimination was necessary in the name of public order and decency — the equivalent of saying that laws against libel or spreading false news are a reasonable democratic limit on freedom of expression.

But on appeal, the Monroe County Court obliged the Ten fully at last, ruling that the "gender classification" in the anti-exposure law (no naked breasts below the top of the areola, with nursing mothers excepted) violated the equal protection clauses in constitutions of both the United States and New York State.

A few years later, a Canadian crusader got to the first stage of topfree success, which she apparently has found sufficient for her own purposes, despite the fact that the court did not give her toplessness constitutional protection. On a hot and humid day in Guelph, Ontario, during the summer of 1991, Gwen Jacob, a university student, strolled around topless downtown, drawing a crowd of teenagers with binoculars and even momentarily stopping a bus. Like the Topfree Ten, Jacob asserted that she had as much right as men to walk around topless on a hot day, and indeed shirtless men passed on the street as the police arrested her. But the Ontario Court of Appeal acquitted her on the more technical basis that she had done nothing to offend community standards. "There was nothing degrading or dehumanizing in what the appellant did," Justice Coulter Osborne wrote for the majority. "The scope of her activity was limited and was entirely non-commercial. No one who was offended was forced to continue looking at her. I cannot conclude that what the appellant did exceeded the community standard of tolerance when all of the relevant circumstances are taken into account. It follows that what the appellant did on July 19, 1991, did not constitute an indecent act."

Justice Karen Weiler dissented only on the law, agreeing that Jacob was not guilty of indecency, but adding that it was dangerous to justify Jacob's conduct on a community tolerance test. "If the term 'indecent' were to mean whatever the community will not tolerate," she wrote, "there is a danger that discrimination by the community will [not] be seen as harmful and [will be] legitimized." One need only think of lynch mobs to see the sense at the heart of this argument. Conduct was criminally indecent, Justice Weiler said, if it was unduly sexual. For an act to be "indecent" under the Canadian *Criminal Code*, Justice Weiler concluded, it "must be a sexual act in the sense that the act is done for the sexual gratification of the accused or others. In this case, a reasonable bystander, fully informed of all the circumstances, would not conclude that this was the case."

69 Wave if you want to see my etchings

In 1988, Philip Monk, Curator of Contemporary Art at the Art Gallery of Ontario in Toronto, estimated that one-half the gallery's collection was subject to regulation or prohibition by a proposed anti-pornography bill under consideration by the Canadian parliament. Monk described, among other things, a painting at Toronto's Harbourfront (federal government property) depicting a middle-aged woman in a ball gown standing in front of the Washington monument. Police were called in because of the painting's caption, "'Neath my arm, the rustling of a subaru." But unaccustomed as the police were to using libraries, they could not discover any Japanese dictionary that said *subaru* meant "penis" — probably because it means "big wave."

70 Salome à Montréal . . .

Two female dancers take the stage to music, each dressed in transparent dresses. Underneath, they wear only their brassieres. They kiss passionately. One lies on her back while her companion licks whipped cream off her navel. The second strips off her dress and gets down on all fours. Her companion licks whipped cream and a cherry off her bottom, then gives the cherry to a patron. The dancers perform simulated oral sex at least twice. They lick whipped cream from each other's breasts, then lather a banana with whipped cream, take it into their mouths, and deposit the other ends in the mouths of patrons. One dancer pours water on the buttocks of the other and licks it off. The act finishes when the first dancer rubs ice all over the front of her companion's naked body. And that, said the Quebec Court of Appeal in 2001, did not constitute an indecent performance prohibited by section 173(1) of Canada's *Criminal Code*.

In *R. v. Comeau*, the three-judge panel overturned the convictions of dancers Mélanie Roux and Johanne Comeau. Given the nature of the acts in question, and considering the barroom context as well as modern society's tolerance for such performances, Justices Michel Proulx, René Dussault, and André Forget ruled that the sex show was not criminally indecent.

Roux and Comeau worked as table dancers at Cabaret les Amazones on St. Jacques Street West in Montreal. To earn extra money, they had created the special "erotic show." On first appeal, the Superior Court upheld their convictions in Municipal Court. Society would not tolerate performances, the Municipal Court had ruled, where the audience was meant to derive pleasure from acts that degraded and dehumanized other human beings. The performances were anti-social, the Municipal Court said, in presenting women "publicly as nothing but a sex object and a being stripped of dignity."

The Court of Appeal admitted that the law considers sexualized performances degrading and dehumanizing where anti-social harm might flow from them. However, this harm must be, as a leading case put it, "for example, the physical or mental mistreatment of women by men. . . . Anti-social conduct for this purpose is conduct which society formally recognizes as incompatible with its proper functioning. The stronger the inference of a risk of harm, the lesser the likelihood of tolerance."

Given that people could watch much more graphic and shocking material on their televisions any hour of the day, the appeal court held that Roux and Comeau's performance was well within legal boundaries. Moreover, the dancers "would undoubtedly be astonished to learn that a court would find 'degrading' and 'dehumanizing' a performance for which they took full responsibility."

"It is not enough," the court added, "that, to find indecency the judge, in his own view of things, considers this show 'degrading and dehumanizing.'" In the case before the court, there was no question of "an orgy involving the dancers and the customers, or a degrading spectacle in the primary sense of the word."

Peter Segarkis, the owner of the Amazones, later remarked that he still thought real on-stage sex should be illegal. "I hope the bar owners don't think to try to use the decision to have couples perform real sex on stage," he told a reporter. "I hope I never see live sex on stage."

71 . . . and in Toronto

Where does one cross the line of community tolerance? In Canada, anyway, it seems to be when the performer has physical contact with the patron.

In *Comeau*, the Quebec court did not even mention the Ontario case, *The Queen v. Ludacka*, from five years earlier, never mind that the opinion was written by Ontario's influential chief justice, Charles Dubin, sitting on a panel of five judges where ordinarily only three appeal justices would sit. So when the Quebec court reached an opposite conclusion on exactly the same law, one was left to guess why. Perhaps a sociologist would put it down to the supposed Gallic distinctiveness of Quebec, versus the rest of Canada with its legal and social roots in Britain, Ireland, and Eastern Europe. The relevant test, after all, was what the community would tolerate. And then, of course, there was the matter of more exuberant audience participation, though the Ontario trial judge noted, "no one was offended and if anything the spectators cheered on and encouraged the performers. Hypothetically the same patrons would have reacted in the same way had the activities been real instead of simulated." Otherwise, as Chief Justice Dubin's recital of the facts about the relevant night at Babies Hotel in Welland shows, there was not a lot to choose between the two cases:

"[T]here were thirty to forty male patrons seated throughout the premises. . . . There was an area of seating immediately around the edge of the stage commonly referred to as "perverts' row" (the front row). There were various other tables set throughout the room overlooking the stage. On the evening of April 11, the majority of patrons were seated in the front row. The rest were seated at tables.

"At approximately 9:45 p.m., two dancers, Carin Edwards and Leone Greenland, arrived on stage. They were the feature act for the week, "Opposites Attract."

"The dancers began by taking off their clothes, save for a G-string or T-bar. They each held a small basketball hoop between their breasts. Patrons would attempt to sink a basket by throwing a Nerf basketball into the hoop. When a patron was successful, the dancer would place a sucker in her pubic area, and the male patron would retrieve it with his teeth. After a while, the dancers placed the basketball hoop against their G-strings in their pubic region. If a patron was successful in sinking a basket, the dancer placed the sucker between her buttocks, and the patron retrieved it with his mouth. When he did this, the dancer would bump her buttocks against his face. . . .

"Following the basketball portion of the routine, the dancers removed each other's G-strings, stripping completely nude. They then proceeded to pour some kind of white cream in between each other's breasts; they took turns spreading the cream with their fingers on their breasts and abdomens.

"The dancers then called a male volunteer up on stage, and he came willingly. The dancers stripped him to the waist and had him lie down in the centre of the stage. Carin poured cream on him, and Leone spread it around with her hands. Each dancer took a turn spreading the cream on the patron's chest and stomach with her breasts as she lay across him. They then did it together.

"Leone then reversed her position and began to use her bare buttocks to spread the cream, sliding back and forth sideways across the patron's chest. She changed her position again, straddled him, arched her back, and began sliding on him. The officers observed that her genitalia were in full contact with the patron's chest and abdomen. . . .

"Once the male volunteer returned to his seat, the dancers proceeded to pour the white cream between and on each other's buttocks. They danced around for a few moments on the stage. Then each dancer selected a male patron who was seated in the front row, and backed her creamed buttocks into the patron's face. The dancers pulled the patrons' heads into their buttocks and gyrated with the music for approximately five to seven seconds. The patrons' faces would be covered with cream, indicating that full contact had occurred.

"Each dancer did this with two patrons. Constable MacDonald gave evidence that there was no verbal communication between dancers and patrons. The dancers did not question the patrons whether or not they wanted this contact. The first patron chosen had no idea of what was coming.

"The officers gave evidence that, for the finale, Carin lay on her back with her head towards the audience. Leone straddled her face with her back to the audience and lowered herself onto Carin's face, gyrating her hips to the music as she went down. Both officers testified to full contact between Leone's pubic area and Carin's face.

"Constable McNeil also recalled Leone spreading cream on her pubic area. She spread her legs apart while Carin put her face into the cream. There was a transfer of cream to Carin's face."

Chief Justice Dubin held that this was not a constitutionally-protected form of "expression." "It is purely physical activity," he wrote, "which does not convey or attempt to convey meaning. The activity does not manifest ideals, thoughts, opinions, or beliefs that have inherent value to the community and the individual." Babies' owner "would be hard-pressed to show how the meaning being conveyed relates to the pursuit of truth, participation in the community, or individual self-fulfilment and human flourishing."

And even if such performances amounted to expression, the chief justice added, it was appropriate to censor them to forestall any harm they might cause. Then, Chief Justice Dubin quoted from the same Supreme Court of Canada precedents as the Quebec Court of Appeal would later cite in *Comeau*, to arrive at the opposite conclusion: "'The conduct in issue in this case in the context in which it takes place is harmful to society in many ways. It degrades and dehumanizes women and publicly portrays them in a servile and humiliating manner, as sexual objects, with a loss of their dignity. It dehumanizes and desensitizes sexuality and is incompatible with the recognition of the dignity and equality of each human being. It predisposes persons to act in an antisocial manner, as if the treatment of women in this way is socially acceptable and is normal conduct, and as if we live in a society without any moral values.'

"I think the same can be said about the conduct in issue here."

Where the Quebec court found that the tavern setting helped make such entertainment legal, Chief Justice Dubin thought it added to the risk: "Furthermore, particularly because the activities were carried on in licensed premises, there is a real risk of physical harm to the performers, the harm of unwanted sexual touching, of sexual assault. By reason of the nature of the activities, there is also a risk of spreading infectious diseases by oral and genital contact."

The Supreme Court of Canada effectively affirmed both the Quebec and Ontario decisions, and the ambiguity they left behind, by refusing to hear appeals from them.

72 Charms to soothe the savage scofflaw

The very idea of biology can be legally offensive, depending on the tenor of the times. In a 1918 Rhode Island case, Justice Walter Vincent was so repelled by a contract to sell "adult toy novelties" that he refused to describe the merchandise in his judgment. "To do so," he wrote, "would only serve to extend the knowledge of and give permanency to obscene and indecent devices."

The defendant before Justice Vincent was a novelty store owner who had ordered, but never paid for, the impugned "devices," "Bear Charms," "Bull Charms," "Modern Dancers," and "Naked Truth." The first was a disc, suspended in a metal frame, with a bear depicted on either side; when the disc was spun, the bears seemed to copulate. In a similar fashion, "Bull Charms" depicted the eponymous animal relieving itself. "Modern Dancers" comprised a metal token covered with a translucent material, designed to depict a naked woman doing the "hootchy-cootchy" when a match was played behind it. "The Naked Truth" was a cardboard envelope, protruding from which was a picture, on cardboard, of a woman's legs. When the legs were pulled from the envelope, a mousetrap-style snare was sprung on the puller's hand, and the woman's "chemise" was revealed, printed with the word *Stung*.

As far as Justice Vincent was concerned, a deal to sell such novelties was so outrageous that it was unnecessary to cite any authorities for denying the toymaker the $151.61 the retailer owed him. The problem remained, of course, that the welshing retailer might already have illegally sold some of the toys, himself, and made a 100-percent profit.

73   Not letter perfect

As far as juridical unfairness goes in contracts supposedly having to do with sexual matters, the most astonishing reported instance is *Gardner v. Fulforde*, an upholsterer's suit in 1667 for payment on a "pair of hangings," otherwise described by his lawyer as "gilt skins."

Latin being the language of court pleadings at the time, upholsterer Gardner's lawyer had characterized the skins in papers filed with the court as "*quatuor pictas pellices Anglise.*" Gardner had sold the hangings to Fulforde, who refused to pay. Deadbeat Fulforde's lawyer argued that *quatuor pictas pellices Anglise* meant "four painted whores . . . , for *pellex* signifieth a harlot." As skins, he said, were *pelles*, Fulforde could keep the hangings without paying for them: agreeing to provide someone with four painted English whores was illegal and unenforceable.

This argument prevailed, an outcome that probably says less about the law of contract than about how the most minor deficiencies in court pleadings have sometimes completely hobbled justice. (Sir Robert Megarry reports that, as late as 1849, an action failed because the defendant's middle name had not been spelled out, although the initial would have been sufficient had the middle name begun with a vowel.) In ruling against Gardner, the court suggested that he might have a case under a different cause of action, "trover," which was pleaded where a defendant had "wrongfully converted" property to his own use. A few days later, Gardner renewed his suit in trover, only to be told that no matter how he sued, *pelles* was indeed the "proper word, of a proper signification," not *pellex*, and "similitude is not sufficient." A one-letter "typo," as we would call it today, meant that Fulforde got the skins for nothing. As precedent, the judge cited a case in which someone had sued for the price of six eggs as "*sex ovium* for *ovorum*, and the plaintiff was thereupon nonsuited." His case was thrown out because he used an improper Latin inflection.

74 Of sow bosoms and bovine enceintitude

The famous *September Morn* by Paul Chabas, depicting a naked woman bathing in a pond, started life in the early years of this century as a lithograph for a brewer's calendar. It soon made its way in great quantity into print form. Finding himself saddled with 2,000 copies, a San Francisco art dealer consulted a publicist. Pretending to be a minister of the church, the publicist phoned professional moralist Anthony Comstock to report dirty pictures in the window of an art store on Fourth Avenue "and little boys are gathering around there." Comstock rushed to the art store, where he found a group of wide-eyed children, hired by the publicist at 50 cents each. A magistrate threw an obscenity prosecution out the next morning, remarking, "Mr. Comstock, I think you're nuts." Proving yet again that bad publicity is better than none, *September Morn* soon became so notorious that it sold millions of copies.

Comstock was a ruthless combination of Dr. Bowdler and Joseph McCarthy. As head of the New York Society for the Suppression of

Vice and the U.S. delegate to the International Purity Congress, he proudly boasted of having driven 16 people to early graves. His motto was, "Morals, not art or literature." George Bernard Shaw, whom Comstock called a "smut-dealer," minted the word "Comstockery" in the zealot's honor, and Comstock returned the favor by having the actors and management of the New York production of *Mrs. Warren's Profession* charged with disorderly conduct on opening night.

Comstock is perhaps most famous in literary circles for the 1873 act whose nickname is his legacy — the so-called *Comstock Act* was in fact *An Act for the Suppression of Trade in, and Circulation of, obscene Literature and Articles of immoral Use*. It banned "obscene matter," which it defined to include condoms and pamphlets on birth control, from the mails, with Comstock as sole arbiter of what was obscene. According to H.L. Mencken, the *Comstock Act* inspired a real cottage industry in euphemism. In the Los Angeles *Times*, a *sow-belly* became a *sow-bosom*. The Iowa Farmers' Union decided that in public statements, pregnant livestock would be described as "enceinte," and the police in Chattanooga charged a prostitute's john with the suddenly criminal act of "walking the streets accompanied by a woman."[3]

75 Same old story

While this autocratic approach has become more bureaucratic with time, unusual prosecutions persist. In 1981 in Calgary, Alberta, a man was charged with "sending obscene, indecent, immoral or scurrilous matter through the mails" after he posted abusive correspondence to the Unemployment Insurance Commission. First, there was the matter of his impertinent letter. Then there was "the same type of

---

[3] For more of this sort of euphemism, see number 112 in Chapter Six.

language" (the trial judge said) entered on the commission's "Request for Additional Information." Evidently upset with the time it was taking the commission to process his application, the man had, among other things, called commission workers "assholes," and complained bitterly in terms that included the words "shit" and "fucking." But the law required that to be obscene, the man's language would have had to embody "undue exploitation of sex" — undue in a way that would tend to deprave or corrupt anyone who read the correspondence. The court heard two witnesses from the commission: one said that the language offended her; the other said it more or less came with the territory. The court felt persuaded by the second witness and acquitted the correspondent.

76 Comstockmachen

They say that German authorities prosecuted Beate Uhse some 2,000 times for promoting birth control and selling contraceptives and sexual aids, never mind that she was a war hero. Uhse was a trained pilot who ferried airplanes for the Nazi armed forces during the Second World War, when she was in her early 20s. When Uhse's pilot husband was killed in action, she was left to support herself and her young son. Noting that the privations of military defeat had also left many of her compatriots afraid of pregnancy, Uhse wrote and distributed a pamphlet on the Lehre Knaus-Ogino rhythm method of birth control. (Legend has it that she paid for the printing with five pounds of butter.) Soon she was selling contraceptive devices and, eventually sex toys and aids, through the mails, by catalogue. Soon, too, the police began charging her with indecency, as well as aiding and abetting fornication. From the 1950s until her death in 2001, Uhse's business grew to include two million customers. In 1996 she opened Berlin's "Museum of the Erotic." And she was never convicted of a crime.

77   Anthony rises again

As late as 1997, however, it was clear that the spirit of Comstock lived on. Monica Medlicott, a seventh-grader, had prepared a science project called "Which Brand of Condom Is More Durable?" It showed the packaging from four different brands, but did not include actual condoms. The project earned Medlicott a grade of A, but Carol Blacharski, Medlicott's principal at the Carver Middle School in Palm Beach, Florida, refused to allow her to display the project with the other entries on Parents' Night. Blacharski told Medlicott that she could use a separate room, so that parents would not be forced to see the project if they were offended by its subject. Medlicott's parents sued, alleging that Blacharski had violated Monica's constitutional right of free expression. Their lawyers have pointed out that other projects on general display had sexual subthemes, including one on sexually-transmitted diseases. At last report, the Palm Beach County School Board was mulling over offering to settle the matter for $5,000.

78   Pee-Wee's biggest adventure

As part of society's ambivalence — or hypocritical discomfort — about sex, it is not uncommon for the law to declare communication for the purpose of prostitution a crime, but to leave prostitution itself as a legal activity. More ominously, we hear regularly these days of sexual abuse by clergy, often those sworn to chastity. The notorious indecency prosecution of Pee-Wee Herman, the former stage-name of actor Paul Reubens, throws the hypocrisy into similar highlights.

In July, 1991, undercover police arrested Reubens at the South Trail Cinema in Sarasota, Florida, during a sting operation. The officers alleged that he had been masturbating during the showing of *Nancy Nurse* and *Turn Up The Heat*. Although Reubens initially denied a charge of indecently exposing his penis, and later claimed that videotape showed he was in the theatre's lobby at the relevant time, eventually he agreed to a plea bargain. In return for Reubens' plea of no contest, the prosecution offered to seek a penalty of a $50 fine and 500 hours of community service. As part of the service, Reubens made an anti-drug video for children. Otherwise, his career in children's television and film was destroyed.

He received a great deal of public and peer support, however. Four hundred people, including parents with their young children brandishing Pee-Wee dolls, attended a demonstration in Greenwich Village. Civil rights lawyer William Kunstler told one crowd that Reubens' prosecution reminded him of the time in the 1960s when he defended comedian Lenny Bruce. Bruce was charged with "simulated masturbation with a broomstick in a coffee house," Kunstler explained. "He was convicted, of course, and I think probably it led to his eventual suicide."

The support for Reubens was understandable for reasons beyond celebrity. It is a cliché that Hollywood thrives on grotesque violence and the crudest titillation, both of which can be considered indecent under U.S. law, but never have been. Our children watch this infectious crudity day after day on rock videos and television shows. Robert Altman, the dean of the American *auteur* film, recently issued a *J'Accuse* blaming action movies for helping to foment some of the worst terrorism in the history of the world. None of their makers has been prosecuted. And no one in the *Reubens* case claimed that the comparatively mild, apparently non-violent films shown at the South Trail that day were illegal. If Reubens in fact did what the police alleged, he was sitting in the dark, by himself, harming no one. The defense had contacted an ophthalmologist, in fact, who was prepared to testify that the arresting officer couldn't have seen any indecent exposure because there hadn't been sufficient time for his eyes to dilate in the darkness. (Whether the doctor intended irony is unclear, but his opinion makes an interesting twist on the old wives' tale about the supposed ocular effects of masturbation.) Although even being in the theatre showed bad judgment, it had nothing to do with his working life. The event occurred, as the law might say, on an occasion of quasi-privacy. Unfortunately, Reubens' lawyer rather over-stated this perfectly logical defence, remarking that it was permissible to expose one's penis in the theatre given that it was a place "where nudity is necessarily expected." The prosecutor handily replied, Yes, but. Everyone "clearly expects to see nudity on the screen in an X-rated theatre," but on the screen only.

79   NO 6 PLS

A memorable episode of the television comedy "Seinfeld" included a proctologist whose automobile sported a vanity license plate that read ASSMAN. In many professedly democratic jurisdictions in North America, such expression is banned as indecent or sacrilegious. In Ontario, Canada, for example, it is a matter of administrative law whether you are entitled to call yourself MR HUGE on your car license. A committee of provincial bureaucrats passes judgment on prospective vanity plates, and successful applications are "executed" by inmates at a provincial prison. Rejectees can petition the Minister of Transportation for review. MR HUGE passed muster on the ground that he was a "professional wrestler." MEAT U survived on the basis that the applicant was a butcher, not a call girl. After appeal to the minister, a urologist is happily driving around the province calling himself P P DOC. The hopeful 18 INCHES, however, lost out, even though his real name was Halfyard.

80   Not a blessed event

As recently as 1985, the owner and manager of a bookstore were charged with "exhibiting a disgusting object" after they had turned the store windows over to a display called "It's A Girl."[4] The display had been created by Woomers, a women's art collective, with one of their number explaining that "It's A Girl" was meant to "depict the life of a woman" using "objects we collected from our mothers and grandmothers and ourselves. . . . They weren't surprising items."

The unsurprising artifacts included white bead purses, a Barbie doll, a Pampers diaper box, makeup, a plastic toy machine gun, tampons, white gloves, comic books, plaster casts of penises (ten, one newspaper diligently counted), birth control devices suspended on a mobile over a crib, and Kotex pads spattered with red paint. While it remains unclear whose granny donated the tommy-gun, the accused were acquitted. Under a straight obscenity charge, they might not have been so lucky: traditionally, the proprietors of art galleries, cinemas, and the like have argued that people view the allegedly obscene matter by choice, even paying a fee. In the case of "It's A Girl," passersby pretty well could not help noticing the display if they looked in the window.

Insofar as something is often legally obscene if it offends "community standards," one might say that the better measure of obscenity is the volume of business the store lost or did not lose, not what some paid court witness, an art historian who spends his days in the fetid air of a windowless office, concocted off a survey. If the community were asked to think really deeply for a change, perhaps it might find beer commercials more offensive — maybe less silly, but much more leeringly prurient — than "It's A Girl," less honest in their exploitation than even the most shocking Robert Mapplethorpe photo.

---

[4] The relevant section of the Canadian *Criminal Code* read: "Every one commits an offence who knowingly, without lawful justification or excuse . . . publicly exhibits a disgusting object or an indecent show."

81 Sometimes fighting the virus only spreads it around

The case of the Dead Kennedys, makes the same point. Before they disbanded, they recorded punk music albums called "Frankenchrist," "Plastic Surgery Disaster," "Holiday in Cambodia," "Bedtime for Democracy," and "Too Drunk to Fuck." The Dead Kennedys were going out of their way to shock older people and impress younger ones, at least until somebody genuinely took them up on the offer. To judge by the published pronouncements of Jello Biafra, leader of the Kennedys, proprietor of Alternative Tentacle Records, and known to Mother and Dad as Eric Boucher, one of the reasons the San Francisco group went out of business was that a California mother obliged the band by getting very publicly offended. With "Frankenchrist" in general and "Penis Landscape" in particular, Biafra had finally made the young rebel hit parade, only to find that maybe he didn't really want to be there.

"Penis Landscape" (otherwise called "Landscape +20 Where We Are Coming From") is a painting by the Swiss artist H.R. Giger, who, in 1979, won an Oscar for his art direction on the movie *Aliens*. According to news reports, the painting depicts ten interacting "sets of male and female genitalia" and has been exhibited in several European museums. But when Mary Sierra found a copy of it in her 14-year-old daughter's room, inside the cover of "Frankenchrist," she was not carried away with its aesthetic and semiotic correlatives. In disgust, she wrote David "Fight Back" Horowitz, the TV consumer advocate, and finally, when Horowitz did not reply, Sierra settled for mere mortal authority, the attorney general of California. On April 15, 1986, nine members of the San Francisco vice squad raided Biafra's apartment and the offices and warehouse of Alternative Tentacle Records. Biafra and his manager, Michael "Microwave" Bonanno, were charged with distributing harmful material to a minor — a charge similar to one successfully prosecuted a few years later against a Florida music entrepreneur after he sold tapes of "As Nasty As They Wanna Be" by the rap group 2 Live Crew.

It wasn't that Jello hadn't composed a warning label for "Frankenchrist," somewhat in the spirit of labels recommended a couple of years before at Congressional hearings into rock and roll. If you purchased the record in the U.S., you were advised on the cover, "The inside foldout of this record cover is a work of art by H.R. Giger that some people may find shocking, repulsive or offensive. Life can sometimes be that way." If you bought "Frankenchrist" anywhere else, you didn't even get dust-jacket *Weltschmerz* from a 20-year-old California boy about life being repulsive. In my case, when I eagerly stripped away the cello-wrap to feel the cover coming apart in my hands, I found nothing more than the jacket's perfumey, gray, dead cardboard guts. No "Penis Landscape" on the horizon. Not available in Canada.

There was, however, a funny photograph, filling both sides of the outside cover, showing a clutch of Shriners making spectacles of themselves in full fez, steering their little kiddie-cars down a parade route. The back featured a relatively unshocking graphic, a bat encircled by a chain. It had a cat face and held what looked like a chicken foot in one claw, a comb and a cross in the other. Above the bat, the graphic read "Alternative Tentacles Records." Under the graphic were the words "Virus 45."

This seemed fair enough, given the musical contents of the vinyl. A virus spreads, and is nasty, and evidently that was what Jello had in mind — and what Mary Sierra contemplated when she went to the Attorney General of California. There was nothing attractive about it.

Jello has more or less made the same point in his own defense. On his argument that "Penis Landscape depicts how our commercialized culture dehumanizes sex," the California jury voted a definite maybe. The majority plumped for acquittal, but five, a nearly fatal minority, evidently thought otherwise. When "Frankenchrist" was played in the jury room, one of the jurors hid in the bathroom so as not to be corrupted. Several others bought copies for Biafra to autograph. The young Ms. Sierra had testified that she had bought the album for her brother's birthday. While she found "Penis Landscape" "gross," she did not feel harmed by it.

82 Ardor in the court

Finally, there is indecent exposure where the court itself is an eyewitness, which tends to simplify most of the evidentiary issues while complicating the legal ones: never mind indecency, has there been a "contempt in the face of the court"? Probably the most notorious instance occurred during the mass trial in Florence, Italy, in 1985, of members of Front Line for political terrorism. Front Line comrades Fernando Cesaroni and Maria Cavallo had sexual intercourse in the prisoner's dock. Purportedly, their daughter was conceived in the act, but the parents named her Ramona and not Justitia in honor of the circumstances. Although supporters picketed outside the courthouse with signs reading "You Can't Judge An Act Of Love" and "Love Is Not A Crime," the court sentenced the new parents to two months in prison for gross obscenity.

CHAPTER FIVE

I KNOW IT
WHEN I SEE IT

Pornography and Free Expression

"I shall not today attempt to further define the kind of materials I understand to be embraced within that shorthand definition; and perhaps I could never succeed in doing so. But I know it when I see it."
U.S. SUPREME COURT JUSTICE POTTER STEWART ON "HARDCORE PORNOGRAPHY"
IN *JACOBELLIS V. OHIO*, 1964

"I do not claim to be a literary critic, but I know dirt when I smell it and here it is in heaps — festering putrid heaps which smell to high heaven."
W. CHARLES PILLEY, REVIEWING D.H. LAWRENCE'S *WOMEN IN LOVE* FOR *JOHN BULL*,
SEPTEMBER 17, 1921

"Congress shall make no law . . . abridging the freedom of speech, or of the press."
THE FIRST AMENDMENT TO THE U.S. CONSTITUTION

83   Out of the carton and into "the box"

When authorities in the United States seize something on the basis that it was illegally obtained, they nominally "prosecute" the object, or even a parcel of land. Otherwise unamusing law reports are leavened by cases winsomely named *United States v. Seventy-Five Boxes of Alleged Pepper* (the allegedly pure pepper had been "adulterated" with ground pepper longum); *United States v. 77 Cartons of Magazines*; *United States v. Ten Erotic Paintings*; *United States v. 35 MM. Color Motion Picture Film Entitled "Language of Love"*; *United States v. 25.936 Acres of Land, More or Less, in Borough of Edgwater, Bergen County, N.J., et. al.*; *United States v. Thirty-Seven Photographs*; and *United States v. 12,200-ft. Reels of Super 8 MM. Film*. The last case, from 1973, is otherwise notable for a ringing dissent in which Justice William O. Douglas outlines the surprisingly short history of obscenity prosecutions in Anglo-American law, and makes a powerfully terse argument that "I know of no constitutional way by which a book, tract, paper, postcard, or film may be made contraband because of its contents."

As Justice Douglas points out, outside of religion-based prohibitions on profanity or blasphemy, America had no obscenity laws until the 19th century. "Obscenity" is a matter of taste, the times, and "the neuroses of judges, lawmakers, and of the so-called 'experts' who have taken the place of Anthony Comstock."[1] In this particular instance, customs officers at the Los Angeles airport had seized the alleged pornography, which included color photographs and the eight-millimeter film, and federal prosecutors were asking the courts to make the importer forfeit the material for destruction. Justice Douglas found it "ironic" that "in this nation many pages must be written and many hours spent to explain why a person who can read

---

[1] Regarding Comstock in his own right, see number 74 and following, above.

whatever he desires, may not without violating a law carry that literature in his briefcase or bring it home from abroad. Unless there is that ancillary right, one's [free expression] rights could be realized, as has been suggested," — by Justice Hugo Black, dissenting in *Thirty-Seven Photographs* — "only if one wrote or designed a tract in his attic and printed or processed it in his basement, so as to be able to read it in his study."

Justice Black had written, "The right to read and view any literature and pictures at home is hollow indeed if it does not include a right to carry that material privately in one's luggage when entering the country." In any event, what gave judges the right, Justice Douglas asked rhetorically, "to impose our set of values on the literature of the day? There is danger in that course, the danger of bending the popular mind to new norms of conformity. There is, of course, also danger in tolerance, for tolerance often leads to robust or even ribald productions. Yet that is part of the risk of the First Amendment.

"[First Amendment scholar] Irving Brant summed the matter up: 'Blessed with a form of government that requires universal liberty of thought and expression, blessed with a social and economic system built on that same foundation, the American people have created the danger they fear by denying to themselves the liberties they cherish.'"

The eponymous pictures in *Thirty-Seven Photographs* (1971) had been imported from Europe by a man who intended to use them to illustrate the sexual positions described in an edition of the *Kama Sutra*. In even blunter language than Justice Douglas was to use in *12,200 Reels*, Justice Black decried his judicial brothers' reaffirmation of the obscenity threshold — the judge-made rule that sexually-explicit material was obscene if it lacked "redeeming social value": "Thus, for the foreseeable future this court must sit as a Board of Supreme Censors, sifting through books and magazines and watching movies because some official fears they deal too explicitly with sex. I can imagine no more distasteful, useless, and time-consuming task for the members of this court than perusing this material to determine whether it has 'redeeming social value.' This absurd spectacle could be avoided if we would adhere to the literal command of the First Amendment that 'Congress shall make no law . . . abridging the freedom of speech, or of the press.'"

84 Vile bodies

The technique of prosecuting the inanimate, as it were, was established under the British *Obscene Publications Act* of 1857. Acting on a search warrant, an undercover police officer would buy the alleged pornography and convey it to the magistrates. The seller was then obliged to prove in court why the seized goods should not be destroyed as obscene. According to the anonymous author of *A Lawyer's Notebook*, British police used an unusually subjective test to determine whether a publication was pornographic. A detective read the suspicious material after his dinner. If "he experienced anything in the nature of an unbecoming sensation," charges were filed. As editor of a periodical called *The Free Woman*, the *Notebook*'s author received a visit from a Scotland Yard inspector after publishing "a silly poem" about a woman who took in a prostitute with dirty feet. "'In the Yard,'" the inspector said, "'we don't like pomes about 'ores with dirty feet.'" Apparently the poem escaped prosecution.

85 I know it when I hear it

The American "First Amendment lawyer" Charles Rembar frequently defended his cousin, Norman Mailer, against allegations of obscenity. In 1948, Mailer consulted him about soldiers' language in *The Naked and the Dead*. Rembar suggested that he use *fug*, partly to discourage states from banning the book and partly because the spelling was a truer rendering of how GIs pronounced the now common intensive.

86 I need to examine the evidence more closely

In the 1950s, postal authorities successfully prosecuted New York publisher Samuel Roth concerning flyers advertising his publications, and for the contents of a particular number of his magazine, *American Aphrodite*. The number in question included an unfinished story by Aubrey Beardsley which described the goddess Venus masturbating a unicorn. When Roth's appeal reached the U.S. Supreme Court, Roger Fisher, the justice department's lawyer, filed a box of supporting pornographic "evidence," a selection of allegedly obscene publications available by public sale. The box was purely *in terrorem*: Roth had not published any of it, making its relevance to his case legally suspect. After dismissing Roth's appeal, the court returned the box to Fisher, minus half its original contents.

87 Rules of, um, thumb

Jacobellis v. Ohio (1964) concerned an obscenity prosecution involving the film *Les Amants* ("The Lovers"). It has become famous because of Justice Potter Stewart's words in dissent that, while he wasn't about to attempt to define hardcore pornography, he knew it when he saw it "and the motion picture involved in this case is not that." According to Alan Dershowitz, other judges on the highest court have employed more specific benchmarks. Byron White used what his clerks called "the angle of the dangle" rule, plumping for conviction only if there was "a sufficient degree of erection and penetration." On Justice William Brennan's "limp dick" standard (again, the monicker is his clerks'), anything less than a full erection raised a reasonable doubt. Chief Justice Earl Warren asked himself, "Would my daughters be offended?"

88   I know it when I sleep through it

What, exactly, did Justice Stewart see in *Jacobellis*? Justice Radcliffe in the court below (the Supreme Court of Ohio), remarked: "The film ran ninety minutes. To me, it was eighty-seven minutes of boredom induced by the vapid drivel appearing on the screen and three minutes of complete revulsion during the showing of an act of perverted obscenity. *Les Amants* (*The Lovers*) was not hard-core pornography, i.e., filth for filth's sake. It was worse. It was filth for money's sake." The trial judge had felt the same way. When the one actual sex scene (an act of adultery, apparently) finally arrived, after a great deal of working up to itself, "very little, if anything, is left to the imagination. Lurid details are portrayed to the senses of sight and hearing. After the narrative has reached this carefully built up and long-anticipated climax, it scurries to a hasty conclusion." Although boredom was expressed by the judicial critics all around, only Justice Stewart thought that the film merited constitutional protection.

89   I know it when I smuggle it

In her biography, *The Goossens*, Carole Rosen describes "the tragedy of the conductor/composer Sir Eugene Goossens, who was apprehended at Sydney airport with 1,166 pornographic pictures in brown paper parcels labelled 'Beethoven' and 'Brahms'."

In a chapter titled "Fall of a Titan," Rosen describes how Sir Eugene arrived home in Sydney from a tour in 1956 carrying the photographs, two 9 mm. skin flicks, and a collection of rubber masks in his luggage. A "servant" had fixed pockets into larger envelopes labelled to look like they contained musical scores, then stuffed the photos into the pockets. Goossens was carrying the films, bought at a shop in London's Leicester Square, in his briefcase.

The moral climate in 1950s Sydney, Rosen says, was as repressive as that of Victorian England. "As late as 1970 a Sydney bookshop owner was arrested for displaying a poster of Michaelangelo's David." When it emerged that Sir Eugene enjoyed extra-marital sex in bacchanalian orgies, and that he released his creative energies by indulging in fellatio with a notorious pantheist artist, he was hounded out of the country just a few weeks after pleading guilty to breaching the Australian *Customs Act*. The court had fined him the maximum £100 for importing prohibited material (an offense under the *Customs Act*, not Australia's criminal code) and his highly successful career hit the skids. Although Sir Eugene pled guilty, he quoted *King Lear* to the police: "I am more sinned against than sinning."

90 D.H. Lawrence guilty of non-phallic cerebration

Obscenity prosecutions concerning D.H. Lawrence's *Lady Chatterly's Lover* are well-documented elsewhere, in some cases by the participating counsel.[2] What they don't point out is that Lawrence's defense of the "plain language" he used with religious intensity ("'Th'art good cunt, though, aren' ter? Best bit o' cunt left on earth.' ... 'Cunt! It's like fuck then.' 'Nay, nay! Fuck's only what you do. Animals fuck. But cunt's a lot more than that.' ...") is more obscurantist than the most trying legalese. "I feel that one has to fight for the phallic reality," Lawrence trumpeted in a letter, "as against the non-phallic cerebration unrealities." In an essay, he elaborated, "If I use the taboo words, there is a reason. We shall never free the phallic reality from the 'uplift' taint till we give it its own phallic language, and use the obscene words." This was virtually a plea of guilty, but the book has survived prosecutions in England, Canada,

---

[2] See, for example, Charles Rembar's *The End of Obscenity, The Trial of Lady Chatterley*, edited by C.H. Rolph, and *The Lady Chatterley's Lover Trial* (Bodley Head, 1990), which reprints the transcript of the English proceedings.

and the U.S. It might have been otherwise if performers acted out the offending passages on a stage. But, as Aldous Huxley has pointed out, once the actions are "verbalized and discussed, it becomes an ethical problem, a *casus belli*."

And some of Lawrence's defenders have convicted him of the graver crime of hypocrisy. In a famous *Chatterley* passage, he tones down the verbalization, writing of "burning out the shames . . . in the most secret places" and "the last and deepest recess of organic shame," with Lady Chatterley completely submissive "like a slave." The English Crown took no particular exception to this passage in the 1960 trial, and several of the world's greatest literary critics testified in Lawrence's defense without referring to it. Only two years later did the critics begin pointing out that "the practice approved by Lawrence is that known in English law as buggery," anal intercourse (a crime at the time), and that his euphemistic description of it belied his stated artistic intention.

The Canadian *Chatterley* case was the only one to go all the way, so to speak. The English Crown did not appeal the acquittal at trial, and the U.S. conviction was struck down by a first-level appeals court. But in Canada Lawrence won only at the country's Supreme Court, and then by just a single vote: all of the Catholics on the court dissented, joined by one of the five Anglicans. The prosecution was brought in 1959 against three Montreal newsstand owners. At the time, the law of the province was heavily influenced by the pervasive Catholic ethos. During the trial, the defense called the American Lawrence specialist Harry Moore, who testified that the "dominant characteristic" of *Chatterley* was not sex, which would have helped make it obscene under Canadian law (if the sex were exploited "unduly"), but the sterility of post-Victorian England. "Would you give me a definition of 'expurgated?'" Crown counsel asked Moore, cross-examining him on what might have been left out of the book had Lawrence cooperated with his publisher on a textual "clean-up." Moore said that "expurgated" meant "castrating a book." The trial judge, Justice T.A. Fontaine, leaned toward the court clerk and asked, "What does he mean by that?" When the clerk explained, Fontaine blushed and — according to the news agents' lawyers — looked "upset."

The news agents' appeal to the Quebec Court of Queen's Bench is notable for the fact that one of the appeal judges makes the counterargument to what Justice Douglas asks rhetorically in *12,200 Reels*: who are judges to dictate popular taste? "Ours is a Christian civilization," Justice Paul Casey wrote on the Quebec appeal. "We the judiciary must not defer to or appeal to one section or another of the population by extending the definition [of obscenity] beyond what was intended [by Parliament in the *Criminal Code*] or by reading into it reserves and exceptions that were not envisaged. We must not allow an articulate minority to impose its will and its standards on the majority.

"In this case the yardstick is the restraint of word and action that we the people [note the switch from 'we the judiciary'] hold necessary for the preservation of our morals and of the civilization that we have inherited. We have the right to insist that these restraints be respected and this right is greater than that of the individual to say what he thinks should be said or what he wants to say."

Justice Casey seemed to take his reading of the majority opinion from English reviewers who had excoriated *Lady Chatterley* as "most evil outpourings," a "literary cesspool" and "beastliness" written under the "shameful inspiration" of "sewers of French pornography" by a "muddy minded pervert," "bearded satyr," and "poisoned genius." The critic for *John Bull* was aggrieved that there was "no law at present under which he [Lawrence] may be ostracised more completely for a good stiff spell" in prison.

Lawyer F.R. Scott memorialized his work on the Canadian

appeals in his delightful poem, *A Lass in Wonderland* — "I went to bat for the Lady Chatte / Dressed in my bib and gown" — and therein provides the rebuttal to Justice Casey. The *Chatterleys* in issue were what publishers call "mass market editions," cheaply-made paperback books priced, in this case, at 50 cents apiece, and clearly meant for extraordinary sales — sales, that is, to the subway readers and Molly Blooms of the world. It particularly troubled the Quebec judges that the book was so readily available to the ordinary working person. Justice Casey wrote: "Those to whom this publication is addressed will take from it only what they themselves find. They will not have the benefit of expert advice [unlike the courts in England and Canada]: they will have no one to tell them what the author had in mind, to explain why the story was developed in this manner, to indicate the real purpose and message of the book.

"...The vast majority of readers will not buy this edition for, nor will they find in it, the high moral quality claimed by the appellant. They will buy it for its by now well advertised eroticism and for no other reason."

Scott poetically responded:

> *Then too the sales made in the paper-back trade*
> *Served to aggravate judicial spleen,*
> *For it seems a high price will make any book nice*
> *While its mass distribution's obscene.*

Ironically, one of the most notorious moments in the English prosecution came when the Crown tried to make this same dubious point. The Crown prosecutor, Mervyn Griffith-Jones, had attended Eton and Cambridge and ran in aristocratic circles. In what some lawyers now regard, with the benefit of hindsight, as a serious misstep in his opening address, Griffith-Jones invited the jurors to ask themselves: "Is it a book that you would even wish your wife or your servants to read?" Three of the jurors were women. And it was more likely, of course, that some of the jurors worked as servants than that they could afford to hire them.

To illustrate how shocking or suggestive the book might be, at least to the lower classes, Griffith-Jones regaled the jury with some math in his opening, totting up evidence that *Lady Chatterley* "abounds in bawdy conversation." "These matters are not voiced normally in this court," he modestly advised the jurors, "but when it forms the whole subject-matter of the prosecution, then we cannot avoid voicing them. The word 'fuck' or 'fucking' occurs no less than thirty times. I have added them up, but I do not guarantee to have added them all up. 'Cunt' fourteen times; 'balls' thirteen times; 'shit' and 'arse' six times apiece; 'cock' four times; 'piss' three times,' and so on."

91 We already know what you are; now we're just discussing the price

Mind you, the high-price, limited-distribution argument had already been essayed in France, where it failed just as miserably. "Damned if you do, damned if you don't" might be the motto and legacy of the Pauvert-Marquis de Sade case, in more ways than one. In 1956, French authorities prosecuted Paris publisher Jean-Jacques Pauvert for offending public morals through the publication of four works by the Marquis de Sade, *The 150 Days of Sodom*, *The New Justine*, *La seconde*, and *The Story of Juliette*. Pauvert's barrister, Maurice Garçon, admitted that the works were unremittingly obscene, but contended that there was no criminal intention — no deliberate effort to offend public morals. The books had literary and scientific importance, he said, in documenting psycho-sexual pathology long before Freud and Krafft-Ebbing had done the same. As well, the publication was essentially "private," Garçon argued, by expensive subscription. "When a licentious work is broadly diffused and available to everyone, it should be subject to condemnation. But it is another matter when such work is published for a distinct category of readers, physicians, philosophers, and literary scholars who seek only to inform themselves in the course of their work on psychological problems."

Literary notables such as Jean Cocteau and André Breton testified in support of these points. "The dime-store detective novel of prudish America is more pernicious than the most audacious pages of de Sade," Cocteau asserted. Still, the court held that, even if Pauvert intended a very limited distribution to the intellectual élite (which the court doubted, given the advertising Pauvert ran for the books), this was "insufficient to establish" his purportedly pure motives. In any event, the central issue was not motive, but whether Pauvert intended to publish something morally outrageous, of which there was no doubt. In other words, the French civil law adopted the Anglo-American common law approach of the day: if a work was obscene, its literary or intellectual merit was irrelevant. The court sentenced Pauvert to pay a 120,000-franc fine plus court costs, and ordered the destruction of the de Sade works.

92   Short-sighted ruling

The scientific approach has occasionally fared better across the Channel, but it remains a gamble. In his memoir, *Clinging to the Wreckage*, retired barrister John Mortimer describes how, for a time in England, a lawyer could defeat an obscene publications charge by pointing out the putative therapeutic value of the offending work: that is, private self-stimulation with the help of the impugned book or magazine (videos were unavailable) was a safe substitute for public acts or attacks on unwilling partners. It became usual in such cases, Mortimer says, to hear an old psychiatrist's joke about a boy who asked his mother, "Mummy, if it makes me go blind, can I do it just until I'm short-sighted?" On one occasion, the joke made it all the way to the House of Lords. But the law lords decided that such "therapeutic" evidence itself was obscene and inadmissible.

93 Keep on litigatin'

In an aside to his "therapeutic masturbation" story, Mortimer remarks that it was an epiphany in his legal career to be tricked out in wig and gown and summoned by a high "official in full evening dress" to lecture five ancient law lords "on the virtues of masturbation." Witnesses report the same sense of the absurd, as in an obscenity prosecution concerning cartoonist Robert Crumb in 1973. Crumb is notorious for his "bulbous homunculi and their appalling adventures," as one critic has put it, particularly the bulbous homunculus walking down the street in a sort of reverse Groucho Marx galumph over the caption "Keep on truckin'." Aging hippies remember Crumb more generally and fondly as the progenitor of the "head comic" (adult comics of and from the age of Timothy Leary), designer of the down-and-dirty album cover for Janis Joplin's "Cheap Thrills," and creator of the highly-sexed Fritz the Cat. Crumb and his repulsive homunculi — lumpy men engaged in sexual intercourse with headless women; a "Leave It to Beaver" family, in the infamous and highly prosecuted *Zap Comix No. 4*, practicing incestuous love, with the parents remarking afterwards that they really should spend more time with the kids — were no strangers to obscenity prosecutions. In 1995, British Customs and Excise banned Crumb's *My Troubles With Women* because two out of 200 pages showed oral sex. English media lawyer Geoffrey Robertson persuaded the Uxbridge magistrates to lift the ban, partly on the argument that, far from being pornographic, the sex in the comic was studiously unappetizing. The magistrates ordered the government to pay the comics' vendor, Knockabout Comics, £6,000 — about $15,000 U.S. — for damages caused by the ban.

The 1973 prosecution found another news agent in the dock for selling a copy of Crumb's *Nasty Tales* to an eight-year-old. George Perry, an expert on comic book history, appeared for the defense with feminist academic Germaine Greer, who, Perry says, bored the jury senseless by comparing Crumb to Juvenal, Aristophanes, and Alexander Pope. According to Greer, "the cartoon 'Dirty Dog' was an example of repressive desublimation" and "an orgiastic Crumb spread was a satire on collective sentimental expectation." Perry himself introduced Breughel and Rabelais, and was obliged to explain why Crumb gave all the police officers in *Nasty Tales* pigs' heads.

The jury acquitted the news agent, and Perry found the whole business surreal. "There can be few more curious experiences," he reminisced in the *Times*, "than speaking up for those whose lifestyle may seem bizarre in front of bewigged, berobed persons bobbing up and down and muttering 'If your lordship pleases' with unconcealed venom."

94   Jody's city, uncensored

J.D. Salinger, J.K. Rowling, Kurt Vonnegut, and Joseph Heller have all seen their fiction banned from school libraries. But probably the most significant battle against such censorship was fought in 1978 over a 17-line poem by a teenage girl.

Jody Caravaglia was a 15-year-old middle school student in Brooklyn, New York, when she saw her poem, *The City to a Young Girl*, published by the Dial Press in a school text called *Male and Female Under 18*. Sonja Coleman, the librarian at Chelsea High School in Massachusetts, purchased the book, an anthology of writings by adolescents, as part of a package of one thousand paperbacks offered under a special publisher's promotion. Before buying *Male and Female* Coleman had read some of the material in the book, but not Caravaglia's poem. The poem described "the city" (presumably,

New York) as a million "horny lip-smacking men" who were "screaming" for her body. The men were begging, the poem said, for

> *a lay*
> *a little pussy*
> *a bit of tit*
> *a leg to rub against*
> *a handful of ass*
> *the connoisseurs of cunt.*

The parent of a student at Chelsea High read the book and complained, causing a furor at the Massachusetts School Committee. Although there was nothing else objectionable to anyone about the book, except perhaps a single word in another poem, the committee voted to have the volume pulled permanently from the school library, and some of the members considered transferring Coleman out of the facility. Several students, the parents of one student, Coleman, and some teachers and public interest groups took the committee to court.

Noting that the school had an undisputed right not to buy the book or to reject it for the library or curriculum, the court said that pulling it from the library, or cutting Caravaglio's poem out of it, was different. District Court Judge Tauro ruled that the book was protected by constitutional guarantees of free expression and should stay in the library, fully intact. That is, free expression included the students' right to read what some in the community might find offensive. Yes, the poem might be shocking, Judge Tauro allowed, but if the law protected only "cognitive" over "emotive" language, a dangerous precedent would be set: "The prospect of successive school committees 'sanitizing' the school library of views divergent from their own is alarming, whether they do it book by book or one page at a time.

"What is at stake here is the right to read and be exposed to controversial thoughts and language — a valuable right subject to First Amendment protection."

Judge Tauro concluded: "The library is a 'mighty resource in the marketplace of ideas.' . . . There a student can literally explore the unknown, and discover areas of interest and thought not covered by the prescribed curriculum. The student who discovers the magic of the library is on the way to a life-long experience of self-education and enrichment. The student learns that a library is a place to test or expand upon ideas presented to him, in or out of the classroom.

"The most effective antidote to the poison of mindless orthodoxy is ready access to a broad sweep of ideas and philosophies. There is no danger in such exposure. The danger is in mind control."

95   Ah, honey, you turn me on, I'm a radio

> *She ain't jivin' 'bout no 'rogenous zones,*
> *Mistah FCC, don't ya mess with Sarah Jones!*

That's the gist of a lawsuit filed in early 2002 by a New York poet-musician. In 1999, KBOO-FM in Portland, Oregon, played Sarah Jones' rap song, "Your Revolution," between 7:00 and 9:00 p.m. Hammering home the caveat that "your revolution will not happen between these thighs," the song, Jones explained, quotes hip-hop hits to attack their misogyny, "images of women as groupies and playthings." On a censorship mission of her own, the poet opts out of fellatio, "doing it" in the back seat of jeeps (with or without condoms), drug-use, sexually-transmitted disease, and the other preoccupations of hip-hop culture.

The FCC fined KBOO the minimum $7,000, ruling that, whatever "Your Revolution's" sociological merits, KBOO violated commission rules against broadcasting indecent material when children could have been listening. In a rare and characteristically assertive move, Jones has fought back as an individual artist, complaining in her lawsuit that the FCC has violated her rights of free expression and due process. She is not seeking damages, however, only a declaration that "Your Revolution" is not indecent.[3]

In the past, the FCC has attempted to impose complete bans on similar material, but the courts intervened, saying that if the material was offensive but not legally "obscene," it was protected by the U.S. constitution. The FCC was limited to banning only until bed-time for minors. The same year that *Male and Female Under 18* went to court, the U.S. Supreme Court had occasion to consider a radio broadcast of George Carlin's stand-up routine about the "seven words you couldn't say on the public airwaves." The court below — the Court of Appeals for the District of Columbia — had held that the Federal Communications Commission exceeded its authority by preventing radio stations from broadcasting such routines before 1:30 in the morning.

The commission produced evidence that, until that hour, there were still at least a million children watching television. It also proved that, at about two o'clock in the afternoon of October 30, 1973, a New York radio station broadcast a talk show about "contemporary society's attitude toward language." The show's host warned the sensitive that they might want to turn the program off

---

[3] Jones' case bristles with the irony that, for more than a decade, state and federal authorities have cast about vainly for means of censoring rap and hip hop. In 1990, notorious prosecutions over "As Nasty as They Wanna Be" and associated live performances by the rap group 2 Live Crew foundered when the authorities could not show that the performances were obscene. The prosecutions marked "the first time that a court of appeals has been asked to apply the [common law obscenity] test to a musical composition, which contains both instrumental music and lyrics" — *Luke Records Inc. v. Navarro*, 960 F.2d 134 (11th Cir. 1992). More recently, the FCC withdrew citations against a radio station in Colorado which had played Eminem's "The Real Slim Shady." On reconsideration, the commission decided that the sexually-charged, and some say misogynistic, lyrics were not "patently offensive."

for 15 minutes. Then he played "Filthy Words," a 12-minute cut from the record album, *George Carlin, Occupation: Foole*, which, as Judge Bazelon of the district appeals court put it in his dissent, featured "the persistent, almost lavishly loving reiteration of the special words." A man driving with his 15-year-old son heard the broadcast over the car radio, and he complained to the FCC. The FCC ruled that the broadcast violated the U.S. Code where it prohibited broadcasting of "obscene, indecent, or profane language."

The speech was vulgar, the D.C. court held, but, as everyone agreed, it was not obscene, even though, by the end of Carlin's act, the word list actually ran to ten terms describing sexual and excretory organs or functions: "shit, piss, fuck, cunt, cocksucker, motherfucker, and tits," as well as fart, turd, and twat. Carlin, the majority found, had engaged in social commentary, not titillation. And that, of course, is the crux of Sarah Jones' case.

"Despite the commission's professed intentions," the D.C. appeals court held, "the direct effect of its order is to inhibit the free and robust exchange of ideas on a wide range of issues and subjects by means of radio and television communications." Quoting an earlier judgment of the court, Judge Tamm wrote in the Carlin case, "the radio can be turned off."

Unfortunately for Jones, a bare five-judge majority of the Supreme Court disagreed. "Because the broadcast audience is constantly tuning in and out," Justice John Paul Stevens wrote, "prior warnings cannot completely protect the listener or viewer from unexpected program content. To say that one may avoid further offense by turning off the radio when he hears indecent language is like saying that the remedy for an assault is to run away after the first blow. One may hang up on an indecent phone call, but that option does not give the caller a constitutional immunity or avoid a harm that has already taken place.

"Second, broadcasting is uniquely accessible to children, even those too young to read. Although Cohen's [sic] written message might have been incomprehensible to a first grader, [the] broadcast could have enlarged a child's vocabulary in an instant." Noting that the broadcast ban was limited to the specific "nuisance" of broadcasting "patently offensive references to sexual and excretory activities" before the wee hours of the morning, Justice Stevens coined a graphic metaphor from an earlier case: a "'nuisance may be merely a right thing in the wrong place, — like a pig in the parlor instead of the barnyard'...We simply hold that when the commission finds that a pig has entered the parlor, the exercise of its regulatory power does not depend on proof that the pig is obscene."[4]

Because the broadcast was "vulgar," "offensive," and "shocking" — albeit, not "obscene" and therefore still protected by the First Amendment if it were used in other media or at other times of the day — it did not warrant constitutional protection against the FCC's regulatory authority in the particular circumstances (i.e., at a time and on a medium available to anyone tuning in, whether they wanted to hear it or not, and despite whether they wanted their children to hear it.) The fact that Carlin intended social commentary, not titillation, was irrelevant, the majority said. The U.S. Code gave the FCC the power to regulate indecent broadcasts, and a broadcast could be indecent without being sexy.

In his sometimes sneering dissent, Justice Brennan virtually accused the majority of racism and class bias, pointing out that, for some people, the seven deadly words were part of everyday speech[5]: "I find the court's attempt to unstitch the warp and woof of First

---

[4] On the other hand, the Supreme Court has found that the FCC sometimes overreaches itself by "burning up the house to roast the pig." See, for example, *Sable Communications v. FCC*, 492 U.S. 115 (1988), quoting Justice Felix Frankfurter in *Butler v. Michigan*, 352 U.S. 380 (1957).

[5] He made special mention of the *Keefe* case, discussed at no. 157, where the U.S. First Circuit Court of Appeals court held that the word "motherfucker" enjoyed constitutional protection as part of the mundane speech of political radicals.

Amendment law in an effort to reshape its fabric to cover the patently wrong result the Court reaches in this case dangerous as well as lamentable. Yet there runs throughout the opinions of my brothers Powell and Stevens [in the majority] another vein I find equally disturbing: a depressing inability to appreciate that in our land of cultural pluralism, there are many who think, act, and talk differently from the members of this Court, and who do not share their fragile sensibilities. It is only an acute ethnocentric myopia that enables the Court to approve the censorship of communications solely because of the words they contain."

"Taken to their logical extreme," Justice Brennan concluded, the majority's "rationales would support the cleansing of public radio of any 'four-letter words' whatsoever, regardless of their context. The rationales could justify the banning from radio of a myriad of literary works, novels, poems, and plays by the likes of Shakespeare, Joyce, Hemingway, Ben Jonson, Henry Fielding, Robert Burns, and Chaucer; they could support the suppression of a good deal of political speech, such as the Nixon tapes; and they could even provide the basis for imposing sanctions for the broadcast of certain portions of the Bible." In a footnote, Justice Brennan provided examples from Ezekiel: "And they committed whoredoms in Egypt; they committed whoredoms in their youth; there were their breasts pressed, and there they bruised the teats of their virginity. . . . Thus thou calledst to remembrance the lewdness of thy youth, in bruising thy teats by the Egyptians for the paps of thy youth."

96 Shushing talk radio

In the last 15 years, live talk, phone-in, and "shock" radio have stimulated a flurry of warnings and "notices of apparent liability" from the FCC. Apparently, and predictably, "shock jock" Howard Stern first inspired the regulatory trend with his regular discussions on daytime radio of "masturbation, ejaculation, breast size, penis size, sexual intercourse, nudity, urination, oral-genital contact, erections, sodomy, bestiality, menstruation, and testicles," and whatever else strikes him as amusing. While this would seem to cover the waterfront of indecency, media law expert Roy Moore has pointed out that "Stern does not use any of the 'seven dirty words,' which, contrary to popular opinion, the FCC never said were specifically banned from the airwaves."

As early as 1973, the commission reacted to citizen complaints about talk radio by issuing a notice of apparent liability to the Sonderling Broadcasting Corporation. The notice concerned "Femme Forum," a radio call-in show broadcast daily from 10:00 a.m. to 3:00 p.m. on Sonderling's WGLD-FM in Oak Park, Illinois. The offensive broadcasts were two shows in February featuring discussions of oral sex. The FCC singled out a call in which a woman described how she habituated herself to fellatio:

> *Female Listener:* . . . *of course I had a few hangups at first about —in regard to this, but you know what we did — I have a craving for peanut butter all that [sic] time so I used to spread this on my husband's privates and after a while, I mean, I didn't even need the peanut butter anymore.*
> *Announcer: (Laughs) Peanut butter, huh?*
> *Listener: Right. Oh, we can try anything — you know — any, any of these women that have called and they have, you know, hangups about this, I mean they should try their favorite — you know like — uh. . . .*
> *Announcer: Whipped cream, marshmallow. . . .*

The commission noted that other callers discussed "aversions to swallowing the semen at climax, overcoming fears as to having the penis bitten off, and so forth." Apparently the "announcer" also responded rudely, on air, to a listener complaint about the discussion, and read a commercial for automobile insurance in a manner "suffused with leering innuendo."

The Illinois Citizens Committee for Broadcasting and the Illinois Division of the American Civil Liberties Union filed suit, complaining that the FCC was unconstitutionally restricting the public's right to "broadcasting alternatives." But the U.S. Court of Appeals for the District of Columbia upheld the commission. "The excerpts cited by the commission," the court ruled, "contain repeated and explicit descriptions of the techniques of oral sex. And these are presented, not for educational and scientific purposes, but in a context that was fairly described by the FCC as 'titillating and pandering.' . . . [C]ommercial exploitation of interests in titillation is the broadcaster's sole end. . . . Moreover, and significantly, "Femme Forum" is broadcast from 10 a.m. to 3 p.m. during daytime hours when the radio audience may include children — perhaps home from school for lunch, or because of staggered school hours or illness. Given this combination of factors, we do not think that the FCC's evaluation of this material infringes upon rights protected by the First Amendment.

". . . The Commission reasonably concluded that the dominant theme of the material broadcast by Sonderling was addressed to the prurient interest and was therefore condemnable. . . ."

97 Love is not in the air

A story from the World War II era has a soldier explaining why he was charged with assault while on leave: "I fucking came home from three fucking years fighting a fucking war only to find my wife in illicit cohabitation with a male not her husband." You would think the point of the joke was obvious: when used as intensives or vague abuse, certain words cease to describe bodily functions, or anything else in particular. But that has not stopped prosecutions for lewdness where sex clearly was not on the agenda. For instance, on a literal interpretation, the button that Timothy Stewart bought in the United States in June, 1980, seemed to encourage an act of love with the entire nation of Iran. But it had been designed to express something less than affection for the country that was then holding 53 people hostage in its American embassy. Generally, the whole western world had begun feeling antipathetic. Yet, although Canada would later be instrumental in rescuing some of the hostages, when Stewart rode his motorcycle across the U.S. border into Sault Ste. Marie, Canada, local customs officers accused him of importing an illegal button. They called the local constabulary, who charged Stewart with "exhibiting a disgusting object."[6]

At trial, Provincial Court Judge J.D. Greco expressed dismay that Stewart's case had made his list. The days when "the word in question" meant sexual congress and nothing else, though "still within the recollection of this court," were long past. This view had already been properly expressed, Judge Greco said, in *R. v. White*, a case of a teenager acquitted of "exposing obscene matter to the public view" by appearing on the streets of a resort town wearing a T-shirt printed with the words "fuck-off." Both Stewart and the T-shirted teenager were acquitted, even though the defense in the T-shirt case did not include a potentially saving point of grammar, namely, that the hyphen might have convinced the grammatically knowledgeable that the young wearer was engaged in nothing worse than honest self-criticism. While acquitting the teenager, a judge couldn't help wondering "what depraved minds would print such words on shirts and offer them for sale." Some might say the obvious answer is capitalist minds.

As in the *White* case, Judge Greco ruled, Stewart's button was not unduly exploiting sex, a key element in the Canadian legal

---

[6] The offense is discussed further at number 80.

definition of obscenity. And the specific charge laid, of exhibiting a disgusting object, was so unusual that one had to research back to 1864 for a precedent, in the case of a herbalist and his window display. Because the display showed a picture of a man whose bare chest was covered with sores, the herbalist was convicted of a nuisance, but not of indecency. "It is so disgusting that it is calculated to turn the stomach," the judge there said. "The object may be innocent and laudable, and there is nothing indecent or immoral in the exhibition." In Stewart's case, Judge Greco found, the button wasn't even disgusting; it was meant to convey something like "'Down with Iran,' or, if I may, 'To hell with Iran.'"

Nearly ten years earlier, a closely similar case went all the way to the United States Supreme Court and has become a cornerstone of free expression law. At a time when criticism of U.S. involvement in Vietnam was nearing its jagged peak, Paul Cohen wore a jacket into a Los Angeles courthouse with the words "Fuck the draft" printed on the back. On entering a courtroom, he removed the jacket and folded it over his arm. Bizarrely, a policeman sent the judge a note requesting that he cite Cohen for contempt of court. The judge rightly spurned the request (the jacket's silent derision for the draft might have been vulgar, but it did not by itself show contempt for the court), so the policeman charged Cohen under the California Code with "maliciously and willfully disturbing the peace or quiet of any neighborhood or person by offensive conduct."

He was convicted at trial and sentenced to 30 days in prison, a very heavy penalty in the circumstances. Although he claimed that he was merely expressing a political opinion peacefully, and while the prosecution admitted that he never said anything offensive or otherwise aloud about the draft, he lost his first appeal. The appeal court held that, while the sentiment was not obscene, it amounted to fighting words: it could easily have promoted violence by inciting some patriot to attack Cohen. But in the U.S. Supreme Court, Cohen's right of free expression prevailed. "At least so long as there is no showing of an intent to incite disobedience to or disruption of the draft," Justice John Harlan wrote for the five-judge bare majority, "Cohen could not, consistently with the First and Fourteenth Amendments, be punished for asserting the evident position on the inutility or immorality of the draft his jacket reflected." Along the lines of what Justice Greco noted in *Stewart*, Justice Harlan wrote, "It cannot plausibly be maintained that this vulgar allusion to the Selective Service System would conjure up such psychic stimulation in anyone likely to be confronted with Cohen's crudely defaced jacket.... How is one to distinguish this from any other offensive word? Surely the state has no right to cleanse public debate to the point where it is grammatically palatable to the most squeamish among us."

And to forbid such speech on the very low probability that it would provoke violence was to start down the road of suppressing all unpopular expression. Unlike those subjected to raucous political pronouncements from sound-trucks, passersby offended by Cohen's jacket merely had to avert their eyes. Besides, how was it justice to censor someone because some scofflaw thug might attack him?

In words that have become frequently cited in obscenity and other free expression cases, Justice Harlan concluded that "much linguistic expression serves a dual communicative function: it conveys not only ideas capable of relatively precise, detached explication, but otherwise inexpressible emotions as well. In fact, words are often chosen as much for their emotive as their cognitive force. We cannot sanction the view that the constitution, while solicitous of the cognitive content of individual speech, has little or no regard for that emotive function which, practically speaking, may often be the more important element of the overall message sought to be communicated. Indeed, as Mr. Justice Frankfurter has said [in 1944], 'one of the prerogatives of American citizenship is the right to criticize public men and measures — and that means not only informed and responsible criticism but the freedom to speak foolishly and without moderation.'"

98   Football fetish

U.S. courts have considered *The Dallas Cowboys Cheerleaders v. Pussycat Cinema* as standing for the proposition that freedom of speech can co-exist with protection of trademarks. But the Dallas cheerleaders were worried less about freedom of speech than about how people might confuse them with the star of *Debbie Does Dallas*, a film distributed by Pussycat's proprietor, Michael Zaffarano, in the late 1970s. According to Judge Van Graafeiland of the U.S. Court of Appeals for Southern New York, *Debbie Does Dallas* was "a gross and revolting sex film whose plot, to the extent that there is one, involves a cheerleader at a fictional high school who has been selected to become a 'Texas Cowgirl.' In order to raise enough money to send Debbie . . . to Dallas, the cheerleaders perform sexual services for a fee. The movie consists largely of a series of scenes graphically depicting the sexual escapades of the 'actors.' In the movie's final scene Debbie dons a uniform strikingly similar to that worn by the Dallas Cowboys Cheerleaders and for approximately twelve minutes of film footage engages in various sex acts while clad or partially clad in the uniform.

"Defendants [Pussycat Cinema] advertized the movie with marquee posters depicting Debbie in the allegedly infringing uniform and containing such captions as 'Starring Ex Dallas Cowgirl Cheerleader Bambi Woods' and 'You'll do more than cheer for this X Dallas Cheerleader.'"

In footnotes, Judge Van Graafeiland noted that 1) the Dallas Cowboy Cheerleaders were also known as the "Dallas Cowgirls"; 2) Bambi Woods "is not now and never has been a Dallas Cowboys Cheerleader"; 3) whether the movie was obscene was irrelevant. All the same, he could not agree with defendant Zaffarano that the uniform the Dallas cheerleaders wore was purely functional and "generic." The Cowboys had a common law (that is, unregistered) trademark, Judge Van Graafeiland ruled, in the "particular combination of colors and collocation of decorations of the uniform" — white vinyl boots, white shorts, a white belt decorated with blue stars, a blue bolero blouse, and a white vest decorated with three blue stars on each side of the front and a white fringe around the bottom.

In affirming the Cowboys' injunction against Pussycat, Judge Van Graafeiland concluded that "it is hard to believe that anyone who had seen defendants' sexually-depraved film could ever thereafter disassociate it from the plaintiff's cheerleaders."

99 Jewels not all in the family, brother

That same year, another U.S. appeal conjoined pornography with sexual invective, but in a foreign and nearly dead language. In *California v. Arno* the Los Angeles Municipal Court had convicted the appellants of dealing in films such as *Hard Core Girls* and *Raped Rectum*. The appeal focused on evidence gathered by police officer Johnson while he was on a hilltop opposite Arno's offices in the Playboy Building on Sunset Boulevard.

Johnson swore that, through ten-power binoculars and from a distance equal to two or three football fields, he had seen "Arno and others handle a distinctively marked flip-top box displaying a label with a picture of a nude woman." Associate Justice Thompson, for the majority, held that the binocular evidence was inadmissible because it derived from an invasion of privacy: the handling of the box was meant to be "protected from the uninvited eye." He allowed the appeal.

In his dissent, Justice Hanson wrote that "pornography, narcotics, prostitution, pimping, bookmaking, and the like" are not victimless crimes. "There are no victim-less crimes. Society is the victim. The majority opinion in my view unduly restricts law enforcement officers from protecting society's interests." Justice Thompson replied, in his footnote number two,

> *We feel compelled by the nature of the attack in the dissenting opinion to spell out a response:*
> 1. *Some answer is required to dissent's charge.*
> 2. *Certainly we do not endorse "victimless crime."*
> 3. *How that question is involved escapes us.*
> 4. *Moreover, the constitutional issue is significant.*
> 5. *Ultimately it must be addressed in light of precedent.*
> 6. *Certainly the course of precedent is clear.*
> 7. *Knowing that, our result is compelled.*
> *(See Funk & Wagnall's* The New Cassell's German Dict.*, p. 408)*

The section in question of *Cassell's German Dictionary* seems to be the entry for *schmuck*, or at least that is what some readers have deduced from "spelling out" the first letters of each of the footnote's numbered sentences.

According to Gerald Uelmen, writing in the *American Bar Association Journal*, Justice Hanson "protested that press accounts of the footnote used the Yiddish definition" found in *Webster's*, not the German one in *Cassell's*. The *Cassell's* meaning is "ornament, decoration, jewels." How this became the *Webster's* Yiddish meaning of penis or "prick," may have something to do with our English expression "family jewels," and also with German or Jewish *hausfraus* admiring their young sons at bath.

100 That frigging clothing company

Then again, *fuck* can be legally offensive even when it is only present by inference. In the late 1990s, the clothing multinational French

Connection UK discovered that its gross profits rose by 84 percent after it began using the acronym FCUK. It placed ads on Vancouver buses in 2000 which showed a young man running beside the jumbled words "hot dash must date," and a small FCUK logo in one corner. Unjumbling was the idea, of course, but only the bus drivers complained, asserting that the acronym amounted to workplace sexual harassment. One woman driver was concerned that the ads might encourage rowdyism. To forestall a dispute at the provincial human rights commission, head office pulled the ads.

In the past, censorship has only inspired French Connection. Its first FCUK campaign in 1997 featured the slogan "Fcuk fashion." When the British Advertising Standards Council objected, French Connection replaced the slogan with "Fcuk advertising."

THE WAGES OF SIN

Prostitution and the Sex Trade

"I believe that sex is one of the most beautiful, natural, wholesome things that money can buy."

STEVE MARTIN

"There are a number of mechanical devices which increase sexual arousal, particularly in women. Chief among these is the Mercedes-Benz 380SL convertible."

P.J. O'ROURKE

101 Paying the price

We all have our price, and the law on prostitution reflects this ambivalence. In many jurisdictions, it is a crime to "communicate for the purposes of prostitution," but not actually to have sex for money.

In 1957, the British *Report of the Committee on Homosexual Offences and Prostitution* elaborated: "Prostitution in itself is not, in this country, an offence against the criminal law. Some of the activities of prostitutes are, and so are the activities of some others who are concerned in the activities of prostitutes. But it is not illegal for a woman to 'offer her body to indiscriminate lewdness for hire,' provided that she does not, in the course of doing so, commit any one of the specific acts which would bring her within the ambit of the law." The committee saw the law's function as regulating the nuisances and criminal activity surrounding prostitution, but not the activity itself. Where the Danes more baldly accept prostitution as an inevitable part of the social fabric, the tribal Taliban of Afghanistan hanged prostitutes specifically because their trade "corrupted society." Las Vegas legalizes and carefully regulates prostitution in the name of free enterprise where once American pilgrims worked hard to deter it in the name of freedom generally. Under the statutes of the Massachusetts Bay colony, proprietors of brothels were "severely" whipped with 30 lashes "at the cart's tayle," then imprisoned and "kept with hard fare [bread and water, so to speak] and hard labour, by dayly Task, and in defect of their duty to be severely whipt every night with Ten Stripes." At least once a week the law further compelled the jailers to chain the convicted pimps to a hand-cart, fit them with "hair Frocks and blew Caps," and set them to "draw all the filth laid up in the Cart through the Streets, to the Sea side going to the Gallows." This sentence "to be alike kept with hard Fare and Labour" was for an indefinite term.

102 Transporting gulls across staid lions

The most notorious anti-fornication law in the Anglo-American legal world is the *Mann Act*, passed in 1910 by the United States Congress. In its original form, and speaking generally, it forbade the "transportation" across state lines or internationally of "any woman or girl for the purpose of prostitution or debauchery, or for any other immoral purpose." Although it was intended to regulate prostitution, moralists, many of them judges, began using it to punish sex outside marriage. And the penalty could be heavy — "a fine not exceeding five thousand dollars, or . . . imprisonment of not more than five years, or . . . both such fine and imprisonment, in the discretion of the court."

The law invited widespread ridicule, even early on, and spawned a pun known to every U.S. high school student as late as the 1970s or '80s. The set-up joke varied, but generally concerned a scientist performing research on aging. The scientist experimented on dolphins, the joke usually went, which he fed baby gulls or mynah birds. For security, he also kept a couple of lions in his lab. The police inevitably charged him with "transporting gulls [or mynahs] across staid lions for immortal porpoises."[1] In 1917, however, the United States Supreme Court was not amused, upholding *Mann Act* convictions against two California men who simply took their girlfriends for a naughty weekend in Reno, Nevada.

The lower courts had sentenced Drew Caminetti to 18 months in prison and a $1,500 fine. Maury Diggs, who stood accused of arranging the interstate holiday for both couples, fared even worse, with two years in prison and a $2,000 fine. It was an aggravating circumstance, of course, that the men were married while practicing this recreational "concubinage." Their lawyers pointed out to the high court that the *Mann Act*'s author, Representative James Mann of Illinois, specifically stated in a report to Congress that the legislation "is not needed or intended as an aid to the states in the exercise of their police powers in the suppression or regulation of immorality in general. It does not

---

[1] The author's report of this joke is not to be taken as his endorsement of the view that a dolphin is a porpoise.

attempt to regulate the practice of voluntary prostitution, but aims solely to prevent panderers and procurers from compelling thousands of women and girls against their will and desire to enter and continue in a life of prostitution." As well, Chief Justice Oliver Wendell Holmes and two other justices dissenting with him noted that the act itself stated that "this Act shall be known and referred to as the 'White-slave traffic Act,'" meaning that it was "commercialized vice, immoralities having a mercenary purpose," and not general fornication or adultery that it prohibited. Mann himself, the dissenters said, had told Congress that the act was "so drawn that [prosecutions] are limited to cases in which there is the act of transportation in interstate commerce of women for purposes of prostitution."

The dissenters admitted that "any measure that protects the purity of women from assault or enticement to degradation finds an instant advocate in our best emotions." But "everybody knows that there is a difference between the occasional immoralities of men and women and that systematized and mercenary immorality epitomized in the statute's graphic phrase 'White-slave traffic.' And it was such immorality that was in the legislative mind and not the other. The other is occasional, not habitual — inconspicuous — does not offensively obtrude upon public notice. Interstate commerce is not its instrument as it is of the other, nor is prostitution its object or its end. It may, indeed, in instances, find a convenience in crossing state lines, but this is its accident, not its aid."

This seeming good sense did not hold sway for decades to come. While even the majority in *Caminetti* admitted that using the statute against mundane extra-marital sex opened the statute to be exploited by blackmailers (jilted mistresses or cuckolded spouses, for example), they contended that this was for the legislature to worry about. The words of the *Mann Act* were plain, and they forbade interstate transportation of females "for debauchery or any other immoral purposes," which included fornication and adultery.

103 Trampling the Little Tramp

The same interpretation in 1944 helped drive Charlie Chaplin out of America. The FBI spearheaded a *Mann Act* prosecution against Chaplin, whose "citizen of the world" stance the bureau characterized as communism. The federal attorney general alleged that Chaplin had paid for actress Joan Barry to travel all the way from Hollywood to New York City for one night of intimacy. Barry was mentally unstable and later won a paternity suit against Chaplin, never mind that blood tests showed he was not the father. Chaplin said that Barry had burst into his home with a gun, threatening to commit suicide. He denied any sexual intimacy, and though his lawyer pointed out that it was ridiculous to assume Chaplin would have transported Barry three thousand miles for one sex act when "she would have given her body to him at any time or place," it took the jury nearly three hours to acquit Chaplin.

As late as 1962, the pop musician Chuck Berry was convicted of violating the *Mann Act* by abetting international debauchery. He had brought a 14-year-old prostitute from Juarez to check coats at his St. Louis bar. When he fired her, she went to the police. Apparently there is no evidence that Berry knew her age, but he was sentenced to two years in prison for violating the *Mann Act*.

In the next two decades Congress brought the law more in line with the times. A 1978 amendment included "minor boys" with the "women or girls," and in 1986 more politically-correct wording forbade the interstate transportation of an "individual" for illegal sexual activity. The legislature excised all gender-based allusions, as well as all references to debauchery, "other immoral purposes," and "white slavery."

104 When you call me Mistress Fanny, smile

The debate over who is a prostitute is not confined to whether it includes women who choose wealthy men over the more soulful.

Does it include men selling their bodies for money? In 1972, a county court judge thought not.

One early morning in downtown Windsor, just across the Canadian border from Detroit, a man named Patterson flagged down a car. Patterson was dressed as a woman. After a brief conversation, he got into the car and the driver agreed to pay him ten dollars for what was probably fellatio. County Court Judge Clunis is spartan with the details, while characterizing them as "abhorrent" and "revolting." Patterson began undoing the driver's trousers when a police officer appeared. Only after the officer arrested Patterson did the driver learn that he was a man.

His sex — or "gender" as semantic prudery puts it these days — proved decisive. Patterson argued that under Canadian law only women could be prostitutes. Therefore, even though he was cross-dressed at the relevant time, he could not be convicted of soliciting for the purpose of prostitution. As the Canadian *Criminal Code* did not define "prostitute," Judge Clunis felt obliged to resort to dictionaries. He discovered there that it had two meanings: "First, the offering of her body by a woman to indiscriminate acts of lewdness for hire. Secondly, the selling of a talent or capacity for an unworthy purpose."

The second meaning, Judge Clunis wrote, could have included Patterson's conduct. But it was "dangerous indeed to permit the interpretation of a statute to be based upon the figurative use of the words contained in it. If this is so, it would be unthinkable that one should adopt such an approach to the interpretation of penal statutes."

Besides, the "vernacular of the times" had a separate phrase for Patterson: "*male* prostitute," expressly. The court acquitted Patterson, but the law has not generally accepted the proposition that only women can be prostitutes.

Then again, not to put too fine a point on it, was it "prostitution" when Holden Caulfield, of *The Catcher in the Rye*, paid a prostitute just to talk to him? A preliminary hearing in Ontario in 1991 raised something like that point.

Joseph Polyak stood charged with living on the avails of prostitution. He had hired Therese Mercado to fulfill, as his ads for customers said, "fetishes and fantasies," and to provide "massage." Coitus, Polyak and Mercado both testified, was not necessarily part of her job description. "If it happened, it happened." And in fact, although Mercado worked in Polyak's apartment for several weeks, charging customers nearly $175 an hour for her ministrations, she never once had intercourse with a customer.

Instead, she spanked and dominated, allowed herself to be tied up, and otherwise fulfilled hearts' or other physiologies' desire, usually in matching underwear or "a plain teddy," depending on the desire to be fulfilled, no cheques please. Polyak would be standing, or sitting, by elsewhere in the apartment in case a customer alleged frustration of contract. All clients would reach sexual climax, Mercado admitted, but often "by themselves." It was not necessarily a boast: Mercado was in the room, but her appearance, however expensive and thoughtfully styled in the appropriate underwear, was pretty well incidental. Nonetheless the court evidently did not find it necessary to infer that sex is often more an affair of the mind than of fact, rather like legal advocacy.

Mitchell Chernovsky, Polyak's lawyer, argued that as Mercado did not actually have sexual intercourse with her customers, she was not a prostitute. And if she was not a prostitute, any money she gave his client ($50 out of every $160 she earned) could not amount to "the avails of prostitution." The court disagreed. The woman's services, Judge Young held, constituted prostitution insofar as they involved "the performance of physical acts of indecency for the sexual gratification of others in return for payment." Polyak was obliged to stand trial on the charges.

Judge Young based his opinion on law that was three quarters of a century old. In 1918, the British crown charged a West London prostitute named De Munck with pimping for her own daughter, Kathleen, who was younger than 16. Witnesses saw mother and daughter, and sometimes Kathleen alone, "accosting men in the street" and taking them back to their room in a nearby building. While medical evidence showed that Kathleen was "virgo intacta," Judge Atherley Jones directed them "that the term 'prostitute' was not necessarily confined to a woman who for gain offered her body for natural sexual intercourse, and that if the jury came to the conclusion that the appellant procured her daughter to offer her body for gain for the gratification of the sexual passions of any man by any unnatural and abnormal act of indecency, they would be justified in finding her guilty." The jury in fact convicted De Munck.

105 Desperate for rhyme and reason

The combination of easy sexual accessibility and low social status makes prostitutes the frequent target of the homicidally deranged. A 1954 example caused a storm of protest in the legal world when a troubled 18-year-old was convicted of murdering a prostitute.

Alec Bedder was a confused young grocer's assistant. He had quit school at 16, worked briefly in a factory, then joined the army only to be turfed out after two months because of bad eyesight. Attracted by women, but impotent with them, he admitted to homosexual encounters that had frightened him. Because of these bad experiences, he had taken to carrying a knife.

On March 12, 1954, he met Doreen Redding, a prostitute, in the streets of Leicester, England, and arranged to have sex with her in a nearby courtyard. When Bedder couldn't perform, Redding mocked him. Bedder apparently held Redding very tightly. He told a court at the Leicestershire Assizes that in retaliation she slapped him, then punched him in the stomach. He pushed her. Then: "She kicked me in the privates. . . . After that, I do not know what happened till she fell." What happened was that he had stabbed her twice. The court convicted him of murder and sentenced him to death.

The trial judge had told the jury that Bedder's crime could be reduced to manslaughter only if a reasonable person would have acted as he did. That reasonable person, the judge explained, is not "a drunken one or a man who is sexually impotent." The rule for many years was "that an excitable or pugnacious person is not entitled to rely on provocation [as a defense to murder] which would not have led an ordinary person to act as he did." The reasonable person was not an impotent 18-year-old.

Of course, it is doubtful that a perfectly reasonable person of any age would commit manslaughter under any "provocation." If he committed homicide — if, say, he were starving to death or could save the life of his young child by killing an old woman — he would think about it very hard. A reasonable person would never act on the sudden, before his passion had time to cool, as the law requires. And premeditated homicide is murder (unless, of course, the killer acts out of necessity or duress).

The legal community could not see what was to be gained by hanging a young man who was experiencing immense difficulty in growing up. Where was the justice? Bedder's execution would not deter anybody in a similarly deranged state. It would not redress Redding's suffering and horrible end. It would not offer society any catharsis.

In fact, the reasonable person standard was proving itself decidedly undemocratic. In the emerging global village, the common law of the great democracies declared that a person was reasonable only if he was an average, white, heterosexual male, probably a clerk at an insurance company or an import-export house — "the man on the Clapham omnibus." The Home Secretary commuted Alec Bedder's death sentence to life in prison.

Still, the law on provocation and the reasonable person stood for another quarter of a century, until the *Camplin* case.

Fifteen-year-old Paul Camplin had been blackmailing a laborer of about 50. The man was pursuing a homosexual relationship with one of Camplin's school friends and Camplin had threatened to "shop him" to the police. Some time later, Camplin showed up drunk at the man's apartment. The man sodomized him — raped him, Camplin told a trial court — and then laughed at him. In a rage, Camplin — in the vivid words of Lord Diplock of the House of Lords — had "split the man's skull" with two blows of a handy chapati pan, a heavy, rimless fry-pan comparable to a pancake skillet.

Relying on *Bedder*, the Director of Public Prosecutions argued that our criminal law's "reasonable person" does not include a boy of 15, nor anyone else who is not ordinarily a balanced, physically normal adult. "A one-eyed man driving a car would not be heard to say that he did not see the other vehicle." But the House of Lords took the opportunity to overturn *Bedder*. The reasonable person, they said, "is a person having the power of self-control to be expected of an ordinary person of the sex and age of the accused, but in other respects sharing such of the accused's characteristics as they think would affect the gravity of the provocation to him."

Such a rule meant that both Alec Bedder and Paul Camplin, though teenaged killers with special problems, might qualify as ordinarily reasonable people.

106 The wages of sin are taxable

The government might outlaw bawdy houses and pimping, but that doesn't stop it taxing the illicit gains. The argument that this amounted to living off the avails, itself, failed to impress the Exchequer Court of Canada in 1964, although taxpayer Olva Eldridge was allowed many deductions, including legal fees and money for strong-arm men.

Her operation was sophisticated, with nine full-time employees: two dispatchers and seven prostitutes. Its sophistication, in fact, lubricated its downfall: the police found detailed call-sheets in the "workplace," which they turned over to tax inspectors. In business from 1953, Eldridge began filing returns in 1957, when, according to Exchequer Justice Angus Cattanach, tax officials "pointed out the advantages and necessity of maintaining complete records." At issue now were claims pertaining to taxation years 1959 and 1960, during which Eldridge had grossed, at the very least, $77,661 and $80,749 — very high income for the time. Revenuers had allowed her more than $53,000 in deductions for 1959 — "salaries," commissions, telephone costs, room rentals, refreshments, taxis, bad debts (bad checks, etc.) — and almost $60,000 for 1960. When the tax appeal board allowed her another $11,860 and $9,700 for those years, the Minister of Revenue appealed to the courts.

Justice Cattanach affirmed the appeal board's allowance of deductions for room rentals, lawyers' and bodyguard fees ($1,925 and $100 respectively), and $5,400 in bail bond commissions Eldridge had paid to get her "girls" out of the slammer. (Justice Cattanach saw such a service as part of Eldridge's "contractual obligations" as an employer.) But because Eldridge did not produce receipts, she was disallowed

> — $1,000 *supposedly paid to a moonlighting telephone company serviceman who checked her phones for wire-taps;*
> — $16,750 *ostensibly paid to the police as "protection money";*
> — $4,600 *allegedly provided, in the form of liquor, to city government officials;*
> — over $4,300 *in rent and utility bills;*
> — nearly $1,700 *supposedly paid to "casual employees" for a "Penthouse party";*
> — $500 *expended to buy up an entire print-run of a sensationalist newspaper that described Eldridge as a Czarina of the underworld*

with enemies who "subjected her to loathsome indignities" (charges strenuously denied by the taxpayer before the tax appeal board);
— *and* $1,000 *paid in commission to a bail bondsman to secure the taxpayer's own freedom.*

The Exchequer Court would have allowed this last as a legitimate business expense had Eldridge not been run directly *out* of business near the time of that transaction, upon being convicted of living off the avails of prostitution. Catch-22 proved operative, though it went under a different name and number in the *Income Tax Act*.

Twenty years later, prostitutes in London picketed the law courts to make the "government is a pimp" argument in support of Lindi St. Claire. St. Claire was a madam of extravagant proportions, a "retired bondage queen with the 62FF chest and a mission to decriminalise prostitution," the *Sunday Times* said of her in 1991. When she founded the Corrective Party to run for Parliament in 1997, she was still known as Miss Whiplash, and she claimed to possess intimate knowledge of governmental workings through the 72 sitting MPs who had been her professional clients. To whip up business, she once took out a classified ad reading, "Nymphomaniac blonde, short, fat, slut, aged 33, 55-45-55, wishes to marry titled aristocrat."

The Inland Revenue began pursuing St. Claire in 1984 for about $100,000 in unpaid taxes on her prostitution earnings. As she addressed the judge in the ensuing litigation, several of her professional colleagues paraded outside the courthouse in black silk masks. "They prosecute me for being a prostitute, they have fined me hundreds of pounds," St. Claire told reporters, fruitlessly. "They also stopped me from setting up a company because it would be to carry out an unlawful business. Yet they want me to pay tax. It's totally unfair. If I pay anything toward the keep of my boyfriends, they can be had for poncing, that's why I say the tax men are pimping."

By 1997, St. Claire's debt to the Inland Revenue had increased by another $10,000 and she complained that "I've had to give them my £25,000 Corrective Party campaign funds, the deposits for my 50 candidates, straight away. Otherwise they will prosecute me for wilfully avoiding taxes." Thus ended her political mission to legalize prostitution, bring back caning, televize the execution of criminals (never mind that the death penalty had been abolished in Britain), and provide "therapeutic" sex courtesy of the National Health Service.

107 Everything's in working order

The cases continue to show that the tax game is the same for prostitutes as for any other business people — a struggle by the taxpayer, on one hand, to score deductions from taxable income, and by the taxing authority, on the other hand, to accumulate maximum revenue. In 2001, the Danish stripper and porn star Lia Damen told the Danish National Tax Council that her breasts constituted work tools and that the law therefore permitted her to deduct implant surgery to enlarge them. The argument was not without precedent, at least in Britain. During the Second World War, a court stenographer who fell ill, ostensibly because of unhealthy conditions in the justice buildings, pressed a claim for deductions under the "wear and tear of plant" section of the British *Income Tax Act* — the section that normally applies to depreciation of industrial equipment. Perhaps inspired by the advocacy he had witnessed during working hours, he presented evidence of lost work-time and medical expenses. While Lord Greene was sympathetic, especially considering that business- and tradespeople usually enjoyed more tax breaks than "professional men" like court clerks, the judge held that "your own body is not plant." A horse might be plant, or at least a horse had been held to be a plant under the *Employer's Liability Acts*, Lord Greene admitted, but no one had ever held a person to be plant.

Without mentioning anything about horses (which was probably just as well), the Danish Tax Council reached a similar conclusion about Damen's chest: although she exploited it earnestly to gain her daily crust, it was not a work tool.

108 Clothed in morality

Never mind that government collects massive "sin taxes" while advising us sternly that prostitution, smoking, and drinking are bad for us: prostitutes, and tobacco and distillery magnates must live, too. We have already seen that the courts sometimes refuse to enforce contracts that "assist fornication" — the landlord might whistle for his unpaid rent if he knows that his property is rented by a man for his mistress. The lease amounts to a "contract for an immoral purpose," so that the landlord cannot turn to the courts for help. But with the rise of capitalism, moral gray areas blur against the black bottom line. This has become especially clear in cases about prostitutes as consumers.

The leading case (quoted, in fact, in the landlord case at no. 8) is *Pearce v. Brooks*, 1866. Brooks was a "woman of the town" who had refused to pay a premium on a rented carriage when she defaulted on the rent and damaged the vehicle. The law seemed to say that if the carriage-owners knew that Brooks was renting the carriage to pick up johns, *and* knew that she would pay for the carriage out of her ill-gotten gains, the contract for its use was illegal and the carriage-owners could not get the courts to make her pay.

This rule was set originally by one of the most influential judges in Anglo-American history, Edward Law, first Baron Ellenborough. In the 1808 case of *Bowry v. Bennet*, Lord Ellenborough, as chief justice of England, had ordered a prostitute to pay for clothes delivered to her. The contract was good, it seemed, because the woman would not necessarily wear the garments only in the course of her illicit business. A long line of such disputes had ended in similar victories for the plaintiff-merchants and prostitutes' landlords.

Generally, unless a landlord knew that lodgings would be used exclusively for prostitution, the prostitute-tenant had been held liable for her rent. As one judge bluntly put it in the case of a working girl who was a minor, "both an infant and a prostitute must have lodging." In order to stop prostitutes from getting off rent-free, the courts were obliged to make a chameleon distinction between a prostitute's workplace and residence, forced to assert that her "office" turned back into a residence between clients — as though, if you made your living as a doctor or dentist out of your house, your office there was not really an office. By such reasoning, prostitutes have of course also been held liable for plumbing repairs, phone bills, and so on, even though it could be said that someone providing those services was furthering an illegal enterprise. A prostitute (or a doctor or dentist) requires heat and water even when she isn't on duty.

(On the other hand, a madam can win damages from a landlord who throws her out, even if she rented the rooms under the pretence of using them for a legitimate business — a perfumery, for instance, as was the front in an 1854 case. There, the court found that the tenant's lie about the nature of the business had nothing to do with the lease *per se*, and so the landlord could not evict her without proper notice.)

In one widely-quoted case, while ordering a prostitute to pay a laundry for cleaning flashy dresses as well as men's nightcaps, Justice Buller asked the prostitute's lawyer, with exasperation that survives on paper from 1798: "What do you mean by the expression 'clothes used for the purposes of prostitution?' This unfortunate woman must have clean linen, and it is impossible for the court to take into consideration which of these articles were used by the Defendant [the prostitute] to an improper purpose, and which were not." The court did not speculate as to what proper purpose a single woman might have for men's nightcaps.

Lord Ellenborough had attempted to fashion a two-sided rule from such precedents. In ordering the prostitute in *Bowry v. Bennet* to pay her couturière, he held that even if the couturière knew of her customer's way of life, the contract was enforceable unless the couturière also expected to be paid directly from the customer's ill-gotten gains.

From that time until the carriage case nearly 60 years later, Lord Ellenborough's rule had been making judges fidget and fumble: in practice, if prostitutes simply relied on their own turpitude or notoriety, asserting that everything they wished to buy or rent would be paid for by whoring, the rule could make it laughably easy for them to welch on their debts.

For nervous Victorian judges, the complementary problem with the rule was that merchants could get away with furthering prostitution simply by turning a blind eye, or at least pretending ignorance: as far as they knew, they would say, Mistress Quickly bought her dresses out of the innkeeping part of her business, not the whore-mongering part. It was too difficult, the judges soon realized, to prove both that the seller knew that the buyer was engaged in immoral or unlawful enterprise *and* that she would pay out of the tainted proceeds. So, very carefully professing not to contradict anything the redoubtable Lord Ellenborough had declared, the later judges contradicted him anyway. In his observation that a seller should not be paid with dirty money, Lord Ellenborough, the later judges hedged, had not been making a hard and fast rule, but was merely talking about the weight of evidence. If the seller knew that merchandise was to be used exclusively, or at least primarily, for something unlawful or contrary to public policy, that was enough to render the contract void. If it could be shown that a seller expected to be paid out of ill-gotten gains, this simply added weight to the evidence that he knew the buyer was making the purchase to carry on her evil ways.

109 Occupational hazard

In 1994, the Federal Court of Australia had occasion to consider a more refined question about business administration in the sex trade: What if you perform innocuous, non-sexual services in a brothel? Can you collect workers' compensation if you are "injured in the course of your employment?"

In this case, Heather Farnell was a babysitter for two prostitutes in New South Wales. They told her that the brothel where they worked needed a receptionist. Farnell took the job, which required her to open the "studio," answer the phone, meet customers and conduct them to the waiting area, perform some elementary bookkeeping, and clean some of the premises. Arriving at work one day, she fell and broke her arm.

A magistrate ruled that she could not claim compensation because her job contract was void as "illegal, contrary to public policy or prohibited by statute." She was helping to run a "knocking shop" and living on its "avails." But on second and third appeal, the courts said that Farnell might have a legitimate claim, which they sent back for arbitration. Two of the judges in the Federal Court (the highest body) admitted that Farnell had "aided" the offense of keeping a common bawdy or disorderly house. One even said that the non-menial work she performed amounted to participating in the brothel's management. But this did not make her employment contract void or contrary to public policy. She knew what was going on, but within its own context her behavior was not illegal. At worst, another judge said, to the extent that Farnell herself did something criminal, the illegality was technical and insignificant. And there was no proof that her pay amounted to "avails of prostitution." Federal Court Justice Higgins even worried that to say otherwise would allow criminals to get out of legal contracts by claiming the contracts furthered criminal purposes. In other words, in 1994, he voiced the same alarm that judges felt a century earlier about Lord Ellenborough's rule. In any event, market forces and promotion of the "Protestant work ethic" prevailed.

110 Nice work if you can get it

A 1948 case from New York provides a variation on the workers' compensation theme. What if the worker in question is a prostitute's customer, visiting her workplace, but on his own off-hours?

On shore-leave in Yugoslavia from his duties as fireman and coaltender on the *S.S. John N. Robins*, Eino Koistinen had met a woman in a bar "whose blandishments," according to New York City Court Justice Frank Carlin, "lured him to the room for purposes not particularly platonic." It turned out that his spirit was more than willing but his flesh wasn't up to it. So, on the basis of non-performance, albeit his own, he refused to pay. Though the prostitute insisted on her "dinner" ("the court erroneously interpreted the word as showing that the woman had a carnivorous frenzy," Justice Carlin wrote, "which could only be soothed by the succulent sirloin provided at the plaintiff's expense"), Koistinen remained adamant.

Of course, had sex-for-money itself been a lawful enterprise, the prostitute could have staked a solid legal claim on the contract. Forced to resort to her own manner of enforcement, she tried to take the money from Koistinen, but failing at that, locked him in her room. Koistinen kicked at the door without success and had gone to the window, which was between six and eight feet from the ground, when another man "formidably loomed at the lintels" of the door, armed with a knife. Koistinen jumped out the window.

He sustained injuries that put him in the hospital in both Yugoslavia and the United States. But when he sought compensation, his employer, American Export Lines, argued that his "immoral intent" nullified their obligation to pay; randiness, not anything legitimately covered by his contract of employment, was the true "proximate cause" of his fall — or leap — from grace. Justice Carlin admitted that the sailor had not gone to the prostitute's room "for heavenly contemplation," but held that the "ticklish situation" he found himself in just before his defenestration "was not a reasonably foreseeable consequence of his original situation." Koistinen, himself, in other words, had not been negligent in seeking the woman's services. The proximate cause of his injuries was not the visit to the brothel, *per se*, but "the concurrence of the locked door . . . and the subsequent looming threat of the man with the menacing mien."

While the law would disallow maintenance to sailors who contracted venereal diseases, injured themselves while drunk, or were otherwise reckless or indiscreet, it did not inquire into the morality of their behavior during the shore-leave portion of their employment. Shore-leave was part of the sailor's contract and Koistinen was entitled to worker's compensation: sailors, after all, will be boys — an allowance, as we have seen, not accorded landlubbers such as ranch-hands.[2] The life of a sailor was unusually stressful, and according to the common law, seamen were "wards of the court" to be "treated with the tenderness of a guardian."

111 The barber never charged this much

What if there is a "contract" for actual sex with a prostitute, but the sex never takes place?

In 1993, Eric McFarlane, a pimp, came before the English Court of Appeal with that question. Police had charged McFarlane with

---

[2] See number 5. Comparing the two cases demonstrates that since the Second World War it has become more difficult for employers to avoid provisions of employment contracts by impugning a worker's private "moral turpitude." Even in contract law, sexuality has come out of the closet since the days of *Denham v. Patrick*.

living off the avails of prostitution. His defence was that, although he had lived "as man and wife" with a woman in the sex trade, the woman was not a prostitute, not someone who "offered her body for lewdness for reward," as the trial judge put it in convicting McFarlane. She was a "clipper" — someone who promised sex for money, but took the money and absconded without keeping her part of the bargain.

In the spirit of the *De Munck* case, perhaps,[3] the Court of Appeal said that McFarlane was still a pimp. "The crucial feature in defining prostitution," the court held, "was the making of an offer for sexual services for reward." The customer probably would have defined something rather more basic as the "crucial feature," just as McFarlane was saying. But the court affirmed the conviction, finding that clipping was commensurate with prostitution.[4]

112 Calling a working girl a lady of the evening

Working the streets; going on the stroll; looking for dates. English is full of euphemisms for prostitution, including legal English. On December 3, 1891, for example, Reverend Frederic Wallis, a vice-chancellor of Cambridge University, had thrown Daisy Hopkins in the "spinning-house"[5] for 14 days after the Vice-Chancellor's Court

---

[3] Number 104.

[4] The court does not discuss the origins of "clipper" in this bait-and-switch context. Perhaps it derives from "to clip" in the sense of "to cut short," or "to disable," as in "to clip the wings" of a bird. Then again, it may well derive from "clipper" describing someone who absconds quickly, as fast as a clipper-ship. Or, considering that "to clip" can also mean "to embrace" (or so says the *Oxford English Dictionary*), maybe it's some vague combination of all these meanings, describing someone who hugs and runs.

[5] "Spinning-house" meant prison (and was one) at Cambridge from at least the turn of the 19th century. *Hotten's Slang Dictionary*, 1879, defines it as "the place in Cambridge where streetwalkers are locked up, if found out after a certain time of night." It had a similar, but evidently more limited, usage outside the university, deriving in all cases from the Dutch *spinnhuis*, apparently describing enforced labor performed in workhouses and prisons.

had convicted her of "walking with a member of the University."

A charter granted to Cambridge in 1561 by Queen Elizabeth I had given the university the right to prosecute anyone found on university property who was a vagabond or "suspected of evil." If those accused were convicted, Reverend Wallis enjoyed the awesome power to fine and imprison them without statutory limit. Daisy, as far as Rev. Wallis was concerned, had been collared in flagrant violation of the charter. He, himself, after all, had done the collaring.

A lesser working girl might have been daunted by such eminent opponents. But Daisy applied right over the vice-chancellors' heads, to Queen Victoria's justices, for a writ of *habeas corpus*. She didn't care what Rev. Wallis had seen or said; merely walking with someone was not an offense known to Her Majesty's law. For all Rev. Wallis knew, "a person simply walking with a member of the university ... might be that member's mother, or sister, or wife, or friend."

As far as the justices at Queen's Bench were concerned, Daisy and her lawyer were picking nits: everybody involved had a fair idea what Daisy did for a living. The justices were also more than a little embarrassed to declare that a common streetwalker had bested the vice-chancellors of Cambridge University at their own game of casuistry. But no lesser eminence than the Chief Justice of England, Lord Coleridge, felt compelled to agree that Daisy had been convicted of an offense unknown to English law. Daisy was entitled to her freedom. It was no answer that, as Rev. Wallis put it in his evidence, "walking with a member" was a charge "repeatedly to be found in the records of the Vice-Chancellor's court, and is frequently adopted when the offence charged is that a woman is in company with an undergraduate for an immoral purpose, and I intended to make that charge in this case."

A person could not be called to answer for perambulating and then be told that her accusers had meant whoring. If Daisy was suspected of "walking with a member of the University for immoral purposes," then she should have been charged in those words, Lord Coleridge said, so that she could have replied in kind.

On the strength of this victory, at the Ipswich Assizes the following spring the irrepressible Hopkins brought a civil action against Rev. Wallis for false imprisonment. For reasons not recorded in the law reports, her suit failed.

113 Let your fingers do the walking

In 1960, the British Court of Queen's Bench practiced a more liberal brand of philology, if not of law, in ruling that a woman could be a "streetwalker" even while lounging on her balcony a story or two above the pavement.

To attract the attention of men passing in the street, working girl Marie Smith had tapped on her balcony railing "with some metal object" and then hissed at them. The balcony was eight or ten feet in the air. If the men looked up, Smith became hospitable, calling out, "Would you like to come up here a little while?"

Later at night, she would turn more circumspect, tapping at a street-level window behind a pavement railing. Once she had attracted notice, she would signal her prices "by extending three fingers of her hand and indicating the correct door of the premises." A watchful policeman saw one of Smith's prospective johns make a counter-offer "by extending two fingers," but the counter-offer was declined and "that man walked away."

Hearing these facts, the Court of Queen's Bench held that "taking into consideration the mischief" addressed by the British *Street Offences Act*, "projecting" invitations into the street, though from hearth, chaise longue, or armchair, constituted streetwalking. A person was a streetwalker even if it was her prospective client doing the perambulating.

114 Caveat emptor

In 1993, an Alberta judge further refined the tricky legal definition of what exactly amounted to "communicating for the purposes of prostitution." The prosecution alleged that Lloyd Swift had driven into a Calgary parking lot and sounded his horn to attract the attention of a person he thought was a prostitute. Swift asked the woman if she were "a talented lady" and informed her he wanted "some head." Then he inquired respecting the dimensions of her breasts and asked her to show them to him, suggesting that this would prove she was not "a cop."

The woman replied, "Business first, pal," and Mr. Swift inquired, "Forty dollars for head?" The woman agreed and instructed Mr. Swift to drive around the block and pick her up. Instead, he drove up the street and then away from the area entirely. He was arrested anyway, perhaps proving he was right: you should always see the merchandise before offering to purchase. The woman was, in fact, a police officer.

And, indeed, Judge C.L. Daniel of the Alberta Provincial Court acquitted Swift. She held that, as Swift had driven away from the officer instead of following her directions for an assignation, he did not show the necessary intent to communicate *for the purpose* of engaging in prostitution with her.

115 It takes a heap o' livin'

About 20 years ago the Ontario Court of Appeal broke linguistic ground by holding that "any defined space" — including a parking lot, bare asphalt painted with parallel lines — could be a common bawdy house. Despite the fact that the principal word of the term, the noun of the noun phrase, was *house*, a "common bawdy house" did not need to be covered or enclosed as long as prostitution had been taking place within a "substantial" portion of it.

The inspiration for this unusual philology was an indictment against two women charged with being "keepers" of a particular stretch of asphalt in downtown Toronto, and "common" seems a fair description of an otherwise nocturnal no-person's-land behind a building in the seedier reaches of Richmond Street. The Crown alleged that the women would approach johns in their cars at other locations on nearby streets and then accompany them to the lot, whereat the police had found incriminating tissues. While this was enough to make the lot a common bawdy house under Canada's *Criminal Code*, it would not support a charge that the women were "keepers": keepers could be trespassers, as the accused prostitutes had been at the lot, but they must also have at least attempted real control over the premises. Here, the prosecution had produced no evidence that the women directed their customers to the lot or that they had the slightest interest in which space the customer used, much less a rental agreement with the lot's owner.

116 Caveat vendor

Then, of course, there is the other party to contracts involving the sex trade. Shortly before this book went to press, Greg Bonnett of Coquitlam, British Columbia, filed a lawsuit against a bar, a stripper it employed, and her agent, alleging that the stripper negligently broke his nose.

Bonnett had a front-row seat for the performance at the Barnet Motor Inn in Port Moody, and when the stripper swung herself around a pole she inadvertently kicked him in the face. Bonnett says that he was left with chronic pain and blurred vision, and he claims that, if the hotel was going to put its patrons in the way of such danger, it should at least have posted warning signs.

No doubt the defendants will argue that with your "cover charge" and refreshment payments, you bargain for food, drink and the opportunity to see naked women at work. If you get hurt during a conventional performance, it amounts to what lawyers call voluntary assumption of risk, and you cannot get damages for it.

Bonnett can take some heart, however, that the courts in neighboring Alberta rejected this view in 1983 when Colin Edwards tripped over the steps at Tracy Starr's restaurant in Edmonton and ended up crippled for the rest of his life. On the other hand, Edwards made for an unusually sympathetic plaintiff. He had held security guard and administrative jobs in Prince Albert, Saskatchewan, having been rendered unfit for other sorts of work after an army accident in 1954, when premature detonation of an explosive tore away his left hand and the use of his left eye. He had recently retired, and was visiting his daughter and son-in-law in Edmonton at the time of his mishap at Starr's. By the end of the evening there with his son-in-law (the wives were at bingo), he had ruptured the quadricep muscles in both his legs and would require braces and canes to walk.

It was true that both he and his son-in-law had used the aisle where he would fall, and that the entertainers, waitresses and other patrons navigated it night after night. Edwards had consumed two, maybe three drinks, but also dinner: the court accepted his testimony that he was not "impaired." The bill had been paid. Edwards and his son-in-law had returned from the men's room and were about to leave when he tripped over a step obtruding into the aisle. The step led up to the stage, where a stripper was honoring her contract of employment and Edwards was directing his attention. The way the court saw it, "there was an unfortunate combination of an existing obstacle or hazard and a distraction at the crucial time. Both were provided by the proprietor." In other words, it was Tracy Starr's fault that Edwards was not looking where he was going.

"He was not doing so because he was distracted by the nude female on stage," Justice Cavanagh of the Alberta Court of Queen's Bench found. "The occupier [Starr's] put her there to be looked at and, in my view, cannot say the visitor should not have allowed himself to be distracted." Distraction was on offer as part of the contract. Justice Cavanagh awarded Edwards something around $195,000, including $15,000 in trust for his wife in return for the care she had provided Edwards during the four years between the accident and the trial. On appeal, his total damages increased by nearly $58,000, not counting interest. It is open to debate, of course, whether the courts would have been so generous had Edwards been distracted by a hockey game on the bar television, or a gambling machine near the stage.

CHAPTER SEVEN

CRIME AND CONTROVERSY

117 Delilah in Nigeria

Although a man can live without his sexual organs, and earn a good living as a classical singer, the organs are highly prized, culturally and individually. Our word *testify* derives from the fact that the Romans sometimes put their hands over their groins — their *testis* — when they made oaths, swearing on the lives of their progeny, their good names through time. In modern-day Nigeria, police have had to quell riots over supposed genital thefts by citizens with magical powers. Purportedly, the thieves would distract a man with a handshake or by asking the time, and before the victim knew it, his private parts were spirited away. Fear of such thefts at markets and bus stops in Lagos led to rioting in the early 1990s, and some supposed thieves were lynched in October, 1990. Police in Lagos claimed that the urban myth itself was a distraction, created by common criminals as an excuse to attack and rob the purported magicians or others.

118 Implied consent

There are two basic defences in prosecutions or civil actions for sexual assault: the defendant denies it (or, in the case of rape, denies that penetration occurred, as the law puts it), or says that the complainant consented to what took place. Such formalities were strictly observed in the early days of the common law. In 1313, a 30-year-old woman identified in the legal yearbooks as Joan alleged that a man had impregnated her, but she forgot to add that he took her by force. Although the woman had a babe in arms because of the rape, the court sent her to prison "for bringing a bad charge." Then, the Crown began its criminal prosecution on the same facts. The attacker escaped again when Joan admitted that he was the child's father. "This is a wonderful thing!" the judge said, because a child "cannot be engendered without the consent of both parties." That is, because a child was born of the sexual act, the law (probably conjoined with "religious" superstition) assumed consent.

A conviction could bring extreme penalties, which perhaps explains, at least partly, the tendency to look for loopholes. As barrister R.G. Hamilton has remarked, a rape victim could choose to marry her assailant, who was then bound to respect her wish. But if he or she already was spoken for, "she was entitled to tear out his eyes and cut off his testicles."

119 Demonstrative evidence

In 1985, a Florida court refused to allow John Ted Wright to enter his allegedly nine-inch penis directly into evidence.

Wright stood charged with kidnapping a 14-year-old girl and

raping her twice in his truck. Part of his defense was that his penis was nine inches long in its flaccid state, and five inches in circumference. Given such dimensions, he said, he could not have committed the crimes without seriously injuring the girl. Medical evidence showed that the girl experienced only "some redness due to engorged blood vessels," and Wright's wife and girlfriend testified that sexual intercourse with him caused them to bleed and suffer pain.

Although Wright's lawyer wanted to have his client show his private parts to the jury, the trial judge, James L. Harrison, refused to allow it. Judge Harrison made the same ruling respecting photographs and a wooden model, but allowed the photographer and an investigator to attest to the length of Wright's member. The model was "a wooden stick eight-and-a-half inches long and five-and-a-half inches in circumference."

The jury convicted Wright of kidnapping and two counts of sexual battery. Judge Harrison then imposed three terms of 20 years in prison, which Wright was to serve concurrently (that is, as a single 20-year term). Florida's sentencing guidelines required life imprisonment for such crimes, but Judge Harrison explained his "leniency" by noting that "the victim in this case was not chaste," seemed mature beyond her years, and remained untroubled by the facts as she recited them in court. Despite the jury's verdict, her story was not totally credible, Judge Harrison added, and the evidence suggested that Wright's size defense was believable. In other words, Judge Harrison thought the jury was wrong.

The state appealed and Florida's District Court of Appeals sent the case back to Judge Harrison for re-sentencing. The appeal court ruled that if Judge Harrison believed that the state had presented insufficient evidence against Wright, he should not have sent the matter to the jury for final reckoning. Otherwise, Judge Harrison's own doubt about Wright's guilt was "not a clear and convincing reason for abandoning the recommended sentence." The jury was the ultimate arbiter of the evidence.

On reconsidering the sentence in accordance with what the appeal court said, Judge Harrison sentenced Wright to three concurrent life sentences. But Wright ultimately prevailed, at least in the sense that he was sentenced to no more than 20 years' imprisonment. It turned out that at the time he was originally sentenced to the 20-year term, Florida's sentencing guidelines were unconstitutional. So, the life terms were not mandatory after all: the math remained flexible.

120 Let me hear your body talk

"The responses of a penis to audiotaped scenarios cannot be interpreted to be a 'statement made by the accused during the course and for the purposes of an assessment.'"

That, anyway, is what the prosecution argued about "phallometric testing" of a man the law reports identify only as D.K. Facing sexual assault charges, D.K. testified that he consented to the testing during a court-ordered psychological assessment. A psychometrist measured D.K.'s penile response as he listened to audiotaped scenarios depicting consensual sex, sexual assaults with extreme violence, non-sexual violence, and no sex or violence whatsoever. The facts behind the charges are not reported, as they were not relevant to the motion.

The complication was that, according to section 672.21 of the Canadian *Criminal Code*, where a court or review board orders an assessment of an accused person's mental health, what the person says for the purposes of the assessment is a "protected statement." Justice Robert Weekes made what looked like the only reasonable decision: in the context of criminal law, "the responses of a penis" during a *Criminal Code* assessment were protected statements. Otherwise, Justice Weekes observed, those sent for assessments would refuse to cooperate or would tailor their responses where they could. As Justice Weekes put it, "There is no philosophical reason for Parliament to have intended a distinction between verbal and written communications and the analysis of bodily responses to external stimuli."

But as the prosecutor in the case apparently observed, this does not seem to square with long-settled law that constitutional protection from self-incrimination does not cover phallometric testing, or bodily substances and secretions. Arguably, as lawyers like to say, bodily responses and substances amount to circumstantial evidence, not statements at all, at least outside the assessment setting.

121 Extreme measures for extreme abuse

Older law, even under our supposedly civilized system, frequently mandated mutilation for serious sexual crimes. Colonial Virginia occasionally castrated slaves convicted of rape. During the 1640s in Massachusetts, three servants had sexual intercourse with their master's nine-year-old daughter. The prosecution argued for execution, but the General Court held that the extreme penalty was unavailable: there was no precedent or written law on the subject, biblical or secular. The court fined the ringleader, and ordered that officials slit and sear his nostrils, then place a noose around his neck, apparently for public display. The court fined the man's accomplices, and ordered that they be whipped. It then set the "missing precedent," ordering that, henceforth, such crimes were to be punished by death.

122 Stealing an heiress

During the renaissance in England, it seems that if a single woman came into money, golddiggers might hunt her down and force her into marriage. This unorthodox method of redistributing wealth was sufficiently widespread that the law reporters developed a category for it, "stealing an heiress," in breach of a law passed under Henry VII in 1486:

Anno tertio Henrici VII, A.D. 1486
Cap. ii

The Penalty for carrying a Woman away against her Will that hath Lands or Goods.

Item, Where Women, as well Maidens, as Widows, and Wives, having Substances, some in Goods moveable, and some in Lands and Tenements, and some being Heirs apparent unto their Ancestors, for the Lucre of such Substances been oftentimes taken by Mis-doers, contrary to their Will, and after married to such Mis-doers, or to other by their assent, or defoiled [sic], to the great displeasure of God, and contrary to the King's Laws, and Disparagements of the said Women, and utter Heaviness and Discomfort of their Friends, and to the evil Ensample of all other: It is therefore ordained, established, and enacted, by our Sovereign Lord the King, by the Advice of the Lords Spiritual and Temporal, and the Commons, in the said Parliament assembled, and by Authority of the same, That what Person or Persons from henceforth that taketh any Woman so against her Will unlawfully, that is to say, Maid, Widow, or Wife, that such taking, procuring, and abetting to the same, and also receiving wittingly the same Woman so taken against her Will, and knowing the same, be Felony; and that such Mis-doers, Takers, and Procurators, to the same, and Receitors, knowing the said Offence in form aforesaid, be henceforth reputed and adjudged as principal Felons. Provided alway, that this Act extend not to any Person taking any Woman, only claiming her as his Ward or Bond-Woman.

The offense was complete if the woman was kidnapped *and* forced into marriage or "defilement" for "lucre" (or if one "received" a woman in such circumstances, the women being comparable to chattels, as stolen goods!). Both the "taking" and the marriage or fornication had to occur, more or less together in time and place. The most notorious case, *Lady Fulwood's*, featured a debate about jurisdiction: if you kidnapped the heiress in town A, and forced her into marriage in town B, how was the heiress-kidnapping law broken? "For the taking without marriage," Matthew Hale puts it in his *Pleas of the Crown* (1800), "nor the marriage without taking, make not felony."

Happily, the judges did not altogether buy this argument, possibly because it would have encouraged general rape and pillage. The evidence showed that Sarah Coxe, a maid and orphan, inherited part of a £1,300 legacy. Although the law reports are ambiguous about the details, apparently Roger Fulwood and two other men kidnapped Coxe at sword-point in Middlesex at 8:00 p.m. on August 23, 1633. Although Fulwood was the son of a titled lady, he seems to have been desperate for funds. The kidnappers brought Coxe to the Bishop of Winchester's house in Surrey. On the pretext of showing the terrified Coxe around the house the next day, Fulwood conducted her to the chapel, where the couple went through a form of marriage. The judges ruled that "if the jury found that she was taken with force in Middlesex, and carried in a coach unto Strand-bridge, and brought by them into Surrey, it is a continuing force." In other words, Fulwood and his accomplices broke the law, even though the kidnapping and marriage occurred in different towns.

Apparently running out of arguments, the kidnappers' lawyer asserted that there still was no breach of the old heiress-stealing law because the marriage was invalid: Coxe herself said that she was so terrified she didn't know what she was doing. The judges admitted that the marriage might be invalid under the law on holy matrimony, but it was close enough to fall within this criminal statute forbidding the defilement of heiresses.[1] The judges sentenced the kidnappers to death, but exonerated Lady Fulwood on the basis that she played no part in the plot. (Apparently the authorities had suspected her of being an accomplice to the crime.)

123 No appeal or mercy

While the heiress-stealing legislation presumably acted as a deterrent, the courts were practicing the same rigorous summary justice under it 47 years later. Law reporters Ventris and Keble record the case of John Brown, accused of kidnapping another "city orphan," Lucy Ramsy. Lucy was 14 years old and the heir to a £5,000 inheritance. As Ventris describes the case, Mrs. P., "a confederate" of Brown "inveigled [Ramsy] into Hide-Park . . . to take the air in an evening, about the later end of May last, and being in the park, the coachman drove away from the rest of the company, which gave opportunity to Brown, who came to the coach-side in a visard-mask [a mask hiding his face], and addressing himself first to Mrs. P. soon perswaded her out of the coach, and then pulls out a maid-servant there attending [Lucy Ramsy]; and then gets himself into the coach, and there detains her [Ramsy] until the coachman carried them to his lodgings in the Strand, where the next morning he prevails upon her (having first threatened to carry her beyond sea if she refused) to marry him, but was the same day apprehended in the same house."

Apparently Brown never "deflowered" Ramsy, but the forced marriage ceremony was sufficient to seal his conviction. (Again, as the marriage was made under duress and there was no consummation, church law would not have recognized it.) On Friday, June 13,

---

[1] The courts have also said that a statute forbidding sodomy can include oral sex, even though that is not generally what sodomy means in law. See number 39 and following.

the court pronounced Brown guilty of violating Henry VII's statute. On Saturday the 14th it sentenced Brown "to dye." And three days later he was executed in Southwark.

124 "A little still she strove, and much repented, And whispering 'I will ne'er consent' — consented."

Like the rest of society, the law once assumed that sometimes "no" signified yes — that propriety obliged a woman to resist at least a little at first. This meant that some men got away with rape, and that in more modern times we occasionally have over-corrected and convicted the innocent. In light of this swing, comments by Justice William Maule in the mid-19th century are both of his time and ahead of it, at least insofar as he deplored "political correctness." After considerable nudging by his lordship to the effect that a rape complainant was more than willing, the jury had acquitted the accused man. Justice Maule then told him: "Let me, my man, give you a bit of advice. The next time you indulge in these unseemly familiarities, I recommend you to insist on your accomplice giving her consent in writing, and take care that she puts her signature to the document. Otherwise, it seems to me, you may get before a jury who will be satisfied with nothing else."

Fully a century and a half later, a case came before the British Columbia Human Rights Commission on the following facts:

In the summer of 1990, Linda Dupuis arrives in British Columbia to begin work on her master's degree in zoology. Dale Seip, an employee at B.C.'s Ministry of Forests and an adjunct professor at Dupuis' university, is to supervise Dupuis' summer work in the Queen Charlotte Islands. After Dupuis and Seip spend some friendly time getting acquainted in Vancouver, Seip tells Dupuis that she can travel with him in the project truck to the remote work site, or she can take a ferry with the other students. Dupuis chooses to travel with Seip. *En route*, Seip arranges single rooms without consulting Dupuis, but at this point she does not complain or resist his advances. In fact, although there are two beds in the first room, she joins Seip on his bed and tells him that she finds him attractive. Later that night, they have consensual sexual intercourse.

A sexual relationship persists during the first week at the site, although Dupuis is moody with Seip and seems increasingly angry with him. By the second week she rejects his further advances, and his apparent presumption that they are "an item." Though Seip accepts her rejection without pressing himself further on her, Dupuis goes so far as to change her thesis topic to avoid him, and then files a complaint against him and the forestry ministry with the B.C. Human Rights Commission. Never mind that she is 26, well-educated, and has lived and traveled on her own internationally, she seeks $17,000 to $20,000 for sexual harassment.

In an age and society that touts the equality and independence of women, in a time that acknowledges that adults frequently regret but must assume responsibility for their own missteps, one might think that the complaint is ill-founded. One would not be the B.C. Human Rights Commission, which awards Dupuis $5,000 for emotional injury, $14,976 for lost wages, and $594 in extra tuition for school time lost due to emotional upset.

125 Death for gold-digging

There is precedent for this approach, but from times with radically different mores, and times when women had little social leverage and could be much more compromised if they became single mothers or were viewed as unchaste. If a man had ulterior motives or seduced under a promise to marry that he did not intend to keep, the law sometimes regarded consensual sex as fornication, or even rape.

Professor Lawrence Friedman gives some interesting U.S. examples. During the late 18th century, a New York statute provided special, if condescending, protection to wealthy women, specifically targeting those expecting large inheritances and women with substantial "goods moveable" or "lands and tenements." Somewhat in the manner of Henry VII's law against "stealing an heiress" (see no. 122 above), the New York law made it a capital crime — an offense punishable by death — for a man to seduce or "defile" such a woman and then marry her for her money. It is unclear how the prosecution would safely prove this, however; people have always married for money, and many cultures view the practice as astute.

126 Third time's no charm

Even under the sway of such stereotypical views of female weakness, however, lines were drawn. In 1776, a Michigan trial court convicted Walter Clark of seducing Alice Morey three times under a promise of marriage. But when Clark appealed, the court ordered a new trial, suggesting that Morey had to take some responsibility for serial hanky-panky. The three "seductions" occurred over a short time, the court noted. By the second and third trysts, Alice could not honestly say she was still "chaste," or had restored herself to chastity. The appeal court also noted that Morey's parents had been pressuring Clark to marry their daughter, and that Walter had presented medical evidence at the trial to show that one of the supposed "connections" — in a buggy, the Moreys claimed — was "highly improbable if not impossible." (This defense succeeded in a later British adultery case, although the vehicle involved was a truck: see number 30.)

127 Maybe it's the Calvinism

The Scottish case of *Ross v. Macleod*, from 1861, suggests that, just as women say, men will promise anything for sex. Donald Macleod went so far as to give Jessie Ross a signed, sworn statement: "I hereby declare that I shall make you my lawful wife, before God and man, within three months from this date." Ross's lawsuit for breach of promise to marry failed on the surprising basis that she and Macleod were *de facto* married, never mind that there was never a wedding. Until the British Parliament passed the *Marriage Act* in 1939, this meant that there was no such thing (legally, anyway) as fornication between unmarried Scots: sexual intercourse between unmarried people amounted to automatic marriage. Lest there was any doubt, the court elaborated:

"Finds, that by force of such promise *subsequente copula*, the pursuer and defender became in law married persons: Therefore, finds and declares that the pursuer, Jessie Ross, and the defender, Donald Macleod, are married persons, husband and wife, of each other; and decerns [decrees] and ordains the said defender to adhere to the said pursuer as his lawful wife, and to treat, cherish, and entertain her at bed and board as such, and to perform towards her all the conjugal duties of a husband to a wife, and in nowise to leave or desert her in time coming."

Twenty-seven years later, in Michigan, the absconding cad was able to turn this logic on its head and escape prison as well as his "conjugal duties," deliberately using marriage as his defense. Finding herself pregnant by William Gould, Kate Morrow brought a prosecution against him for "seducing and debauching her." A state law made Gould liable to as much as five years in the penitentiary. The case went to the Shiawassee County Circuit Court in April, 1887, but at the luncheon recess Gould offered to marry Morrow, and the couple found a justice of the peace who immediately performed the ceremony at the home of Morrow's parents. Gould had nothing more to do with Morrow. That same evening he fled town by train. He was eventually arrested for disorderly conduct and brought back before the Shiawassee court. Although Morrow deposed that she did not want to prosecute any longer, her mother pressed the matter on, and the circuit court convicted Morrow of the old "seduce and debauch" charge. The jury seems to have relied on the judge's instruction that "if the marriage was resorted to as a piece of legal trickery to stop the voice of the girl, Kate, and prevent her from being a witness . . . the offense would be one against public decency and order, and would not be condoned by such marriage."

The Supreme Court of Michigan overturned the verdict, acquitting Gould. The crime, they said, was not whether he married Morrow in bad faith. It was whether he seduced and abandoned her — whether, in terms of public policy, he was leaving her an unwed mother with an illegitimate child. The marriage, although a sham in all but formality, made the child legitimate (the law always presumes legitimate births, and has usually gone out of its way to assure them), and it "cured" both Gould and Morrow of the taint of illicit seduction. Justice Long, writing the majority judgment, put it graphically:

"Debauchery and carnal intercourse, without seduction, is no offense under this statute. The offense which this statute is aimed at is the seduction and debauchery accomplished by the promises and blandishments the man brings to his aid in effecting the ruin and disgrace of the female; and where the seduction and debauchery is accomplished by promises of marriage, upon which the female relies, and thus surrenders her person, and gives to the man the brightest jewel in the crown of her womanhood. It is the broken promise which the law will regard as the *gravamen* [essence] of the offense."

128 An honest, if deserted, woman

These fine distinctions arose partly because of the severity of the penalty for seduction under promise to marry: in Texas, for example, W.C. Wright was sentenced to four years in prison for seducing "Miss Nesbitt."

Nesbitt, according to Judge W.A. Blackburn sitting on Wright's appeal, "was highly esteemed, and visited by other young gentlemen, and [she] moved in the best social circles, with a good reputation for chastity and virtue." Wright pursued her so ardently, pledging marriage, "that all other gentlemen were compelled to cease attendance" and her family regarded him as a faithful suitor. Nesbitt yielded, and apparently Wright broke his promise of wedlock.

On the stand, however, before the jury, witnesses, and the trial judge, he produced a marriage license and swore that "in good faith" he would marry Nesbitt then and there if the trial judge agreed to perform the ceremony. Unlike the Michigan law, the Texas penal code stated that if a defendant offered in good faith to marry "the female" bedded under a false promise of matrimony, the court could not prosecute him for seduction. The good faith offer retroactively erased the fornication. Before Nesbitt could reply, the district attorney objected, insisting that the court allow the state to test Wright's good faith in offering matrimony. The judge sustained the objection, and the D.A. called witnesses who testified that Wright had told them he would not voluntarily marry or live with Nesbitt. Wright then testified for himself, and again made his marriage proposal, promising not to desert Nesbitt. But she responded, "I most positively decline to marry you or to live with you. I would not marry any man who treated a woman as you have done me." The trial judge refused to dismiss the charge, and the jury convicted.

The appeal court reversed the conviction, however, ruling that an offer of marriage was sufficient if the offer itself was made in good faith, no matter that Wright might soon have deserted his new bride. The fact of marriage, even if just for show, was sufficient (as in *Gould*) "to make an honest woman" of Nesbitt. "Of his good faith [in his eleventh-hour offer of marriage, specifically] there can be no earthly doubt," the appeal court ruled. "The penitentiary towering above him was the strongest guaranty of the sincerity of his offer, and the [trial] court erred in permitting the district attorney to question the *bona fides* of an offer that was patent to all." After all, by suggesting that the trial judge perform the marriage ceremony, Wright was assuring that Nesbitt would again be "an honest woman," no matter what kind of husband he proved to be.

129 Another Hollywood epic

Since 1975, acting in the civic interest, San Francisco's Court of Historic Review has decided, among other things, that "Casey at the Bat" was written and the martini was invented in San Francisco, Enrico Caruso did not flee the 1906 earthquake there in cowardice, Wyatt Earp fixed a local boxing match so that a man who was knocked out won, and the hot dog was invented not in Frisco, but in New York. More recently, the court (which, speaking of hot dogs, sits during lunch hours and does not necessarily require its judges and advocates to be members of the bar, although they often are) has handed down a once-and-for-all exculpation in the 1921 Roscoe "Fatty" Arbuckle rape-homicide case. In the event there was any doubt, Arbuckle — who rose from a knockabout childhood to a five-buck-a-day Keystone cop to $3,000 a day as the world's richest, best-loved movie comedian (even his dog made $300 a month) — absolutely didn't do it.

Arbuckle stood accused of causing the death of starlet Virginia Rappe in the course of raping or attempting to rape her with a soda bottle at an impromptu party at San Francisco's St. Francis Hotel. The charges were trumped up by Rappe's companion that day, Maude Delmont — who (according to David Yallop's book on the scandal) had attempted 40 past extortions — and Rappe died of natural causes aggravated by hard living to the last. But the case was whipped up in the press for a public that in those earliest Prohibition days put a premium on puritanical morality. D.A. Matt Brady, ever political, was only too happy to oblige, trying a spirited prosecution in the newspapers.

According to Bernard Averbuch, the San Francisco public relations man who founded the Court of Historic Appeals, "This was the period of... *The Front Page* style of journalism. Newspapers put out as many as eight editions a day and sometimes there were half-a-dozen stories of the trial on the front page. Many of the photos of the trial were composites or were doctored by newspaper artists to portray events that later were shown to have never happened." The media circus reflected Rappe's own sad attempts at a life of celebrity: to give her career flair, she had added the e to her name, *sans accent*, then gave the game away by pronouncing it RaPAY.

After immediate conviction by the press for murder, Arbuckle faced three jury trials for manslaughter. Both the grand jury and a police court refused to send him to trial on a murder charge, despite extortionate pressure from Brady's office. The first two trials ended in deadlocked juries. Arbuckle would have been acquitted by the first had the panel not included a Daughters of the American Revolution blueblood whose husband had business dealings with the D.A. She refused to discuss the case in the jury room and put her hands over her ears so as not to be swayed by argument.

Only during the third trial did the court allow the jury to hear that Brady had badgered two witnesses into perjuring themselves at the inquest, and that Rappe's medical history supported Arbuckle's plea of innocence. The attending doctor had stated the cause of death as a ruptured bladder and peritonitis, but at the earlier trials the jury did not know of her history of chronic and progressive bladder disease; they accepted as virtually unchallenged the prosecution claim that Arbuckle's 266 pounds had crushed Rappe's bladder. Not until the third trial did the jury learn that Rappe was pregnant at the time of death (she had asked Arbuckle, who hardly knew her, for money for an abortion), suffered from active gonorrhea (Arbuckle never contracted it), had five abortions between the ages of 13 and 16, and bore one "illegitimate" child (the accepted legal term of the day) when she was 16. The press had made her out to be a vestal virgin.

Although Delmont instigated the murder charge, she was never called to testify — not at the inquest, the grand jury hearing, or any of the three trials. She had drunk ten double scotches on the afternoon of the alleged crime (Rappe had been drinking as well, despite doctors' warning about aggravating her bladder trouble), and during the very moments it was supposed to be taking place, Delmont was in a separate room changing from her dress into a man's pajamas (the man was in the room with her) while, in a third room, the party had shifted into noisy high gear.

When Rappe became ill, screaming in pain and finally tearing at her own clothes, the partygoers stripped her and "treated" her by dangling her nude, upside-down, by her ankles, dropping her in cold water, feeding her bicarbonate of soda, and putting ice cubes all over her body. Two doctors who checked on her in Arbuckle's room did nothing but catheterize her, using glass catheters that are now considered highly dangerous, and inject her with morphine and atropine, which masked her symptoms.

Although Rappe passed blood in her urine, the two doctors diagnosed her principal problem as drunkenness. When she died five days later, an illegal autopsy was performed, evidently to hide malpractice and possibly an illegal abortion. The evidence seems clear that the only time Arbuckle touched her was to steady her as she vomited, to help her lie down, and (sad to say) to play with an ice cube some drunk had placed between the poor woman's legs.

The five months of legal proceedings comprise a monument to injustice, with some few light moments. During the last trial, one of the jurors developed an acute tooth problem. To prevent jury tampering, the judge sent the entire panel and two bailiffs to the dentist. During the second trial, Arbuckle got locked out of the courtroom.

When he knocked, the bailiff called through the door, "Are you attached to the court?" Presumably Arbuckle took a long breath before replying, "Not very deeply."

The final jury heard 31 days of evidence and acquitted immediately, issuing an extraordinary statement: "Acquittal is not enough for Roscoe Arbuckle. We feel a great injustice has been done him. We feel also that it was only our plain duty to give him this exoneration, under the evidence, for there was not the slightest proof adduced to connect him in any way with the commission of a crime." But Arbuckle was ruined. He remained the moralist's scapegoat, even among his colleagues, for Hollywood's corrupting influences. His films were banned and he was barred from performing. When the bar was lifted, the damage was irreparable.

He died broke and early, at 46, eclipsed by then by Chaplin, Keaton, and Harold Lloyd, whose careers he had helped establish. Ironically he is better known today for his influence on contract law than for his films or the Rappe case. The clause in Hollywood contracts warranting that the actor is of "good morals" and character first appeared after Arbuckle was charged with murder. It is still known familiarly — a final injustice — as "the Arbuckle clause."

130 French beetle disguised as a Latin bluebottle

Learning the Spanish fly legend, or "urban myth," is a rite of passage among teenagers. A high-school Lothario and his girlfriend are at the drive-in, the story goes. (In better neighborhoods, the protagonists are college students.) He slips the substance in question into her cola and then goes to the washroom. When he returns, he finds her dead from desperate coitus with the gearshift lever.

Cantharis vessicatoria, or cantharides, a.k.a. Spanish fly, has nothing to do with flies. And the legendary high school hot-shot could well have been liable in battery, if not negligence, as well as guilty of

Criminal Code provisions having to do with administering a noxious substance and even manslaughter. Cantharides is called Spanish fly after the green beetle that gives up its life in the cause of love and urology. The *Oxford English Dictionary* says that it was once "used externally as a rubefacient and vesicant" — something that irritates living tissue and causes blisters. One could get the same effect, in other words, by rolling around in a charcoal barbecue pit.

Taken internally, cantharides is also a diuretic which stimulates the genito-urinary tract. Physicians once used it to treat problems there, and to procure abortions. But intemperate application blisters the plumbing, and instigates vomiting and internal bleeding. It is rather the opposite of an aphrodisiac.

In the wrong hands, it becomes the date rape drug that isn't. French authorities prosecuted the Marquis de Sade in 1801 for sickening prostitutes on candied almonds laced with the stuff. In England and America, others have been convicted of battery for similar use. In 1838, Edward Button, a waiter at the Crown in Butcherhall Lane, London, slipped two scruples (one-twelfth ounce) of cantharides into the staff's breakfast coffee. He claimed that "he did it only for a lark," but, despite the small quantity, two barmaids (one of them his employer's wife, apparently) became "sick, sore and diseased, and disordered in their bodies, insomuch that their lives were despaired of." Mrs. Campbell, the boss's wife, was too ill even a month later to testify at Button's trial. Button went to jail for a year after the jury convicted him of assault.

In 1845, three men put thrice as much cantharides into the beer at a wedding party, and several guests took sick. Possibly uncertain which charge would stick, the Crown threw every possible misdemeanor and felony at the spikers — assault, conspiracy to assault, attempted manslaughter, conspiracy to administer a noxious and dangerous substance, and common assault. Like Button, the accused men disclaimed any intent to harm; they were only fooling around, they told the Liverpool Assizes. In the end, nothing stuck, because Baron Parke, the trial judge, instructed the prosecution that *Button* was wrongly decided: as everybody had recovered from the prank and there was no intention to cause real harm, there was no assault or battery. However, Baron Parke added that "a very serious manslaughter" would have made the court's docket had someone died.

131 They didn't care a fig what happened?

Perhaps in the spirit of the Revolution, a Massachusetts court in post-colonial America ruled that *Button* was *rightly* decided. In *Commonwealth v. Stratton*, 1873, two young men were convicted of assault and battery after they gave a girlfriend figs laced with cantharides. They explained that their supplier told them the drug was "love powders" and "perfectly harmless." An appeal court upheld their conviction, noting that they still "knew it was not ordinary food," and tricked the girl into ingesting it. This amounted to "a fraud upon [the girl's] will equivalent to force in overpowering it. . . . Although force and violence are included in all definitions of assault, or assault and battery, yet, where there is physical injury to another person, it is sufficient that the cause is set in motion by the defendant, or that the person is subjected to its operation by means of any act or control which the defendant exerts."

By this time, in any event, the British courts had found a way around their doubts that administering the noxious beetle powder was assault. In 1861, again at the Liverpool Assizes, Baron Martin heard the case of Wilkins, a man who lodged with the victim. Unknown to the victim-landlady, Baron Martin elaborated, Wilkins "put into a cup of tea which she was about to drink, a quantity of cantharides; she drank the contents . . . and suffered much pain, and was very ill in consequence. . . . The jury found that the prisoner administered the cantharides to, and caused it to be taken by, the prosecutrix [the landlady], with the intent to excite her sexual passion and desire, in order that he might obtain connexion with her." The Court of Criminal Appeals confirmed that Wilkins was guilty of the statutory offense of administering a substance with the "intent to injure or to aggrieve or to annoy."

132 Before Viagra

As late as 1954, a London office manager was convicted of killing his secretary and her colleague with cantharides. Arthur Ford worked for a pharmaceutical manufacturer. A customer's question about the use of cantharides to remove warts — a persisting use that demonstrates the chemical's real effect — reminded him of army stories about Spanish fly. When Ford consulted a staff chemist about using cantharides in rabbit breeding, the scientist warned him that the chemical was dangerous. Ford anyway sneaked some of it from the lab into ice cream which he shared with the secretaries, who died the next day. On convicting Ford of manslaughter, the court sentenced him to prison for five years.

How is it, then, that the popular mind has conceived cantharides as an aphrodisiac? Ambroise Paré, a 16th-century physician, reported that a man in Provence had taken a huge quantity of cantharides to cure a fever. "His wife swore to us by her God that he had been astride her, during two nights, eighty-seven times, without thinking it more than ten . . . and even while we were interviewing him, the poor man ejaculated thrice in our presence, embracing the foot of the bed." In other words — and assuming that the poor ancient was not simply trying to relieve himself of the blistering pain — as with the *droit de seigneur* (see number 2), the male mind persists, century after century, in wishful thinking. Then again, one male author on aphrodisiacs suggests the safer alternative of lettuce, formerly used as an aphrodisiac in German brothels.

133 The kissing bandit

Occasionally, women have turned the tables with so-called Mickey Finns — adulterated drinks — or similar subterfuge. In 1985, the newspapers reported a bold variation on the spiked-beverage ruse in the case of 22-year-old Margarita Delos Santos. Santos was a thief working the clubs and casinos of Atlantic City, New Jersey. Her modus operandi was to pose as a prostitute and slip a "knockout pill" into her "johns'" mouths while kissing them. When the men were senseless, she robbed them. Three victims reported losing a total of $52,000 in jewellery and cash. The state charged Delos Santos, whom the police nicknamed "the kissing bandit," with three counts of theft over $500 and three counts of reckless endangerment.

134 Uninformed consent

The lover-impersonation theme titillates the popular imagination. Ballads, folk tales, and movies such as *The Return of Martin Guerre* tell of the woman who makes love with a complete stranger, mistaking him for her lover or mate. But these are not mere projections of subconscious feelings or of fantasies. The motif is shockingly common in everyday life and in our law reports. The reasons for judgment of Lord Justice Edmund Davies of the English Court of Appeal relate an instance from 1972.

An 18-year-old woman was sleeping naked very near an open window. At about three-thirty or four o'clock on a Sunday morning, she was awakened by a figure crouched at the window in the moonlight. In court, she could not recall whether the figure was already in the room, or on the part of the sill outside it. "The young lady," Edmund Davies found, "then realized several things: first of all that the form in the window was that of a male; secondly that he was a naked male; and thirdly that he was a naked male with an erect penis." Thinking it was her boyfriend "paying her an ardent nocturnal visit," the young woman invited the man into her bed.

She did not discover until after she had sex with the man that he was not her boyfriend but 19-year-old Stephen Collins. Collins testified that he was acquainted with the young woman because he had done odd jobs around her mother's house. He had a drinking problem, he told the court, and on the night in question, he was inebriated. He had seen a light in the woman's window and moved a ladder to it. When he climbed up, he saw her sleeping naked in the room, descended, and removed all of his clothes except his socks. Then, he climbed back up to the window. Apparently "he took the view," Justice Edmund Davies said, "that if the girl's mother entered the bedroom it would be easier to effect a rapid escape if he had his socks on. . . . That is a matter about which we are not called upon to express any view, and would in any event find ourselves unable to express one."

The police claimed that Collins had told them he had meant to have sex with a woman by force, if necessary. He denied this at the Essex Assizes, although he admitted that when the woman invited him into her bed he "was rather dazed because I didn't think she would want to know me." A trial court convicted him of burglary.

It seems an odd and inappropriate charge, but it was historically based. Reading the law reports, it sometimes appears that, before the days of electric light and fastidiously bolted doors and windows, confusion over who was who and in whose bed was an everyday occurrence. Occasionally a bold rapist would climb in next to the husband and children. Often, a sleepy wife wouldn't comprehend what was what until it was all over but the crying.

A rule grew up around these cases that signals what contemporary society views as the law's shameful treatment of women as property. The rule said that a person consented to something if she understood the "nature and quality" of what was done to her. That, in part, was why Collins was charged with burglary instead of some particular sexual assault. (Under English statute law, burglary also denotes illegal entry with intent to rape.) The girl knew that he wanted to have sex with her, and she knew what sex was.

Nevertheless, the Court of Appeal ultimately acquitted Collins, even on the charge of burglary. If his victim had been able to say that he was on the part of the window-sill *inside* her bedroom before she invited him into bed, he would have been a trespasser, and thus a house-breaker. But because she might have beckoned to him when he was outside the room (under the misapprehension that he was her boyfriend), he was not a burglar. She had "invited him in." Still, according to the leading British textbook on criminal law, all was not lost:

> *The common law rules relating to [illegal] entry were developed with not a little ingenuity and a fondness for technicality. . . . Collins . . . does seem to involve a rejection of the common law rule that the entry of any part of Defendant's body sufficed. To that extent it has been welcomed for otherwise: "burglary may well . . . vary with the length of a part much more private than the prisoner's foot."*[2]

135 Quality of what, exactly?

The leading "nature and quality" case is *Williams*, known to lawyers as the "choirmaster case." At the Liverpool Assizes in 1922 (when by

---

[2] Note that the judges did not consider that if you invite B in thinking he is A, you are not really inviting B in. The court rejected the argument that only the girl's mother, as tenant, had the absolute right to allow anyone into the house. As to "the prisoner's foot," historically the law was divided into the common or king's law (the law as adjudicated in the common law courts) and equity, the courts that were established later, under the lord chancellor, as a more flexible alternative. Sometimes equity was criticized for its unpredictability or arbitrariness: "Tis all one as if they should make ye Standard for ye measure wee call A foot, to be ye Chancellors foot; what an uncertain measure would this be; One Chancellor has a long foot[,] another A short foot[,] a third an indifferent foot; tis ye same thing in ye Chancellors Conscience."

and large young adults were more innocent than they were 50 years later), Owen Williams was convicted of having carnal knowledge of two of his female singing pupils, ages 16 and 19. The prosecution proved that Williams had undressed the younger girl and earnestly "examined" her with an aneroid barometer — which "was not in working order" — before telling her he was going to make an air passage so she could sing better. He then had sexual intercourse with her, still under the pretence of treatment, assuring the girl that her parents knew all about it and approved. He even swore to God that he would not harm her.

The court found that Williams had obtained the girl's consent fraudulently. Because the fraud concerned what he intended to do to her, and not who he was, the court found him guilty of rape and sentenced him to 12 years at hard labor.[3]

---

[3] Williams' appeal to the Court of Criminal Appeals makes an interesting footnote to the case. According to the London *Times*, the Court of Criminal Appeals heard *Williams* on the afternoon of December 11, 1922. That morning, it had reviewed the case of a man convicted of pimping for a 17-year-old girl. The trial judge had sentenced the pimp to 21 months at hard labor and 15 strokes with the cat'o'nine tails. Appealing the corporal punishment, the pimp wanted the court to hear a prison warder testify that he was subject to epileptic seizures.

The appeal court refused to hear the epilepsy claim, while coldly suggesting that those responsible for the whipping might want to consider it. The chief justice emphasized that this was not an endorsement of mercy by the court, and added, "If ever there was a case in which a prisoner deserved corporal punishment, this is it." (The pimp, a married layabout, had picked the teenager up at a dance hall, promising to marry her. He took her from Nottingham to London and after three weeks of cohabitation cajoled her out to the streets, where she earned him £10 a week.)

When *Williams* came on that afternoon, the chief justice remarked, "It may be that before long persons who are found guilty of this sort of offence will run the risk of suffering the same punishment as that which we have had to deal with this morning." The choirmaster seems to have escaped whipping, but the Court of Criminal Appeals affirmed his 12-year sentence.

This genre of prosecution obviously concerns the most craven breach of trust, and, human nature being what it is, the law reports bulge with similar cases. In other instances, adult women will go to doctors or quack-doctors who obtain putative consent for sex by disguising an assault as treatment. The cases date from the 18th century until as recently as yesterday. In *Doc*, published in 1989, journalist Jack Olsen shows that virtually every woman in Lovell, Wyoming, was sexually assaulted by the town physician — who played on the women's religious piety and innocence, and on their habit of equating the family doctor with God and parent. (Like Williams, Doc claimed great therapeutic value for routine "dilation.") In another recent American case, a surgeon sutured closed the vagina of his own ex-wife.

In older examples, market-stall quacks play on simple ignorance and desperation, promising to cure a young woman's seizures by "breaking her string" in the snug of a pub or offering to ease menstrual problems with "dilation." Fortunately, in most of these cases assailants can be convicted of rape, because the fraud lies in what they are doing, not in who they are. On the other hand, the sleeper *au naturel* in *Collins* understood the nature and quality of what Collins did to her. The law therefore says that he might have been guilty of assault, but not of rape. The absurd presumption in this is that sex with a drunken stranger has the same "nature and quality" as intimacy with a loved one.

136 Not what we mean by "lovesick"

Of course the judges who formulated these rules were men — often old, rigid, sexually frustrated men. In an Irish case from 1878, a woman pleaded that had she been aware her common-law husband was infected with venereal disease, which he knew about but didn't tell her, she would not have consented to sex with him. When she sued the man for infecting her, the judges said that her consent was valid, and because she was "living in sin" she had no right to complain in the first place.

And *plus ça change*, in the late 1980s a Virginia woman attempted to sue her estranged husband for infecting her with genital herpes before they were married. Ruling that fornication was a crime in that state, the supreme court refused to award damages to the woman, even though she had been unaware of her future husband's condition.

137 De Sade's compliments to the chef

The legal shillyshally in the *Collins* case — that sex with an imposter is not rape, *per se* — is even more bizarre when you consider that the law might be willing to cry rape, or something like it, in situations where the so-called victims are quite clear on who does what to whom. In the Massachusetts case of *Appleby*, the accused man claimed that he had picked up a male prostitute who, he said, eventually became his live-in "slave." The "slave" begged to be beaten with a bullwhip Appleby used to train guard dogs, and Appleby eventually obliged, because it gave his partner pleasure and made him otherwise sexually pliant. The two later designed a "torture chamber" together. In October, 1975, Appleby beat his partner with the bullwhip and a baseball bat, fracturing his knee. The pair told staff at the emergency ward, as well as a trial court, that the injured man had fallen during an epileptic fit. Appleby was acquitted.

In February, 1976, Appleby was charged with beating his partner with a bullwhip "because of displeasure with a sandwich" the partner had prepared. He was again acquitted, apparently for lack of evidence.

Appleby was finally convicted, and sentenced to *eight to ten years* in prison, after his "slave" served him some melted ice cream and Appleby simply tapped him with a riding crop. This was at last too much for the supposed masochist, who fled Appleby's house in his underwear and took refuge in a nearby monastery. (Another suggestive aspect of the story is that Appleby refused to let his lover move in with him unless the man promised that they would go to church together every Sunday.) Apparently he was at last willing to testify fully and candidly. The trial court found that although generally the law stays out of the bedrooms (and kitchens) of the nation, in cases of this sort of violence, consent was no defense. The Supreme Court of Massachusetts agreed: "The fact that violence may be related to sexual activity . . . does not prevent the state from protecting its citizens against physical harm."

The same rule had been applied in a 1934 English case, when a 17-year-old girl agreed to be spanked with a cane, only to discover that it wasn't that pleasant after all. At trial, the spanker was convicted and sentenced to 18 months at hard labor. The Court of Criminal Appeal eventually acquitted him, but merely because the trial judge had failed to direct the jury to convict only if "the blows were likely or intended to do bodily harm." The judges were evidently loathe to punish an old public school tradition.

138 Self-absorbed, honestly

Judges are constantly forced to admit that what may seem reasonable to one jury may strike another as scandalous. This has caused some egregious problems in the criminal law of mistake when judges and juries attempt to assess intent and consent to sexual activity. In the case of *Morgan*, for example, an army officer told three strangers in a bar, young colleagues below him in rank, that his wife would enjoy sex with each of them in succession. The men were incredulous, but Morgan provided them condoms and remarked that although his wife would resist, this was kinky pretence, to make the experience more thrilling.

The truth was that the Morgans had been sleeping apart for some time and Daphne Morgan had been involved in at least two extramarital affairs (possibly encouraged by her vengeful husband). All three of the men had intercourse with her, as did Morgan after them. The three men testified that Mrs. Morgan resisted when they dragged her out of a room she shared with her 11-year-old son, but subsequently masturbated them, licked their genitals, and "moaned in pleasure." In fact, Mrs. Morgan had called out for her son to call the police. What the men called "masturbation" she described as digging her nails into their private parts to fight them off.

The men contended that they had honestly believed that Mrs. Morgan had consented to sex. The courts decided that she very clearly had not and convicted all four defendants of rape. But on appeal, the English House of Lords left a door open for others accused of the crime. The law lords held that the men would have been blameless if they honestly believed Mrs. Morgan had consented, *even if only a thoughtless, self-absorbed brute would make that mistake.* In rape, an honest mistake of fact meant there was no criminal intent, even if reasonable people would not have made the same mistake.

This approach was followed in Canada, in (most influentially) the case of George Pappajohn, a man who had sex with his real estate agent. After a long, bibulous lunch, Pappajohn and the agent retired to the house Pappajohn wanted the woman to sell. One of Pappajohn's friends testified that upon seeing the couple *en route*, he thought the woman was "handing it to George on a platter." Eventually, her hands bound with a bathrobe cord and a bow-tie around her mouth, the agent fled naked to the nearby home of a priest, crying rape. Pappajohn claimed she had consented to three acts of intercourse, but had suddenly gone hysterical when he attempted amorous bondage to overcome their mutual inability to reach climax. Indeed, the police evidence was that the woman's clothing had all been neatly folded, and there were no signs of violence on her body. But the man was found guilty on the same basis as Morgan. The Supreme Court of Canada ultimately held that if the man had *honestly* believed the agent was consenting (and evidently they felt he had *not* believed she was), his belief did not have to be based on reasonable grounds.

139 Lust has its own illogic

One day in the early 1960s, a Yukon Territories man named Ladue got drunk and began feeling amorous. He had sex with his girlfriend, even though she was inanimate, apparently asleep. The girlfriend did not awaken or respond. This was because she was dead. Ladue was charged with "indecently interfering with a dead human body," also known under the Canadian *Criminal Code* as "offering an indignity to a corpse."

Ladue pleaded that he was too drunk to know the woman was dead. In other words, he had made what lawyers call a mistake of fact (versus a mistake of law, which is usually no excuse). Because he didn't *intend* to have sex with a corpse, he claimed he wasn't guilty of that crime: how could he interfere with a dead body if he didn't know the person was dead?

This logic failed to impress the justices of the Yukon Territories Court of Appeal. Ladue knew that the woman was not conscious, they found. He knew, in other words, that she was not consenting to sex. If the woman had been functional, the chief justice remarked, Ladue would have been "raping her." As commentators have pointed out, this conclusion itself is not strictly logical: insofar as a corpse is not a person, you cannot rape a corpse. (An "alive corpse" is obviously a contradiction in terms.) While Ladue could not commit the impossible, he could certainly try to, making his crime *attempted* rape. (But even this is not always clear in law: see number 44). Still, relying on the argument that Ladue would have been forcing sex on his girlfriend had she been alive, the court held that "it is impossible for him to argue that, not knowing her to be dead, he was acting innocently. An intention to commit a crime, although not the precise crime charged, will provide the necessary *mens rea*" — illegal intent — under the law.

The court's disgust is manifest in its apparent determination to convict, despite legal illogic. The charge was interfering with a dead body. Yet the chief justice concludes, "I do not consider knowledge that the body is dead to be a specific ingredient" of interfering with a dead body. And he does not tell us how the intent to (attempt) rape can be the same as the intent to offer an indignity to a corpse.

140 Reckless eyeballing

What if you're *just looking* without consent? A law professor once wrote of sexual politics that "there's no harm in asking." But is there harm in reckless eyeballing?

Ishmael Reed has written that "black folklore is full of tall tales about black men walking up the side of buildings in order to avoid colliding with white women on the street." An article in *Ebony* in the 1950s recounted a case in Mississippi, he says, of a man arrested for "reckless eyeballing" — looking at a white woman. All of this was the raw material for *Reckless Eyeballing*, Reed's novel about a black playwright under siege by feminists. In an attempt to win their favor and restore his grants, he writes a play about a man who is lynched for recklessly eyeballing a white woman. The woman demands that the corpse be exhumed and put on trial. The play's producer, a black woman, remarks that "because he leered at [the woman] the black was just as guilty as the white men who murdered him."

In correspondence, Reed has commented that, during the 1990s, charges of reckless eyeballing seemed to be making a comeback among feminist students where he taught in California — or at least that "white feminists are giving black men the evil eye" there. In 1989, a student at the University of Toronto made headlines for months by lodging a complaint of the type Reed might have had in mind.

During her regular swim at the pool in Hart House — until fairly recently, an athletic and social club restricted to males — a professor harassed her, the student told the university's sexual harassment board, by swimming near her in a snorkel mask and flippers, and ogling her. The board upheld the complaint and banned the professor from the pool for five years. As well, it ordered the professor to take counselling. The professor admitted looking at the student, but denied harassment. He said that he was a keen student of human nature and the human form, especially in athletic pursuits.

141 "Vasectomies do not constitute mayhem." (Headnote, *Jessin v. The County of Shasta*, 1969)

Sado-masochists, or the merely curious, can legally consent to spankings, whippings, or even "torture," at least to the extent that they are not really hurt. Nowhere in the Anglo-American world, however, can you legally consent to mayhem.

According to Lord Coke, Attorney General to Elizabeth I,

> *"Mayhem,"* mahemium, membri mutilatio, *or* obtruncatio, *commeth of the French word* mehaigne, *and signifieth a corporall hurt, whereby hee loseth a member, by reason whereof hee is less able to fight; as by putting out his eye, beating out his fore-teeth, breaking his skull, striking off his arme hand or finger, cutting off his legge or foot, or whereby he loseth the use of any of his said members.*

Mayhem, in other words, is a battery, and a close etymological relative of *maim*. Originally it signified "an atrocious breach of the king's peace, an offence tending to deprive him of the aid and assistance of his subjects" — especially in military endeavors.

Under common law, ears and noses didn't count as members capable of mayhem because severance did "not weaken but only disfigure him." Arms, legs, and fingers always counted. So did, in Blackstone's words, "those parts, the loss of which in all animals abates the courage." More recently, this has been jurisprudently called "disabling the testicles."

Perhaps because the punishment on conviction of mayhem was an eye for an eye, Coke's list has never been definitive. And as Blackstone points out, "upon repetition of the offence the punishment could not be repeated." In any event, the punishment for castration by mayhem was not a testicle for a testicle, but death.

In 1980, the California Court of Appeals declared involuntary tattooing mayhem after two thugs beat a woman and tattooed "MFFM" ("Misfits Forever, Forever Misfits") on her breast, "Property of G.P." on her abdomen, and "Mine Too," with an arrow, on her left thigh — pointing, one presumes from the sensitivity and wit here displayed, north.

One thug contended that although California courts had said knife wounds could amount to mayhem, tattooing was different because its purpose was not injury and many people even paid money to have it performed on them. "That argument," the judges pointed out, "is the equivalent to saying that a defendant who cuts off a person's leg against his will is not guilty of mayhem because some people voluntarily have their legs amputated for medical reasons." Although the other hoodlum likely had never heard of Lord Coke, he argued that the breast and abdomen are not "members" of the body. The court replied with a contrary ruling from an especially gruesome California case, in which a woman's heart had been cut out and her mutilated external genitalia were found to be a "member."

While probably any permanent disfigurement can now amount

to mayhem, the courts have specified that voluntary vasectomies are an exception. In 1969, the California county of Shasta tried to rely on the old "disabling the testicles" argument to avoid paying for the vasectomy of a "qualified medical indigent" — a man who could not afford medical care, partly because he already had several children to support.

Lawyers for the county unearthed an old opinion of the state's attorney general that, except in cases of extremity such as grave illness, sterilization of prison inmates could amount to mayhem. Apparently they concluded from the opinion that if sterilization was mayhem, it was a criminal medical procedure, just as abortion can be criminal in certain circumstances. But the California District Court called the opinion "archaic and illogical." This is perhaps extreme: it takes little effort to imagine situations where a prisoner might find it easier to submit to sterilization than risk offending authorities by refusing. (There persists a view that crime is in some senses genetic, and more than one would-be reformer has proposed the sterilization of the "lower orders of society.") In any event, consent by coercion is no consent.

In the Shasta County case, the district court found that county-funded vasectomies were an "acceptable method of family planning" that would hardly "render the patient impotent or unable to fight for the king." A perhaps stronger answer would have been that if the court declared vasectomies to be mayhem in welfare cases, they would be mayhem for all other purposes. That is, no one, no matter how rich or poor or overawed with children, could obtain one (nor could any doctor perform one), because you cannot consent to mayhem.

142 Taking the law into your own hands

It was in 1994 that "to Bobbitt" became a synonym for castration. Twenty-four-year-old manicurist Lorena Bobbitt became a celebrity that year during her trial for malicious wounding. The jury heard how she cut off her husband's penis as he slept. Lorena explained that John Wayne Bobbitt had assaulted her repeatedly during their four years of matrimony and, on the June evening in question, had raped her for the second time in five days. The cumulative abuse made her snap, she said: after the supposed rape, she went to the kitchen for water, where sight of the knife instigated an "irresistible impulse" to revenge. She testified that only once she had fled the scene did she realize she was still clutching what police witnesses called John's "appendage." She flung the appendage out the car window as she drove, but police (or fireman; reports vary) retrieved it, and it was reunited with its owner in a nine-hour surgical operation. John, a U.S. marine and erstwhile nightclub bouncer, was acquitted of the rape allegation, and went on to star in a pornographic film — *John Wayne Bobbitt Uncut*, a purported re-enactment of the events of June 23, 1993.

The Manassas, Virginia, jury accepted Lorena's defence of temporary insanity, but not before several copycastrations ensued worldwide — from Germany and Britain to Korea and Taiwan to India and Zimbabwe, and back to several of the United States. Some were relatively mundane — a man's pelvis set alight with gasoline, sulphuric acid on the genitals, etc. But in Taiwan, Chien Liu-liang, 51, was sentenced to two years' imprisonment after her husband bled to death when she scissored off his penis and flushed it down the toilet. The Korean victim also bled to death, in frigid weather outside a Seoul motel. In Turkey, Abdullah Kemal Konak, a security guard, testified that he was "too drunk to resist" bobbitting when his girlfriend Zeynep Atici tied him up after he threatened to leave her for another paramour. In Zimbabwe, peasant Shanangurai Tinarwo, 40, spent two months in jail after she arrived home one night to find her husband in bed with a lover. She hit him over the head with a log and then sliced at his member until it hung by a bit of muscle and skin. The girlfriend fled through the window, and, though medical help was a 40-mile drive through the bush, a regional physician saved the husband's penis. In 1995, five Brazilian men were bobbitted in a single three-week period, one of them losing a testicle down the toilet, another contending that his girlfriend castrated him with her bare hands. Mind you, the international toll could have been higher. During Lorena Bobbitt's trial, supporters in her native country of Ecuador threatened to castrate 100 Americans if the jury convicted her.

143 Out of the frying pan

A few months after the jury acquitted Lorena Bobbitt, The Teesside Crown Court in England convicted Diane Sladek of grievous bodily harm for pouring hot wax on her husband's genitals and hitting him in the head with the pan.

Sladek, 49, pled guilty before Judge David Bryant, who suspended her 18-month prison term after her husband, Michael, submitted a petition with 73 signatories urging leniency. Judge Bryant also ordered Diane to pay Michael, 45, £1,500 to compensate him for the suffering she caused him, including three skin grafts, after she melted five candles at the kitchen stove and poured the wax over him at two in the morning, as he slept. Diane explained that she was provoked by the day's mail, which included a pair of her husband's underpants accompanied by a mocking letter from his mistress. Michael said that his philandering did in fact drive Diane to the deed, and that she was not ordinarily violent.

144 "A show about nothing," but very nearly about $26.6 million

It might have happened to George Costanza, the bumbling narcissist on the popular television comedy "Seinfeld." In 1997, when he was

51, Jerold Mackenzie lost his $95,000-a-year job at the Miller Brewing Company in Milwaukee, Wisconsin, after he discussed a "Seinfeld" show with co-worker Patricia Best. In the episode of the sitcom, which parodied itself as "a show about nothing," Jerry (Seinfeld) is unable to recall the name of a woman he has begun dating, and, despite such thoughtlessness, he has the grace to be embarrassed to tell her. Recalling that the name rhymes with a woman's body part, Jerry and his friends speculate on such monikers as Mulva and Mipple. Only after the woman realizes that her "boyfriend" doesn't even know her name and ends the relationship does Jerry remember: Dolores.

Mackenzie, a distributor information manager at Miller, claimed that he discussed the episode with several co-workers because he was surprised that the network censors had allowed it to be broadcast. To avoid pronouncing the offending word, he photocopied a page from the dictionary and, pointing to "clitoris" on the photocopy, showed it to Best, saying, "Patty, look at this. This is the word in question." Best said she didn't want to talk about it, and complained to her supervisor, adding that Mackenzie previously had left a romantic voice-mail message for her and told her that he had dreamed about her. "It was what he did, how he did it, how he looked at me," Best later testified in court. "He knew it was my wedding day. It was about a female sex organ, and I thought there was some kind of weird connection for him, and he was getting pleasure out of that."

Best told the superiors that she didn't want Mackenzie severely disciplined, but five days later Miller fired him, claiming that the "Seinfeld" discussion was just the latest in a series of bad management decisions by Mackenzie — what lawyers sometimes call "the culminating incident." Miller said that Mackenzie had been warned in the past about sexually harassing a secretary, but he denied any harassment. The secretary "alleged I would put my arms around her up to ten times a day," Mackenzie publicly explained, that "I forced myself upon her, touching her breasts and buttocks." Miller had settled the secretary's legal action for $16,000.

Mackenzie, who was unable to find other work, sued Miller, his supervisor, and Best. He complained that Best "improperly induced" Miller to fire him "by fraudulently misrepresenting . . . that she felt harassed" by the "Seinfeld" conversation, and that she "had no purpose or desire independent of intentionally causing [his] termination . . . by exerting moral pressure on Miller in fraudulently misrepresenting" that she felt harassed. Much of the lawsuit concerned whether Miller had "misrepresented" Mackenzie's job status to him (a demotion, but without loss of pay or benefits) long before the "Seinfeld" incident, and whether his supervisor had interfered in his employment contract by telling company executives that Mackenzie was a poor manager. This perhaps confused the jury of ten women and two men, who deliberated for six hours before awarding Mackenzie nothing against Best in compensation for her supposed role in his firing, but anyway ordering her to pay him $1.5 million in punitive damages. Added to what they awarded him against Miller and the supervisor, Mackenzie was looking at a $26.6-million (U.S.) payday. He had been suing for $9.2 million.

However, on appeal he lost everything. Concerning the award against Best, the appeals court ruled that a plaintiff cannot get punitive damages if he doesn't first win damages compensating him for the actual harm done — lost wages, mental distress, or something of that sort. Here, the jury found no actual harm. The appeal judges rejected as merely speculative an ingenious argument by Mackenzie's lawyer that the jury probably was just being over-zealous about obeying the trial judge's instructions. The trial judge properly advised them that they could not give duplicate awards (pay Mackenzie twice for the same injury, even if caused by different people). That led them to think, Mackenzie's lawyer argued, that they couldn't award compensatory damages against Best when they had already awarded Mackenzie such damages against Miller. Therefore (the argument went), they were adding the punitive damages onto the compensatory damages from Miller, but really had found that Best, too, had caused Mackenzie actual harm.

The court also rejected Mackenzie's argument that an exception should be made in his case, allowing the punitive damages to stand, because society had a special interest in deterring the serious damage wreaked by false complaints of sexual harassment. Society had a greater interest, the court concluded, in making certain that people were not deterred by the threat of lawsuits from bringing sexual harassers to justice.

145 Walls do not a prison make

When men complain of sexual harassment, they often face even greater ridicule than women. Other men, for example, will ask them what they're complaining about, why don't they just "give in." This was the situation in the case of Robert Lockley, a senior corrections officer at the Mid-State Correctional Facility in New Jersey.

Ronda Turner, Lockley's colleague, had aggressively expressed a sexual interest in him. He told her that he was happily married, with a family, and was not interested. Turner persisted, and when Lockley would not fold, Turner became vengeful. "She began a campaign," the appeals division of the New Jersey Superior Court ruled, "in which she enlisted her friends, to insult Lockley publicly about his sexuality. [S]he expressed, in the most obscene and vulgar terms, persistent opinions about his alleged sexual preferences or lack thereof, alleged sexual abilities or lack thereof, and physical endowments.

"She also, according to Lockley, subjected him to continuing petty indignities. One of her tasks in Center Control, for instance, was to operate the gates controlling entry to and exit from the prison. Lockley testified that Turner constantly made him wait before opening the gates for him and, on one occasion, almost closed the gate on him as he was passing through."

Lockley's male colleagues wondered why he didn't just sleep with Turner, and for several years he found himself dreading going to work as the abuse continued. He ate lunch alone in the guard tower, and his marriage began to suffer. Mid-State contended that union regulations frustrated it from transferring Turner. It ordered an employee to prosecute Turner vigorously before an internal tribunal, Mid-State claimed, but the employee ignored the instructions and presented no evidence against Turner beyond a letter from a state official concluding that there was probable cause to believe that she had subjected Lockley to sexual harassment.[4] Some of the other staff celebrated the dismissal of the charges against Turner with cake and flowers.

Lockley and Turner settled complementary lawsuits (she sued him for defamation), but Lockley's suit against Mid-State went to trial, where the jury awarded him compensatory damages of $750,000, punitive damages of $3 million and legal fees of $855,350. The appeals court ruled that the trial judge had mishandled the punitive damages issue and sent it back to trial. But they affirmed the trial judgment in all other respects (affirming the rest of the damages

---

[4] According to Justice Wefing, writing the opinion for the appeals court, "A disciplinary hearing was scheduled but was adjourned a number of times with the result that it did not take place until more than six months had elapsed after the probable cause letter was issued. Captain Powell Johnson, who was the administrative captain at Mid-State, was ultimately assigned the responsibility to represent management at this disciplinary hearing. Johnson testified that he was instructed by his superiors to do no more at this hearing in support of the charges against Turner than to present the probable cause letter. Others, however, testified that Johnson was instructed to prosecute the matter fully and present live witnesses. In any event, when the hearing finally did take place, Johnson did nothing to present the management case for discipline beyond introducing the probable cause letter, with the result that the hearing officer dismissed all charges against Turner; the State was precluded from reinstituting the same charges against her."

award), writing that "Lockley was subjected for an extended period of years to a relentless assault on his dignity and inherent sense of self; his superiors provided no assistance or relief. . . . We concur with the trial judge's assessment that the lawsuit did not merely revolve around exposure to obscene and vulgar language. The attacks upon Lockley's dignity are not of lesser import because obscenities were commonly heard in the prison environment. We see no basis to conclude that this award is so excessive that it represents a 'manifest denial of justice.'"

146 You say sex toy, I say weapon

In the spring of 2001, the Ontario (Canada) Court of Appeal held that a cucumber could be a weapon. The circumstances in *R. v. Robinson* are not otherwise amusing. They concern several sexual assaults and acts of degradation, including anal rape and defecation. The cucumber became a weapon after Robinson tied up his former girlfriend and gagged her. The jury rejected his story that he used the fruit to "pleasure" the woman, with her consent.

The court held that it was "open to the jury to find . . . that the cucumber was used or intended for use in causing injury to the complainant or for the purpose of intimidating her." The previous June, the Quebec Court of Appeal held that a dildo was not in itself a weapon in similar circumstances. The accused, Éric Lamy, had purchased the purported sexual aid — in this case, a *godemiché*, a sort of artificial phallus shaped like a baseball bat and made of bamboo — in Mexico. As in *Robinson*, Lamy said he used the object with the victim's consent. But the trial judge concluded that, although the victim was not injured by the device, Lamy had committed sexual assault with a weapon. The judge sentenced Lamy to 48 months in prison minus time served, concurrent with a 36-month sentence for forcing anal intercourse on the same woman.

The Court of Appeal held that the trial judge erred when he did not consider Lamy's intention in using the *godemiché* or its effect on the victim. The court noted that the trial judge had acquitted Lamy of sexual assault causing bodily harm and that the Crown had not appealed that acquittal. "To find the appellant guilty," the court held, "the judge had to conclude, after examining the circumstances, that this object, which was not created to kill or wound, was used to kill or wound the victim or, again, threaten or intimidate her." However, on further appeal, the Supreme Court of Canada re-instated Lamy's conviction on the weapon count. "When an accused knowingly or recklessly applies force and sexually assaults a complainant," Justice Louise Arbour wrote for the court, "if he uses an object in doing so, and if the object contributes to the harm caused to the victim by the assault, the accused cannot escape a conviction for sexual assault with a weapon by claiming that his intention was to sexually stimulate the person that he was otherwise assaulting." Lamy had caused injury, even if the wounds did not meet the legal definition of bodily harm. There was evidence that the victim suffered bleeding, and Lamy could not "exonerate himself from having caused the injury by claiming that the bleeding may have been triggered by a pre-existing medical condition" — a uterine infection — "of the victim. In the same way, it is not open to him to claim, in the circumstances of this case, that the injuries to the complainant may not be attributable to the insertion of the object in her vagina against her will, but may have resulted from the part of the assault in which no object was used."

Of course many objects not normally considered weapons have been thought to intimidate or cause injury, notably the paint brush in *The Queen v. Barber*. *Barber* was decided in the Ontario Superior Court shortly before the Court of Appeal issued its reasons in *Robinson*. Justice Edward Then affirmed that the charges against Madeline Barber, accused of stabbing her husband just below his armpit with a little artist's brush, should proceed to trial. At Barber's preliminary hearing the man could not recall Barber's having attacked him that way, but remembered that they had been arguing about money and that, when he refused to continue the discussion, Barber followed him into the kitchen, where the brush was sitting on a table. The next thing the man knew, the brush was on the floor and he was in hospital for six days.

147 All of me

Journalists tried to "spin" the Mark Peterson case this way: if Peterson had sex with a young woman on the consent of only one of her 18 personalities, was he guilty of rape? Reports of the case protect the woman's privacy by identifying her only as Sarah. By the time of the trial, purported experts were saying that stress had pushed another 28 personalities under Sarah's skin. But the issue was not consent; the issue was whether Peterson had violated section 940.225(2)(c) of the *Criminal Code of Wisconsin*, which prohibits anyone from having "sexual intercourse with a person who suffers from a mental illness which renders that person temporarily or permanently incapable of appraising his conduct, and the defendant knows of such condition."

Twenty-nine-year old Peterson was not known as a bright light in Oshkosh, Wisconsin. He worked for four dollars an hour at Burnstad's Pick 'n Save in nearby Neena, bagging groceries, and he was feeling lonely, he said, in a sexless marriage. He met Sarah on June 9, 1988, while she was fishing with the Reeves family in an Oshkosh park. Sarah was 26 at the time, and living above the Reeveses in a two-story home. Sarah and Gerald Reeves, husband to Sarah's protector Peggy, testified that they explained to Peterson that Sarah suffered from multiple personality disorder. In fact, Peterson believed that he had met someone called Franny. But he professed ignorance otherwise. He would later claim that all the other people

Sarah kept talking about, including the "fun-loving 20-year-old Jennifer," were separate people altogether.

Sarah, or Franny, gave Peterson her phone number, and two days later he invited her to have breakfast with him. Gerald Reeves pointed out to her that she had already eaten breakfast, and told her (Franny?) in front of Peterson to confirm it with Sarah. Sarah agreed that she had eaten corn flakes but decided to go with Peterson for coffee. According to Sarah, Jennifer "took over" at LaSure's Cafe, and Peterson asked her, "Can I love you, Jennifer?" Sarah, or Jennifer, said yes, but six-year-old Emily kept intervening while she had sex with Peterson in the front seat of his car. Emily afterwards "explained" to Sarah what had happened (Sarah said) in childishly graphic terms about wet underwear and the like. Sarah went to the police, who charged Peterson with violating section 940.225(2).

As far as anyone could determine, it was the first time that multiple personality disorder was used in a U.S. court against a defendant. Usually, it was the *defense*: the defendant himself suffered from the disorder, the defendant would claim, and therefore he was unfit to stand trial or was not criminally responsible for his conduct. When Sarah testified, the judge swore in three of her personalities, whom she purported to summon from her psyche. By then, the case had become a media circus, and Sarah a minor celebrity.

Facing as much as ten years in prison, Peterson testified that he thought Jennifer was "a possible promunctuous person" of Sarah's acquaintance. "Promiscuous?" the prosecution asked. "Whatever," Peterson replied. But in his statement to police, he had admitted that "Emily" had been "peeking" while he had sex with "Franny." A defense psychiatrist said that multiple personality disorder was extremely rare but sensationalist talk shows had made it "the disease of the month and plea of the year." His research suggested that 95 percent of the malady was diagnosed by five percent of clinicians. "It's the UFO of psychiatry," he testified. The jury convicted Peterson anyway, but soon afterwards new details surfaced. Sarah, or her Ginger personality, had been intimate with Gerald Reeves and picked up men at bars. Robert Hawley, the trial judge, had ruled that the jury could not hear about such sexual history because the Wisconsin rape-shield law forbade it. But rape-shield laws generally do allow cross-examination on the complainant's sexual history if the defense can prove that the history is crucial to understanding the case before the court. As well, several of Sarah's main supporting witnesses, including the Reeveses and a psychologist who also served as her unofficial press agent, had entered a joint venture agreement with Sarah ensuring them each a percentage "with respect to any movie, book, magazine article, tape recording, phonograph record, radio or television presentation or live entertainment of any kind, arising from or inspired by the personal relationships and associations of the parties." In a fit of conscience, Peggy Reeves bailed out of the agreement and revealed it to Judge Hawley, and the prosecution was obliged to agree that a new trial was necessary. Subsequently, the state decided not to proceed, purportedly because another prosecution would have been too difficult for Sarah. A reporter asked her what she would say to someone who believed that she was ill, but that her illness was desperation for attention and her court testimony was a brilliant one-woman show. "I would not expect the average layperson to understand it," Sarah responded, as Sarah, "because I believe it's a difficult concept to accept, even for me. But I have it."

148 A father's trials

As noted in the section on adulterous provocation,[5] the fact that a defendant simply hears that his spouse has committed adultery will not usually amount to sufficient provocation to reduce a murder

---

[5] See number 35.

charge to manslaughter. A confession of adultery, the law seems to infer, would not stir the blood as much as an eyewitness viewing. A reasonable person would seek more civilized remedy, such as divorce. But what if you hear that someone engaged in homosexual activity with your teenaged son?

On November 1, 1837, Charles Meredith burst into the room of his tenant, James Randall, to find Randall in a compromising position with a 15-year-old boy. "Ah-ha! You wretch!" the landlord bellowed. "I suspected you; now I've got you bang to rights!"

In testimony before a court, Meredith said that, caught in the act, Randall fell to his knees and promised him anything, even £100, if Meredith would forbear turning him in. Meredith scuffled with him, then Randall and the boy fled.

The next day, the boy's father, William Fisher, came to the landlord "in great misery," sobbing, attempting to find Randall. Later that day, William was seen at the head of a mob, beating Randall with a stick. He dropped the stick to stab Randall with a table knife. Randall died the next evening.

The presiding justices suggested strongly to the jury that they find Fisher guilty of premeditated murder. "What a state we would be in," one of the judges remarked, "if a man, on hearing that something had been done to his child, should be at liberty to take the law into his own hands, and inflict vengeance on the offender." There had been no formal accusation, no trial, no presumption of innocence. "The father only heard what had been done from others."

But the jury had heard Fisher's statement to the sheriff "that he had only done what a father and an Englishman would have done under similar circumstances." This probably struck a sympathetic chord. They had heard Fisher's lawyer remark that Fisher was in a dilemma of despair: if he sicced the law on Randall, he would incriminate his own son. The provocation, the lawyer argued, was "far beyond that of adultery; for the adulteress only has to bear the scorn and contempt of society, while the son in this case might have been subjected to capital punishment." (Homosexuality, being "a sodomite," could attract the death penalty.) The more a father brooded over the situation, "the more likely he would be to be goaded into desperation and madness."

The lawyer was hedging his bets, going for a complete acquittal. The jury compromised; where the black letter of the law said Fisher was a murderer, they found him guilty of manslaughter and "recommended him to mercy, on account of the greatness of the provocation."

CHAPTER EIGHT

YOU SAY "COCOTTE," I SAY "HARLOT"

Imputations of Unchastity

Shaw: Would you sleep with me for a million dollars?
Actress: Of course.
Shaw: Would you sleep with me for a hundred dollars?
Actress: What do you take me for?
Shaw: We've already established what you are.
Now we're just negotiating the price.

DINNER CONVERSATION ATTRIBUTED TO GEORGE BERNARD SHAW

149 Pardon my French

Occasionally the law transforms jurors into semi-professional linguists. A 1925 defamation action demanded that New Yorkers translate French, never mind their ignorance of the language. The facts before them were that Elena Rogira worked as a stewardess on the *S.S. Orizaba*, which called at ports in Cuba and Spain. The second steward, Andrew Boget, was so enamored of Rogira, a widow with four children, that he became jealous when she performed shipboard work for the chief steward.

As the *Orizaba* steamed out of Havana one evening for Spain, some of the crew were seated at dinner. Rogira asked Boget to arrange for water to be brought to the table. According to her evidence, Boget replied, "Why don't you go to your friend's room and ask him for ice water?"

"I have no friends," Rogira responded. "I just am nice to everybody, and I have no friends."

"Go ahead," Boget said. "You are worse than a *cocotte*."

"With this, the plaintiff fainted," the New York Court of Appeals reports, "not, however, until she had slapped his face." The court found that the other crew members at the table understood French and that *cocotte* was "a French word meaning a woman who leads a fast life, one who gives herself up for money. The interpreter said it implies to some men the same ideas as the word *prostitute*. In other associations it may mean a poached egg."

The trial and lower appellate court dismissed Rogira's complaint, but the appeal court decided that, as Boget's use of *cocotte* might "impute unchastity" to Rogira, she could have a valid slander action. The court ordered a new trial, but the law remains bereft of a settled definition of *cocotte*. Rogira dropped her lawsuit before it reached a second hearing. Perhaps someone would have pointed out there that *ma cocotte* can mean something like "sweetie-pie," and that the most common usage of the word is to describe a casserole pot.

150 That Gallic cachet

What amounts to an imputation of wrongful or immoral behavior is of course a product of the times. One day in the early 1600s, for example, a man named Knight said to Joan Califord, "Thou art Mutcome's hackney," a hackney normally being a horse, of course, but it could also mean a woman who offered rides for a price. In case there was any doubt, Knight elaborated: "Thou art a thieving whore and a pocky whore, and I will prove thee a pocky whore."

When Joan Califord's husband sued Knight for slander, the justices proved themselves unrelentingly literal-minded. Thieving was not a felony, they noted, so calling a woman a "thieving whore," left no obvious stain on her reputation. To call her "pocky whore" would have been actionable if it implied "unchastity," but "pocky" in itself did not signify the *French* pox "when it is not shewn by any other circumstance, as to say that she was laid of them, or the like." (*The Dictionary of the Vulgar Tongue*, 1811, gives *French disease* as "the venereal disease, said to have been imported from France.")

Forty-three years later, a different court saw the illogic of this when Bridget Marshal's father sued neighbor Chickall. Chickall had called Bridget "a whore, and a pocky-ars'd whore." It was not actionable, the court ruled, to say simply "thou art a whore," and "thou hast had the pox" (again, calling a woman a "whore" did not necessarily mean she was "unchaste"), but to link the allegations — "Thou art a whore and hast had the pox" — was to invite penalty, the implication being that the pox was not chicken- or small-, but French, indeed.

Even within a year of the *Califord* case, an English court seemed to rule that if the "pocky whore" accusation was accompanied by some repulsively graphic details, it could get you money damages. The words there were "Mrs. Miller is a whore and hath had the pox and hast holes one may turn his finger in them. Mr. Ring the apothecary gave her drink for it, and therefore take heed how you drink with her."

In fact, in the even earlier *Levet's Case*, a much tamer aspersion was held to be slanderous. The defendant had said, "Thy house is infected with the pox and thy wife was laid of the pox," which was offensive not because of the words "thy wife was laid of the pox," but because the "house" was an inn. The words were therefore "a discredit to the plaintiff, and the guests would not resort thither." Business was business. The court awarded Levet £50 in damages.

151 Imputations of illegitimacy

By the early 1900s, Anglo-American court rulings reflected society's greatly-increased sensitivity to a woman's good name. A young plaintiff successfully sued for libel when a New York reporter wrote that she was a "dancer at Coney Island." This, the court held, put the woman before "the public gaze not only as unchaste but as belonging to one of the lowest classes of the great army of fallen women." In 1910, the New York courts determined that a local publisher libelled socialite Emilie Snyder merely in reporting that her "Irish maid" allowed a process server to enter Snyder's bathroom as she bathed. The story said that the process server retreated, but delivered a subpoena — concerning an unpaid butcher's bill of $40 — to "a hand which was extended from the bathroom. The fact that the hand was attached to a naked arm led the man to believe he was giving the paper to the woman whom he surprised in the tub." The court summarily decided that the article was fiction and made Snyder the object of public ridicule, never mind that it was the process server who was ridiculous, the maid who was allegedly indiscreet, and Snyder's husband who supposedly had not paid the butcher's bill. Nakedness was all, no matter how innocent.

More surprisingly, the modern cases also say that, even in times when putative illegitimacy could dash one's hopes of property and inheritance, it wasn't very often that *bastard* was an actionable slander, no matter who you were, and no matter the associated "imputation of unchastity." In 1950 a New York couple called their landlady, Mrs. Notarmuzzi, a "bleached blond bastard." She sued but, according to the state's supreme court, it didn't matter that the Shevacks also called her a "lousy tramp," "rotten son of a bitch," "black marketeer," and "bootlegger." Circa 1950 in the U.S., alleged bleached-blondism, not to mention bastardy, did not seriously impugn Notarmuzzi's character.

As with the case of *cocotte* in dictionaries, law reports that predate *Notarmuzzi* translate *bastard* as an endearment. The American journalist Walter Winchell was once prosecuted for criminal libel after using *bastard* in his column. The complainant evidently suspected that the insult would not be defamatory civilly, but his resort to criminal justice was no more productive. Acquitting Winchell, the court found that great men such as Erasmus and Alexander Hamilton were "illegitimate," and that men regularly called friends "you old bastard."

A similar finding was made in South Africa in 1943, arising out of a dispute between two railway foremen. The alleged defamation occurred after "threats of violence were exchanged, interposed with the usual pleasantries" — racial slurs, scatological commands, and a theory that the plaintiff was bred of "half bastard, half yellow-belly." But Justice van den Heever found that railroaders "habitually use strong language spiced with salacious terms subolent [redolent?] of the sewer" and in railway workshops "the word 'bastard' is frequently used as a term of endearment." The plaintiff therefore could not recover damages for that denigration, but was awarded £80 for the observation that "he should have been in an internment camp long ago."

152 The court non-interpreter

The case law also demonstrates that even the most polite language — or at least language not prone to slang interpretations as *cocotte* might be — can be translated into imputations of dastardliness, if not bastardliness. At the Bodmin Assizes in the 1930s Justice Wright had just convicted a farm laborer of bestiality. "Prisoner at the bar," he began, "the jury have convicted you on the clearest evidence, of disgusting and degrading offences. Your conduct is viewed by all right-minded men with abhorrence. The sentence of the court is that you be kept in penal servitude for seven years."

The prisoner had not taken in all of this little lecture, so Justice Wright asked the warder, standing near the prisoner, to repeat it. But apparently the warder found the judge's rhetorical flight high-minded and obscure. He told the prisoner, "His lordship says that you are a dirty old bastard, and he's put you away for 17 years."

Still, the last word belonged to the court. "Warder," Justice Wright said, "I have no objection to your paraphrasing my sentence, but you have no power to increase it."

153 And sometimes they can sing really high

A man, conversely, is bound to sue if someone imputes that he won't or can't be unchaste. A newspaper war at the turn of the last century in Arkansas City, Kansas, illustrates the point. T. W. Eckert edited *The Arkansas City Daily Traveler*, a weekly paper. In an editorial for May 23, 1902, he wrote that he was looking forward to the prospective change of editors at the rival paper, which he called *Greer's Supplement*. Greer's paper was actually called the *Arkansas City Enquirer*, edited by W. W. Van Pelt. Rumor had it, according to Eckert's editorial, that Charlie McIntire was to be the "*Supplement*'s" new editor. "Charlie is all right," Eckert wrote. "In fact anybody would be an improvement on the eunuch who is snorting around in the basement and unable to do anything else."

In his libel claim against Eckert, Van Pelt asserted that "at the time of the said publication he was known and recognized as a man possessed of a due amount of potency, virility, and masculinity, and of all the various members and power which characterized the male portion of the human race, and was a young, unmarried man, 'in the lusty prime of vigorous youth.'"

In his defense, Eckert argued that nowhere did the editorial name Van Pelt, and that no one would have thought that he was necessarily the snorting eunuch. The trial and appeal courts found that Van Pelt indeed was the intended target, although calling him a snorting eunuch was not necessarily libellous. The words could have meant that Van Pelt's editorial attacks on Eckert "were weak [and] barren of thought." But the "primary and general" definition of *eunuch* was "a castrated male of the human species," and the law required that the word "be given its usual and ordinary sense." The courts awarded Van Pelt $700 in damages.

154 Thank you for not joking

Then again, although sexual experience is often thought to be a sign of manliness, men sue for "imputations of unchastity" if they are represented as being unchaste in a crude or perverse way. In 1936, Crawford Burton, a famous steeplechase rider, accused the creators of an ad for Camel's cigarettes of representing him as "guilty of indecent exposure and as being a person physically deformed and mentally perverted," as well as "an utterer of salacious and obscene language."

Burton had agreed to be photographed for the ad, which displayed him in two poses. One photo showed him sitting outside a paddock holding a cigarette in one hand, and his cap and whip in the other. The other showed him carrying a saddle, such that part of it, the girth or strap that goes under the horse's belly to hold the saddle in place, seemed to be part of his lower anatomy. "So regarded," Justice Learned Hand wrote for the Second Circuit Court of Appeals, "the photograph becomes grotesque, monstrous, and obscene; and the legends, which without undue violence can be made to match [the photographs], reinforce the ribald interpretation." The "legends" — that is, the captions to the pictures — read: "Camels restore me after a crowded business day" and "Get a lift with a Camel."

The advertising agency had run the ad without showing the photos to Burton. The court held that "nobody could be fatuous enough" to believe that the ad meant that Burton was deformed or was behaving indecently. It seemed, in fact, that the optical illusion was accidental. But the agency took advantage of the accident to caricature Burton deliberately, and by design they had exposed him to significant ridicule.[1] "A man must not be too thin-skinned or a self-important prig," Justice Hand wrote, "but this advertisement was more than what only a morbid person would not laugh off; the mortification, however ill-deserved, was a very substantial grievance." It was irrelevant that the photograph was a snapshot of a real event in time.

The story goes that, while considering what to rule in Burton's case, Justice Hand brought the ad with him to a luncheon meeting of the Reporters and Advisors of the American Law Institute at the Harvard Club. He based his opinion, say the textbooks on defamation law, on the general hilarity this produced.

155 Garden-variety insults

Baa-lamb. Candy-ass. Chicken. Creampuff. Fraidy-cat. Funker. Girl's blouse. Mary Ann. Panty-waist. Pussy. Tired people. Wanker. Waterboy. Yellowbelly. These are among the 45 synonyms for *weakling* listed in Jonathon Green's *Slang Thesaurus*. Some are *double* or *triple entendres*, signifying homosexuality or masturbation. One is surprised to find

---

[1] Burton's statement of claim used the language still common today in libel pleadings: the photos "exposed him to hatred, ridicule and contempt."

that *pansy* is not among them, particularly given the circumstances of *Thaarup v. Hulton Press Ltd.*

In the August, 1942, number of the British magazine *Lilliput*, there appeared two provocative pictures on facing pages. On the left was, in the words of Lord Justice Scott of the Court of Appeal, "a Home Guard standing in a garden with buildings behind, and holding a garden fork in a minatory position." In other words, the guard was menacing the viewer with his garden fork — a peculiarly English threat, one would think. Under the guard were the words "Keep out of my garden."

On the right-hand page was a picture of the plaintiff, Aage Thaarup, a designer of women's hats. Mr. Thaarup was holding "a model of a woman's head with a hat on and a bunch of snowdrops on the hat." Under him were the words, "I only wanted a few pansies." In a lawsuit against *Lilliput*'s publishers Mr. Thaarup alleged that, taken together, the two pictures libelled him. To see why he took offense, one has to imagine that the pictures are engaged in a dialogue.

Apparently even this would not have clued in most of the judges who heard the case. The trial judge, Justice Cassels, refused to hear evidence that "the word 'pansy' as applied to a man has a slang sense, often used, of an opprobrious character." In those days, homosexuality was a crime with very serious consequences. But evidently believing that the editors of *Lilliput* were referring to horticulture, Justice Cassels dismissed Thaarup's action.

And so things would have stood if it weren't for appeal justice Lord Rayner Goddard, who, indeed, was famous for his red-necked worldliness. After speaking to Lord Goddard, Justice Scott was more than anxious to allow Mr. Thaarup's appeal: "I personally was not alive to the slang meaning of the word, nor, I think, was my brother MacKinnon, but my brother Goddard fortunately was quite alive to it, having had judicial experience as a result of which he had come to know about it." Enlivened by his brother's advice, Lord Justice Scott held: "There must be a new trial. The case must be re-heard, because if the word had the meaning suggested, a very grievous and wicked wrong has been done to the plaintiff." What happened after that seems to have been lost in the garden mists of time.

156 And they call the mechanic Randy

If one has to strain too much to see the insult, it will not likely pass muster as such in court. Notorious in this sense during the Depression was the *Ralston* case. The well-to-do parties had separated in 1916, after six years of marriage, but did not divorce. After separation, Mrs. Ralston set up a garage business. Acting on a tip, she later visited a churchyard to find that her estranged husband, William, had erected a tombstone there, with the inscription, "In loving memory of Jennie the dearly beloved wife of W.R. Crawshay Ralston of the Bungalow Valley. Died 20th May, 1916." Mrs. Ralston sued for libel, claiming that the inscription implied that she was now living in sin, holding herself out as a married woman. (Legally, death ends marriage, of course). The "imputation of unchastity" affected her "credit and character as a trader," she complained. But Justice Macnaghten dismissed her lawsuit, comparing it to *Tinkley v. Tinkley*, in which Mrs. Tinkley's estranged husband falsely accused her of stealing from her employer. As Mrs. Tinkley was in domestic service, any charge of thievery was very damaging, Justice Macnaghten noted. Nevertheless, her lawsuit failed because the law of the day (the *Married Woman's Property Act*) said a woman could sue her husband in tort (that is, for private wrongs such as negligence or trespass) only to protect or secure her separate property. "A charge of dishonesty," Justice Macnaghten wrote, "is surely much more injurious to a domestic servant than is the imputation of unchastity to a garage proprietor. In the occupation of domestic service honesty is a necessary virtue: whereas it cannot be said that chastity is a necessary qualification for the management or ownership of a garage."

157 Up against the wall, Dr. Bowdler

As discussed above (number 97), the Dr. Bowdlers of the world will censor vernacular for sexual activity even when it is used in non-sexual contexts. But they are often frustrated by legal guarantees of free expression. In 1969, for example, Robert Keefe, the head of the English department of a high school in Ipswich, Massachusetts, gave his 12th-grade students an optional assignment to read an article in *The Atlantic Monthly* about young, so-called anti-establishment activists. Because the article used the word *motherfucker* several times, Keefe discussed the word with his class and why the author used it. He then said that students could choose an alternative reading. When Keefe would not promise not to use the word again in class, the school committee purported to fire him. Keefe won a stay of his dismissal from Judge Aldrich of the U.S. First Circuit Court of Appeals. Judge Aldrich took a liberal view of communal versus individual rights that perhaps has not survived Reaganism and neo-conservatism:

> *Hence the question in this case is whether a teacher may, for demonstrated educational purposes, quote a "dirty" word currently used in order to give special offense, or whether the shock is too great for high school seniors to stand. If the answer were that the students must be protected from such exposure, we would fear for their future. We do not question the good faith of the defendants [members of the school committee and two officials at Keefe's school] in believing that some parents have been offended. With the greatest of respect to such parents, their sensibilities are not the full measure of what is proper education.*

Judge Aldrich found that the article was "a valuable discussion of 'dissent, protest, radicalism and revolt'" and in no way pornographic. It was impossible to read it, he added, "either in whole or in part, as an incitement to libidinous conduct, or even thoughts. . . . [T]he word was used, by the persons described, as a superlative of opprobrium." The "general chilling effect of permitting such rigorous censorship" was more serious, Judge Aldrich ruled, than the very low risk of demeaning a proper education.

158 The metaphysics of satire

During the 1980s, so-called "men's magazines" such as *Penthouse* were subjected to persistent attacks by organized groups as well as individuals claiming libel, outrage, and that the publications intentionally inflicted emotional suffering on them. Ultimately, these actions failed because the features under attack were protected by the First Amendment of the U.S. constitution — "Congress shall make no law . . . abridging the freedom of speech, or of the press." Often, the publishers were able to convince higher courts, including the U.S. Supreme Court, that extremely abusive and crude articles, cartoons, or photo features were fair comment, protected opinion, or "could not be reasonably understood as describing actual facts" about those complaining.

In particular, salacious parody and satire enjoyed broad First Amendment protection. In 1979, *Penthouse* magazine published a story by Philip Cioffari, a literature professor at a New Jersey university, about that year's Miss America pageant. The story, labeled "Humor," was called "Miss Wyoming Saves the World, But She Blew the Contest With Her Talent." Its protagonist was Charlene, the pageant contestant from Wyoming. As Charlene prepares to perform her baton-twirling number in the talent segment of the pageant, she, in the words of Chief Judge Seth of the U.S. Court of Appeals, Tenth

Circuit, "thinks of Wyoming and an incident there when she was with a football player from her high school. It describes an act of fellatio when she causes him to levitate."

But such talents do not propel Charlene into the pageant finals. Instead, she is left to fantasize at the pit of the stage, imagining how she would have described to the master of ceremonies her ambition to be a "special ambassador of love and peace," and how she would have admitted enthusiastically that she was willing to save the world from war by performing fellatio on the entire Soviet Central Committee, Marshall Tito, and Fidel Castro. Anxious that the moment might pass with America unaware of her gift, for the TV cameras Charlene performs fellatio on her drunken coach, Corky, causing him to "levitate." The story ends with the coach "having just passed the three-inch mark and still ascending."

Kimerli Pring was the real Miss Wyoming for 1978, and her special talent was baton-twirling. After *Penthouse* published the Cioffari story, some people Pring knew, and a great many people she did not know, began calling her "Miss Penthouse" and making suggestive invitations, sometimes over the phone at four and five in the morning. She began gaining weight and losing sleep, and some of the girls she taught baton stopped their lessons. Pring contacted Gerry Spence — celebrated for the Karen Silkwood radiation-poisoning case — and sued. On her behalf, Spence alleged that the *Penthouse* story suggested Pring "committed fellatio on one Monty Applewhite and also upon her coach, Corky Corcoran, in the presence of a national television audience at the Miss America Pageant. The article also creates the impression that plaintiff committed fellatio-like acts upon her baton at the Miss America contest."

This argument won Pring $26.5 million at trial, but a two-to-one majority of the tenth circuit appeals court overturned the award. It found the *Penthouse* story "gross, unpleasant, crude, distorted," with "no redeeming features whatsoever." But the author was protected under the First Amendment, the majority decided. The story "described something physically impossible in an impossible setting," and it was therefore a reasonable inference that no real Miss Wyoming was portrayed.

159 *1984*, or maybe *Animal Farm*?

In 1984, Jeannie Braun succeeded to a limited extent in her defamation and privacy-invasion lawsuit against Larry Flynt's *Chic* magazine. She convinced the U.S. Court of Appeals for the Fifth District that *Chic* staff had tricked her employers into supplying photos of her swimming with Ralph, The Diving Pig.

Part of Braun's job at the Aquarena Springs Amusement Park in San Marcos, Texas, was treading water in a pool and holding out a bottle of milk topped with a nipple. To drink from the bottle, Ralph would dive into the pool. As promotion for Ralph and the park, Aquarena sold photographs and postcards showing Ralph, as Circuit Judge E. Grady Jolly put it, "in good form, legs fully extended, tail curled, diving toward Mrs. Braun, who is shown in profile holding the bottle."

In 1977, *Chic* editor Henry Nuwer wanted to use one of the photos in the magazine's "*Chic* Thrills" section. As Aquarena's public relations director had never heard of *Chic*, Nuwer told her that it "was a men's magazine containing men's fashion, travel, and humor." On the understanding that *Chic* had "the same clientele that would read a *Redbook* or *McCall's*," the P.R. director supplied *Chic* transparencies of Braun's act with Ralph. *Chic* published one of the photos with the caption, "SWINE DIVE — A pig that swims? Why not? This plucky porker performs every day at Aquarena Springs Amusement Park in bustling San Marcos, Texas. Aquarena staff members say the pig was incredibly easy to train. They told him to learn quick, or grow up to be a juicy ham sandwich."

The trial and appeals courts rejected out of hand *Chic*'s argument that the feature itself was substantially true and should be considered independently of the magazine's contents. In touting the article's distinctiveness, Flynt and his staff were probably motivated by the fact that most of the rest of the 21 "current events" in that month's "*Chic* Thrills" had to do with sex. As well, as the fifth circuit appeals court put it, "on the same page on which Mrs. Braun's picture appeared were stories about '10 Things That Pissed-Off Women' with an accompanying cartoon of a woman whose large breasts are partially exposed; a story entitled 'Mammaries Are Made of This,' about men whose breasts have been enlarged by exposure to a synthetic hormone, with an accompanying cartoon showing a man with large breasts; and a story entitled 'Chinese Organ Grinder' about the use of sexual organs from deer, dogs, and seals as a Chinese elixir. On the facing page is a picture showing a nude female model demonstrating navel jewellery and an article on 'Lust Rock Rules,' about a 'throbbing paean' to sex written by 'the Roman Polanski of rock.' The cover of the issue shows a young woman sitting in a chair with her shirt open so as partially to reveal her breasts, one hand to her mouth and other hand in her tightly-fitting, unzipped pants."

Braun had signed a release authorizing Aquarena to use her photo "in good taste and without embarrassment to me and my family," but she was unaware of the *Chic* feature until a stranger at a grocery store approached her and said, "Hey, I know you." The jury awarded her $30,000 for defamation ($25,000 of which was punitive damages) and $65,000 for invasion of privacy ($50,000 of that amount being punitive), finding that *Chic* created "a false impression as to Mrs. Braun's reputation, integrity or virtue" and acted "willfully and with reckless disregard for her reputation by publishing the photo without a valid consent."

The fifth circuit court did not disturb the findings that *Chic* was liable. However, it sent the matter back to the trial court for recalculation of damages. It held that the jury could compensate Braun for defamation or invasion of privacy, but to compensate her for both amounted to paying her twice.

160 Righteous indignation

Braun was a warning shot over the bow for Flynt, but, as with Kim Pring and *Penthouse*, plaintiffs soon went after his grosser *Hustler* magazine with less success. The courts repeatedly echoed the *Pring* view: "There is no accounting for the vast divergence in views and ideas. However, the First Amendment was intended to cover them all. The First Amendment is not limited to ideas, statements, or positions which are accepted; which are not outrageous; which are decent and popular; which are constructive or have some redeeming element; or which do not deviate from community standards and norms; or which are within prevailing religious or moral standards. Although a story may be repugnant in the extreme to an ordinary reader, . . . the typical standards and doctrines under the First Amendment must nevertheless be applied. The magazine itself should not have been tried for its moral standards. Again, no matter how great its divergence may seem from prevailing standards, this does not prevent the application of the First Amendment. The First Amendment standards are not adjusted to a particular type of publication or particular subject matter."

Flynt was unabashed about fighting dirty against those he considered prudish and censorious. In this sense, the Reverend Jerry Falwell, knight errant for the Moral Majority, made a large target. In 1983, *Hustler* targeted the preacher in a parody of the Campari ad campaign, "My First Time." The Campari magazine ads featured celebrities talking about their personal "first times." The ads were coyly designed to milk the *double entendre*; only near the end did they state clearly that the celebrities were speaking of their first Campari.

The Falwell parody copied the layout and design of the Campari ads, and quoted the parody-Falwell as stating that his "first time" was with his mother in an outhouse, when both of them were drunk.

Fighting fire with fire, Falwell's organization began mailing out copies of the ad, hoping to disgust supporters into a frontal assault on Flynt and his porn empire. Falwell also sued for defamation and various other torts. By the time the lawsuit reached the U.S. Supreme Court, all of his claims had been defeated except his assertion that the *Hustler* parodists had intentionally inflicted mental suffering on him.

Chief Justice William Rehnquist, who is not noted for his liberality, wrote the judgment for the court, in *Hustler*'s favor. The chief justice noted that the parody was "a rather poor relation" to political cartoons such as a colonial one "portraying George Washington as an ass." But Falwell was a public figure open to such attack, as long as it was not defamatory or otherwise illegal. The parody did not state actual facts about Falwell, the chief justice wrote, and no reasonable person would have believed that he actually had drunken sex with his mother, or that he preached only when he was three sheets to the wind.

161 Ludicrous, but lawful

The next quasi-celebrity to take on Flynt was feminist polemicist Andrea Dworkin, notorious for her view that, given male dominance in modern society, even consensual sexual intercourse is rape. In February 1984, *Hustler* published a cartoon which, as Dworkin's complaint put it, "depicts two women engaged in a lesbian act of oral sex with the caption, 'You remind me so much of Andrea Dworkin, Edna. It's a dog-eat-dog world.'" The next month, the magazine published a staged photograph of a purportedly Jewish man having sex with a woman and supposedly saying, "While I'm teaching this little shiksa the joys of Yiddish, the Andrea Dworkin

Fan Club begins some really serious suck-'n'-squat. Ready to give up the holy wafers for matzoh, yet, guys?" And a December feature called "Porn from the Past" showed a man performing cunnilingus on a fat woman. The caption to the photo said, "We don't believe it for a minute, but one of our editors swears that this woman in the throes of ecstacy is the mother of radical feminist Andrea Dworkin."

Dworkin sued *Hustler* and Flynt for $50 million in actual damages and another $100 million in punitive damages, alleging libel, invasion of privacy, intentional infliction of emotional injury, outrage, and that *Hustler* and Flynt deprived her of her constitutional rights.

The court found the latter claim "virtually incoherent," but characterized it as "little more than the unsupported assertion" that *Hustler* and Flynt violated the First Amendment by uttering "unprotected speech" that affected Dworkin in a negative way. Yet all the judges involved had no hesitation characterizing the features as "disgusting and distasteful abuse." Still, Dworkin's lawsuit cracked along the *Pring-Falwell* fault-lines: the features "could not reasonably be understood as expressing statements of fact about Dworkin," and were not malicious in the libel law sense (because Flynt and *Hustler* did not hold out anything to be a fact while knowing it was not true or while being reckless as to its truth). The features amounted to opinion protected by the First Amendment, no matter how crudely expressed. "Ludicrous statements," the Ninth District Court of Appeals said, "are much less insidious and debilitating than falsities that bear the ring of truth. We have little doubt that the outrageous and the outlandish will be recognized for what they are."

The same proved to be true for non-celebrity plaintiffs, two women featured as "Asshole of the Month" for their community organization efforts against pornography. *Hustler* published the women's photographs superimposed on a man "mooning" the camera. Accompanying articles described one of the women as a "tightassed housewife," "frustrated," "threatened by sex," a "fanatic," a "crackpot," as well as a "deluded busybody" and paranoiac who ran a "wacko group" opposed to free expression. Another article characterized the other woman, and her colleagues, as "pus bloated walking sphincters," "sexually repressed," man-and-sex-haters, self-haters, and a frustrated group of "sexual fascists."

"Publication in *Hustler*," one appeals court wrote, "a magazine known for its pornographic content and directed to an audience sympathetic to pornography, creates a context which robs the statements of defamatory meaning because the statements will be taken as statements of *Hustler*'s opinion of [the plaintiff], not as facts about her personal reasons for opposing pornography. We are particularly persuaded to this view because the article appeared in a regular monthly feature routinely devoted to lampooning opponents of pornography and critics of *Hustler Magazine*." Again, while the features were "vicious slurs," they were protected opinion.

162 He that lives by the sword

Another famous plaintiff against *Hustler*, and perhaps the most bemusing one, was Bob Guccione, the publisher of the competing *Penthouse*. In the "Bits and Pieces" section of *Hustler* for November, 1983, Flynt noted that Guccione liked to publish pictures of himself fully-clothed in *Penthouse*, surrounded by nude female models. An accompanying example from *Penthouse* for September, 1983, showed Guccione with a naked woman on his lap. "Considering he is married and also has a live-in girlfriend, Kathy Keeton," Flynt wrote, "we wonder if he would let either of them [sic] pose nude with a man."

Guccione sued and an Ohio jury awarded him $1.6 million in punitive damages for libel, while limiting compensatory damages to one dollar. The disparity between the two amounts suggests, of course, that the jurors did not believe that Guccione really suffered much injury to his reputation. And it was on that basis — the view that Guccione was "libel-proof" in the matter of adultery — that led an appeals court to take the victory away from him.

It was notorious, the appeals court found, that Guccione was married in 1956, separated from Muriel Guccione in 1964, and divorced her in 1979. He began living with girlfriend Kathy Keeton in 1966, 13 years before his divorce. His family, friends, and business associates all knew this, he admitted, and his own publications sometimes advocated adultery. In this sense, the appeal court ruled, Guccione had no reputation to lose. "We have recognized," Judge Jon Newman wrote for the Second Circuit Court of Appeals, "that a plaintiff's reputation with respect to a specific subject may be so badly tarnished that he cannot be further injured by allegedly false statements on that subject. . . . The damage to Guccione's reputation occurred a decade before *Hustler* published its November, 1983 article and stemmed from truthful reporting of facts freely admitted by Guccione himself. Any subsequent reporting accusing Guccione of adultery prior to his 1979 divorce could not further injure his reputation on the subject.

". . . The undisputed facts of this case — the extremely long duration of Guccione's adulterous conduct, which he made no attempt to conceal from the general public, and the relatively short period of time since his divorce — make it fair to say that calling Guccione an 'adulterer' in 1983 was substantially true," and therefore not libelous. "Of course, 'former long-time adulterer'" would have been more precise. But on the facts of this case, to require such a level of accuracy is unreasonable."

Guccione's more earnest aim, it seemed, was to go after Flynt's reputation under the banner of defending his own. The ironies are manifold. Representing Guccione in this modern American version of a not very gentlemanly duel was New York's Norman Grutman, the same lawyer who had represented *Penthouse* against Kimerli Pring in the "Miss Wyoming" case — and who now carried the flag for a whole slate of plaintiffs against Flynt enterprises, including Jerry Falwell in the Campari parody suit and actress Joan Collins, who claimed that Flynt published pictures of another actress participating in an orgy and wrongly stated that the woman was Collins. Grutman's attacks on Flynt personally in both the Collins and Guccione lawsuits were so strong and graphic as to draw a scolding from the bench. The "boisterous trial" in Guccione's case, Judge Newman wrote, "gave new meaning to the term 'adversary proceeding,'"[2] during which Grutman's "melodramatic appeals to jurors' passions and prejudices," criticized by the court just four months earlier in the Collins case, "demonstrated the inadequacy of our prior cautions. Grutman described Flynt as 'the Son of Sam among publishers,' a 'Philistine Goliath' and 'Quasimodo'; he called Flynt's and *Hustler*'s attacks on Guccione 'torture' and 'death by a thousand cuts'; he said those connected with the alleged libel were trying 'to poke Mr. Guccione in the eye with a sharp stick, just as they have been doing for ten years.' At the close of his summation in the damages phase of trial, Grutman urged the jurors, '[i]n the name of the Almighty,' to award Guccione large sums in compensatory and punitive damages."

163 Breach of contract

Even a prison inmate has taken a juridical potshot at Guccione, as well as *Penthouse*'s vice-chair, editor, a writer there, a photographer, and "Paula Jones, one time employee or poser for *Penthouse* magazine."

---

[2] The conventional Anglo-American justice system is called "adversarial" because it works much like a sporting contest of offense versus defense. Each side pushes its case aggressively forward while attempting to destroy the case for the opposing team. Other justice systems, such as that of the Napoleonic Code or of rabbinical courts, use an "inquisitorial system," with the judge actively participating in the questioning of witnesses instead of acting as disinterested referee.

And to add insult to injury, this time it was for not being pornographic enough.

David Joyner was serving 14 years in an Amarillo, Texas, prison when he eagerly opened the December, 2000, edition of *Penthouse*, featuring a centerfold of Jones. Jones was notorious, of course, as the woman who claimed that Bill Clinton had sexually harassed her when he was governor of Arkansas, and whose related lawsuit started his painful and suicidal fall over the rocks of impeachment. Representing himself and suing as minister of law of the Mandingo Warriors (a prison gang, according to Reuters news service), Joyner claimed in the U.S. District Court that he was "very mentally hurt and angered" to discover that there wasn't much of Jones on offer in the pictorial. He sought $500,000 U.S. in damages for his disappointed expectations.

On December 14 the case came before District Judge Sam Sparks, who decided that it was frivolous and vexatious. In very much that spirit, he gave judgment by way of a "poem":

ORDER OF DISMISSAL

T'was the night before Christmas and all through the prison,
inmates were planning their new porno mission.
While the December issue of Penthouse was hitting the stands,
the Minister of the Mandingo Warriors was warming his hands.
For you see, the publishers had promised a pleasurable view
of the woman who sued the President too.
The minute his Penthouse issue arrived
the minister ripped it open to see what was inside.
But what to his wondering eyes should appear
not Paula Jones' promised privates but only her rear.
Life has its disappointments. Some come out of the blue,
But that doesn't mean a prisoner should sue.

As if this wasn't painful enough, Judge Sparks also ordered that, by way of sanction, Joyner was to pay $50 plus another $200 in costs "for filing frivolous lawsuits."

164 Don't have a cow, woman!

On second thought, the director of the National Museum of Science and Technology decided that naming a cow Stephanie did not amount to sexual harassment. In late 1999, Genevieve Sainte-Marie had ordered the Agriculture Museum in Ottawa to stop giving newborn calves names such as Elsie and Roseanne. Instead, the cows were to be dubbed Rhubarb, Cinnamon, and Starburst. Sainte-Marie had said that she, herself, was sensitive to the issue. "Let's say you came in and you found your name on a cow," she remarked to the press, "and you thought the cow was old and ugly."

Her comments led the media to believe that the ban grew out of a complaint by a woman named Stephanie about a cow with the same name. This inspired callers to an Ottawa radio show to suggest that the museum name its cows Genevieve. Shortly thereafter, Sainte-Marie rescinded the ban.

NOTES

The notes below use the following short forms for the more frequently-cited works:

"Blackstone": Blackstone, William, *Commentaries on the Laws of England*, facsimile of first edition of 1765–1769 (University of Chicago, 1979).

"Friedman I": Friedman, Lawrence M., *Crime and Punishment in American History* (Basic Books, 1993).

"Friedman II": Friedman, Lawrence M., *A History of American Law* (Touchstone, 2nd ed., 1985).

"Megarry I": Megarry, R.E., *Miscellany-at-Law* (Stevens, 1955).

"Megarry II": Megarry, R.E., *A Second Miscellany-at-Law* (Stevens, 1973).

Lawyers Weekly refers to the Canadian version, which predates the existence of the U.S. publication of the same name.

INTRODUCTION:

George Steiner: "Night Words," in *Language and Silence* (Atheneum, 1970).

U.S. v. One Book called "Ulysses," 5 F. Supp. 182 (U.S.S.C., 1933).

Tarring and feathering in Calgary: *Toronto Telegram*, Aug. 31, 1939.

Maurice Healy: *The Old Munster Circuit* (Michael Joseph, 1939).

1   Fornication under consent of the king: Hensher, Philip, *The Independent*, Apr. 14, 2000, p. 5.

Blackstone on fornication and bastardy: IV, pp. 64–65.

Charles County prosecutes fornication: "Note: Fornication, Cohabitation, and the Constitution," *Michigan Law Rev.*, Vol. 77, pp. 252–306 (1980).

The real worry of illegitimacy: See, e.g., *Smith v. Minor*, 1 Coxe 19 (Sup. Ct. N.J. 1790).

Colonial whipping for fornication: Friedman I, p. 35–37.

New York law on fornication: Friedman I, pp. 215–16, citing *New York Laws 1848*, chap. 111.

Ohio statute re teachers: Friedman I, p. 219.

Death for *in flagrante* fornication in Afghanistan: Langan, Sean, *Sunday Times* (London), Feb. 18, 2001.

255

Nasira Gulam Dasteghir: Porzio, Giovanni, *Sunday Times* (London), Nov. 18, 2001.

One hundred eighty lashes: Reuters, September 15, 2001.

Safiya Husseini: See, for example, *The Independent* (London), Jan. 5, 2002, p. 14; "Raped, therefore guilty," Wente, Margaret, *Globe and Mail* (Toronto), January 26, 2002; Associated Press, March 26, 2002.

2   *Droit du seigneur:* See, e.g., Boureau, Alain, *Le droit de cuissage: La fabrication d'un mythe (XIII-XX siècle)* (Éditions Albin Michel S. A., 1995).

Wettlaufer, Jörg, "The *Jus Primae Noctis* as a Male Power Display: A Review of Historic Sources With Evolutionary Interpretation," *Evolution and Human Behavior*, 2000, Vol. 21, No. 2, pp. 111–123.

Tenures: Beckwith, Josiah, *Fragmenta Antiquitatis, Or, Antient Tenures of Land, and Jocular Customs of Some Manors*, 1784.

3   *Ibid*, and Megarry 1, pp. 156–7.

4   Moaning tenant: Middlemiss, Jim, "Sexual Practices Grounds for Eviction," *Law Times*, May 28, 1990, p. 1.

Southwark London Borough Council v. Mills, [1999] 4 All E.R. 449.

5   *Denham v. Patrick* (1910), 20 O.L.R. 347.

6   *State v. Snow*, 252 S.W. 629 (Sup. Ct. Mo., 1923).

7   Sex for used car in Wyoming: *Ontario Lawyers' Weekly*, Aug. 3, 1984, p. 5.

Seidler v. Schallhofer, [1982] 2 N.S.W.L.R. 80.

8   *Upfill v. Wright* (1911), 1 K.B. 506.

9   Short-term obsession with this story at the *New York Post* in the summer of 2000 provided the details.

10   Kowalke's cookie settlement: Associated Press, Sept. 9, 1979.

Shaw v. Shaw, [1954] 3 W.L.R. 265.

11   Wallace Beery sued for child support: *Schumm v. Berg*, 224 P.2d 54, 56 (1950).

Fiege v. Boehm, 123 A.2d 316 (1956).

12   One-sided contract quotation: attributed to Lord Evershed.

Dagg v. Dagg (1882), 7 p. 17.

Egyptian marriage contract: *Hussein, Otherwise Blitz v. Hussein*, [1938] p. 159.

13   *Saarnok v. McNeil* (1992), Vancouver Registry No. C900902, B.C.S.C., Sept. 9, 1992. Compare the *Juretic* case, below at number 18.

14   *Welde v. Welde* (1730), 2 Lee 578.

Anderson v. Anderson (1778), 3 Phil. 155.

15   *Brown v. Brown* (1828), 1 Hagg. Ecc. 523.

16   *S. v. E.* (1863), 2 Sw. & Tr. 240.

17   Dangerous surgery: *W. v. H.* (1861), 2 Sw. & Tr.

D.E. v. A.G. (1845), 1 Rob. Eccl. 279.

18   *Juretic v. Ruiz*, [1999] BCCA 417.

19   Shakers and divorce: Friedman II, p. 206, citing *Dyer v. Dyer*, 5 N.H. 271 (1830). In that case, both Mary and Joseph Dyer were Shakers, but only Joseph stayed with the sect.

Mason v. Mason (1980), 11 Family Law 143.

20   *Re Millar*, [1937] 1 D.L.R. 127 (Ont. H.C.); [1937] 3 D.L.R. 234 (Ont. C.A.); [1938] 1 D.L.R. 65 (S.C.C.); [1938] O.R. 188 (Ont. H.C.). Some of the side details about the will are from John Arnup's biography of Justice Middleton, *Middleton: The Beloved Judge* (McClelland and Stewart, 1988).

21   I first encountered Justice Maule's speech in James Parkinson's *Curiosities of Law and Lawyers* (1896, Sampson Low, Maston and Co.), but I have adapted Sir Robert Megarry's report of it, which he describes as an eclectic version combining reports from several sources. Sir Robert's version most clearly describes the circumstances in question. However, on page 366 of his *Miscellany-at-Law*, Sir Robert adds that the case was *R. v. Hall*, prosecuted at the Warwick assizes in 1845, and that Justice Maule has had a little editorial help over the years: "the language of Maule J., though biting, was less polished than posterity has made it."

22 *Bury's Case* (1560–61, 2 Dy. 178b.

23 Widows as bigamists: See, for example, *Year Books* 30 and 31, Edward I, p. 529.

Reynolds v. U.S., 98 U.S. 145 (1878).

Brown's 17 wives: Friedman I, p. 198, citing *N.Y. Times*, July 3, 1888, p. 2.

24 *Willoughby's Case* (1597), Cro. Eliz. 566. The sheriff reported that Dorothy's pregnancy was 20 weeks gone. This report says that she eventually "was delivered of a daughter."

Blackstone, I, 244.

More than ordinarily legitimate: *Ibid.*

Borrowing a baby: *DiLorenzo v. DiLorenzo*, 67 NE 63 (1903).

Ex parte Aiscough (1730), 2 P. Wms. 591.

Theaker's Case (1624), Cro. Jac. 686.

25 Justice MacKinnon and the chambermaid: Gilbert, Michael (ed.), *The Oxford Book of Legal Anecdotes* (Oxford, 1986), p. 209.

26 *Campbell v. Campbell*: Tumim, Stephen, *Great Legal Disasters*, (Arthur Barker, 1983), pp. 97–99.

27 Hamilton, R.G., *All Jangle and Riot* (Professional Books, 1988), p. 181. Compare the language of the soldier on leave, recounted below, in the chapter on pornography, no. 97.

28 Friedman II, p. 502.

29 William Camp on F.E. Smith, Gilbert, Michael (ed.), *The Oxford Book of Legal Anecdotes* (Oxford, 1986), pp. 278–79.

30 *Barnacle v. Barnacle*, [1948] Probate Cases 257.

Love on public pathway: *Mellin v. Taylor* (1836), 3 Bing. N.C. 109.

Love in a truck: *Yuill v. Yuill*, [1945] 1 All E.R. 183.

Manual satisfaction: *Sapsford v. Sapsford* [1954], 2 All E.R. 373.

What constitutes masturbation: *Ontario Lawyers Weekly*, May 3, 1984, p. 2.

31 Justice McCardie v. Lord Scrutton: Pannick, David, *Judges* (Oxford, 1987), pp. 12, 21–23.

Place v. Searle (1932), 48 T.L.R. 428.

32 *Maclennan v. Maclennan*, [1958] Sess. Cas. 105.

33 *Louie v. Lastman* (2001), 54 O.R. (3d), 286, 301. At this writing, the Louies have appealed Justice Benotto's rulings. Apparently the main issue on appeal is whether Lastman owed the sons a fiduciary duty to support them.

34 Friedman I, p. 40. The *Latham* case was prosecuted in 1644, and the New Hampshire statute is dated 1701.

Hutlemyer v. Cox, No. COA98-624 (N.C.App. 06/01/1999).

35 Hawkins, *A Treatise of the Pleas of the Crown*, 1716, Chapter 31, section 36.

Blackstone on provocation: IV, at 191–192.

Maddy's Case, (1671) 2 Keb. 829, 1 Vent. 158; *sub nom. Manning*, T. Raym. 212.

Legislation in Utah, New Mexico, Texas: La Fave and Scott, *Substantive Criminal Law*, West Publishing, 1986, vol. II, pp. 268–270.

Sensobaugh v. State, 244 S.W. 379 (C.C.A. Tex., 1922). In his *Institutes*, Chapter 3, section 62, Lord Coke records a case from 1228 where a man and wife castrated "John the monk" after the man caught the wife and cleric *in flagrante delicto*.

Juries and the unwritten law: See, e.g., La Fave and Scott at 270 and "Comment: Recognition of the Honor Defense Under the Insanity Plea" (1934), 43 Yale Law Journal, 809.

Killing to prevent adultery is justifiable homicide: *Campbell v. State*, 49 S.E. 2d 867 (1948, Ga. S.C.).

Burger v. State, 231 S.E.2d 769 (1977) at 770.

36 *L'Actualité*, September 1, 2001.

37 *Paynel's Case*, 1302: See note to (1554) 1 Dy. 106b; Rot. Parl. I, 140; and Pollock and Maitland, *The History of English Law Before the Time of Edward I*

(Cambridge, 1923), Vol. 2, p. 396. Commoys' name is given variously as de Comeys, de Camoys, etc. I take the spelling from *Dyer's Reports*.

Ann Parsons asks the court to ban her husband: Kenny, Courtney, "Wife-Selling in England" (1929) 1945 L.Q.R. 494.

The price for a wife: *Ibid.*

A second wife-selling report in *The Times*: July 18, 1797.

Observer report of wife-sale: Anstey, Joanna (ed.), *The Observer Observed: 1791-1991* (Barrie & Jenkins, 1991).

38 (1973), 92 Law Notes 171.

39 *R. v. Wiseman* (1718), Fort. 91.

40 Ohio sodomy law: Friedman 1, 128n.

Young v. State, 141 N.E. 409 (1923, Ind. S.C.).

State v. Sundquist, Associated Press, July 10, 2001.

41 Homosexuality under the Taliban: "Un pays en otage," *L'Actualité*, Oct. 15, 2001, p. 28, reprinting an article by Marc Epstein from *L'Express*.

Sodomy in Nigeria: "Nigerian Court Sentences Man to Death," Associated Press, September 14, 2001.

42 *R. v. Wilde*, Hyde, H. Montgomery, *Oscar Wilde* (Farrar, Straus and Giroux, 1975), pp. 257–8.

Homosexuality remains a barrier: Pannick, David, *Judges* (Oxford, 1987), p. 102, citing Skyrme, Sir Thomas, *The Changing Image of the Magistracy* (1979), pp. 137–8.

43 Hogg case: Friedman 1, p. 1, citing Gail Sussman Marcus, "'Due Execution of the Generall Rules of Righteousnesse': Criminal Procedure in New Haven Town and Colony, pp. 1638–1658," in David D. Hall, John M. Murrin, Thad W. Tate, eds., *Saints and Revolutionaries: Essays in Early American History* (1984), pp. 99, 115.

Granger case: Friedman 1, p. 34. Prof. Friedman characterizes the execution of the animals as part of the law of deodand, but, to my knowledge, at common law deodand was limited to chattels, including animals, subject to confiscation by the Crown once they had been involved in the *death* of a human being. The Crown was then supposed to sell the offending chattels and distribute the proceeds to the poor. As E.P. Evans points out in his *Criminal Prosecution and Capital Punishment of Animals* (Faber, 1986; first published in 1906 by William Heinemann Ltd.), legally this is closer to escheat (forfeiture to the state) than deodand, since no pious use is involved. But it is deodand in spirit, I imagine, in the sense that chattels are "sacrificed" in an attempt to appease the godhead and provide catharsis for survivors. The information in my note about termites also derives from Evans' book.

Goad case: *Ibid.* and Friedman II, p. 72.

Slave case: Friedman I, p. 34.

44 *R. v. Brown* (1890), 24 Q.B. 357.

45 *R. v. Cooper, The Times* (London), Apr. 18, 1991, and daily stories by Ian MacKinnon of the *Independent* (London) and Peter Davenport of *The Times*, Dec. 11–14, 1991.

46 *State v. Buble*, Salon.com, Jan. 2, 2001; *Bangor Daily News*, Dec. 7 and 10, 2000.

47 The "Plaster Caster" case was widely reported in the daily press during the last two weeks of April, 1993.

48 "Talk of the Town" article in the *New Yorker*, February 21, 1993. See also *Jones v. Maples*, No. 903N (N.Y. App. Div. 1st Dept. 05/27/1999).

49 One hundred and forty-three bikinis: Canadian Press, June 14, 1984.

Bouwhuis Protective Undergarment: *Globe and Mail* (Toronto), July 16, 1984.

Techno-Bra: *The Times* (London), Oct. 18, 1999 and May 29, 2000; *The Independent* (London), June 28, 1999; *Discover*, Vol. 20, No. 10 (Oct., 1999); *Wired News*, July 1, 1999.

Thief gets stolen underwear back: Associated Press, September 13, 1986.

50 *Herceg v. Hustler Magazine Inc.*, 814 F.2d 1017 (1987, Fifth Circ.).

51 *State v. Stevenson*, WI 71 (Wis. 06/28/2000).

52 Cheerleaders: See, for example, *National Post*, Jan. 11, 2002, p. A16, presumably from an Associated Press story of the previous day and previous press reports; WKYC.com (the "five minutes" remark); *Inquirer* (Philadelphia), August 9, 2001 (phillynews.com).

53 Der Dadjadian, Juan Carlos, "*Le partenaire-symptôme au moment du déclenchement dans la psychose*," conference paper for World Psychoanalysis Association, Yerevan, Oct. 29, 1999; Mantelet, Sandrine; "Les délires chroniques," *Cours de psychiatre des DCEM3*; *The Times* (London), Nov. 20, 1997; Apr. 28, 2000; Nov. 15, 2000; June 7, 1998, July 3, 2001.

R. v. Williams (1993), 140 A.R. 132; sentence affirmed (1994), 149 A.R. 229.

54 Mayer, Jane and Abramson, Jill, *Strange Justice: The Selling of Clarence Thomas* (Houghton Mifflin, 1994).

55 Friedman I, p. 34.

56 *R. v. Jourdan* (1900), 8 C.C.C. 337.

57 *Redd v. State*, 67 S.E. 709 (Georgia C.A,, 1910).

Brigman v. State, 51 S.E. 504 (Georgia C.A., 1905).

R. v. Orchard and Thurtle (1848), 3 Cox C.C. 248.

R. v. Webb (1848), 2 C & K 933.

58 *Curll's Case* (1727), 17 Howell's State Trials 153.

59 *R. v. Read*, Fortescue 98.

Sidley's Case (1663), 1 Sid. 168, *sub nom Sir Charles Sydlyes' Case*, 1 Keb. 620, 84 E.R. 1146.

60 *Evans v. Ewels*, [1972] 1 W.L.R. 671.

61 *In re Lynch*, 8 Cal. 3d 410, 503 P.2d 921, 105 Cal. Rptr. 217 (Cal. 12/04/1972).

62 Immoral gingerbread: Associated Press, Nov. 11, 1981.

63 *R. v. Balazsy* (1980), 54 C.C.C. (2d) 346.

R. v. Borchard, 64 N. (2d) 646 (Ohio C.A., 1972).

NOTES

64   *R. v. Hecker* (1980), 58 C.C.C. (2d) 66.

65   *R. v. Madercine* (1899), 20 N.S.W.R. 36.

66   *R. v. Thallman* (1863), 9 Cox C.C. 388.

67   "Two Virgins": Martin, Linda and Seagrave, Kerry, *Anti-Rock: The Opposition to Rock and Roll* (Da Capo Press, 1993), pp. 187–88.

Barenaked Ladies: Canadian Press, Sept. 21, 2000; September 6, 1994; August 11, 1992; January 7, 1992.

68   Strippers' breasts: See *State v. Jones* 171 S.E.2d 468 (N. Carolina C.A., 1970).

Breasts not "sexual" in New Brunswick: *R. v. Chase* (1987) 45 D.L.R. (4th) 98 (S.C.C.), reversing (1984) 13 C.C.C. (3d) 187 (N.B.C.A.).

Top-Free Ten: *People v. Susan David et. al.*, 549 N.Y.S.2d 564 (1989, Rochester [N.Y.] City Ct.); 585 N.Y.S.2d 149 (1991, Monroe County Ct.); Stern, Jane and Michael, *The New Yorker*, March 19, 1990, pp. 73–98.

R. v. Jacob (1996), 142 D.L.R. (4th) 411.

69   Monk told this story during a public meeting about proposed amendments to Canada's pornography laws.

70   *R. c. Roux*, [2001] J.Q. no. 770 (Quicklaw).

71   *R. v. Ludacka* (1996), 28 O.R. (3d) 19.

72   Rhode Island sex novelties case: *Manes Co. v. Glass*, 102 A. 964. (1918, R.I.S.C.). Record supplied by the Supreme Court of Rhode Island.

73   *Gardner v. Fulforde* (1667), 1 Lev. 204; *sub nom Gardner against Hulford*, 2 Keb. 154. Poor Gardner's second try is reported at 2 Keb. 172.

74   Anthony Comstock: See, e.g., Sifakis, Carl, *Encyclopedia of American Crime* (Facts on File, 1982); Mencken, H.L., *The American Language* (Knopf, 1937), p. 304; Kendrick, Walter, *The Secret Museum* (Viking, 1987); Friedman I, p. 135.

75   *R. v. MacDonald* (1981), 16 C.R. (3d) 91.

76   *The Independent* (London), Sept. 10, 2001.

77 *South Florida Sun-Sentinel;* Aug. 19, 1997; Mar. 19, 1998.

78 Wire service and news reports from the U.S., Britain, and Canada.

79 *Toronto,* February, 1987, p. 9.

80 "Art in the window is not appreciated by all," *Ontario Lawyers Weekly,* June, 29 and Oct. 18, 1985, p. 3.

81 Harmetz, Aljean, *New York Times Service,* Aug. 12, 1987; *National Law Journal,* Sept. 7, 1987, p. 6; Wishnia, Steven, "Rockin' With the First Amendment," *The Nation,* Oct. 24, 1987, p. 444.

82 Reuter news service, Feb. 4, 1985.

83 *Seventy-Five Boxes of Alleged Pepper,* 198 F 394 (1912).

U.S. v. 77 Cartons of Magazines, 300 F.Supp. 851 (ND Cal.1969).

U.S. v. Ten Erotic Paintings, 311 F.Supp. 884 (Md. 1970).

U.S. v. "Language of Love," 311 F.Supp. 108 (SDNY 1970).

25.936 Acres of Land, More or Less, 51 F.Supp. 969 (1943).

U.S. v. Thirty-Seven Photographs, 402 U.S. 363 (1971).

U.S. v. 12,200-ft. Reels of Super 8MM. Film, 413 U.S. 123 (1973).

84 *A Lawyer's Notebook* (Secker and Warburg, 1933).

85 *The End of Obscenity* (Perennial, 1968), p. 17.

86 *Roth v. U.S.,* 354 U.S. 476 (1957) and Wallace, Jonathan and Mangan, Mark, *Sex, Laws, and Cyberspace* (Henry Holt: 1996), p. 34.

87 Jacobellis v. Ohio 378 U.S. 184 (1964); Dershowitz, Alan, *The Best Defense* (Random House, 1982), p. 164.

88 Jacobellis v. Ohio, 179 N.E.2d 123; 175 N.E.2d 123.

89 Rosen, Carole, *The Goosens* (Deutsch, 1993).

90 Lawrence's doublespeak: Hughes, Geoffrey, *Swearing: A Social History of Foul Language, Oaths and Profanity in English* (Penguin, 1998), pp. 191–92.

R. v. Penguin Books Ltd.

Justice Fontaine and castration anxiety: Djway, Sandra, *The Politics of Imagination: A Life of F.R. Scott* (McClelland and Stewart, 1987).

The Quebec appeal: *R. v. Brodie* (1961), 36 C.R. 200.

A Lass in Wonderland, Scott, F.R., *Selected Poems* (Oxford, 1966).

Griffith-Jones's opening address: See, e.g., Rembar, Charles, *The End of Obscenity*, Perennial, 1968, p. 156, and Hyde, H. Montgomery, *The Lady Chatterley's Lover Trial* (Bodley Head, 1990), which provides a transcript of the trial.

91   Pauvert prosecution: The judgment and part of the transcript are reprinted in Hébert, Jacques, *Obscénité et liberté* (Éditions du Jour, 1970), from which I have translated the quoted portions. An appeal court reduced Pauvert's fine.

92   *Clinging to the Wreckage* (Penguin, 1983), p. 241.

93   R. Crumb's bulbous homunculi: Jackson, Kevin, in *The Independent*, June 23, 1995, p. 9 ("Arts and Music").

Knockabout Comics prosecution: *The Independent*, Jan. 31, 1996, p. 2.

George Perry on Crumb: *Sunday Times* (London), July 2, 1995.

94   *Right to Read Defense Committee v. School Committee*, 454 F.Supp.703 (1978).

95   *Jones v. F.C.C.*: Claim and material filed by Jones with the U.S. District Court for Southern New York on Jan. 29, 2002, file no. 02-CV 693.

Carlin case: *Pacifica Foundation v. F.C.C.*, 438 U.S. 726 (1978).

96   Howard Stern: Moore, Roy L., *Mass Communication Law and Ethics*, (Univ. of Kentucky, 1994).

Illinois Citizens Committee for Broadcasting v. FCC, 515 F.2d 397 (U.S.C.A.D.C., 1974).

97   *R. v. Stewart* (1980), 16 C.R. (3d) 87.

R. v. White (1972), 18 C.R.N.S. 279.

Herbalist's window display: *R. v. Grey* (1864), 4 F. & F. 73.

Cohen v. California, 403 U.S. 15 (1971).

98 *Dallas Cowboys Cheerleaders Inc. v. Pussycat Cinema, Ltd.*, 604 F. 2d 200, 205 (2d Circ., 1979).

99 *California v. Arno* 153 Cal. Rprtr. 624 (1979).

Uelmen on "schmuck": *ABA Journal*, June, 1985, pp. 78–80.

100 *Vancouver Sun*, Apr. 7, 2000.

101 Hanging prostitutes: Associated Press, February 23, 2001.

Brothel-keepers in colonial America: Friedman 1, p. 50.

102 *Caminetti v. United States*, 242 U.S. 470 (1917).

More generally, see Friedman 1, pp. 225 ff. and p. 343.

103 David Robinson, *Chaplin: His Life and Art* (McGraw-Hill, 1985), pp. 517–28, and Friedman 1, p. 343.

Martin, Linda and Seagrave, Kerry, *Anti-Rock: The Opposition to Rock and Roll* (Da Capo Press, 1993).

The Rolling Stone Illustrated History of Rock & Roll (Random House, 1992), p. 64.

104 *R. v. Patterson* (1972), 9 C.C.C. (2d) 364.

R. v. Polyak, [1991] O.J. No. 846 (Quicklaw).

The King v. De Munck [1918], 1 K.B. 645.

105 *Bedder v. D.P.P.* [1954] 2 Al E.R. 801. *The Times* (London), April 6, 1954, p. 6; June 22, p. 3; July 3, p. 4; July 24, p. 11, July 29, p. 4, July 31, p. 9.

Camplin v. D.P.P., [1978] 1 All E.R. 1236; London *Times*, July 28, 1977, p. 8; Nov. 11, p. 13; Apr. 11, 1978, p. 11.

106 *Minister of Revenue v. Eldridge*, [1965] 1 Ex. C.R 758. See also, "Prostitutes demonstrate against U.K. tax collector," *Globe and Mail* (Toronto, from Canadian Press story), Nov. 8, 1984, p. 13, and *No. 275 v. M.N.R.* (1955), 13 T.A.B. Cases, 279 (Canada).

107 *Norman v. Golder (Inspector of Taxes)* (1944), 114 L.J. K.B. 108.

Lindi St. Claire: Canadian Press, November 7, 1984; *The Independent* (London), March 17, 1992, February 11, 1997; *Sunday Times* (London), July 21, 1991.

108   *Pearce v. Brooks*, [1866] 1 Ex. 213.

Bowry v. Bennet (1808), 1 Camp. 348.

An infant and a prostitute must have lodging: per Eyre, Ch.J., *Crisp v. Churchill* (1794), cited at 1 Bos. and Pul. 340 (in *Lloyd v. Johnson*, above).

Perfumed lie: *Feret v. Hill* (1854), 15 C.B. 207.

Cleaning dresses and nightcaps: *Lloyd v. Johnson* (1798), 1 Bos. and P. 340.

109   *Barac v. Farnell* (1994), 53 FCR 193 (Australia).

110   *Koistinen v. American Export Lines*, 83 N.Y.S.2d 197 (1948).

111   *R. v. McFarlane*, [1993] E.W.J. No. 5171.

112   *Ex parte Daisy Hopkins* (1891), 61 L.J.Q.B. 240.

Daisy's civil suit: *Ibid.*, 250n.

113   Streetwalking on balconies: *Smith v. Hughes,* [1960] 2 All E.R. 859.

114   *R. v. Swift* (1993), 143 A.R. 173.

115   *R. v. Pierce and Golloher* (1982), 37 O.R. 2d 721.

116   Broken nose: Canadian Press, Nov. 28, 2001; *Globe and Mail* (Toronto), Nov. 29, 2001.

Edwards v. Tracy Starr's, (1985) 33 Alta. L.R. (2d) 115 (Alta. Q.B.); [1987] A.J. No. 1424 (Alta. C.A.).

117   Nigerian genital theft: Agence France-Presse, Feb. 9, 1991, Oct. 30, 1990.

118   Joan's Case: Hamilton, R.G., *All Jangle and Riot* (Professional Books, 1988) p. 46, citing *Eyre of Kent,* 6 & 7 Edward II, 1313-14, Selden Society, vol. 24, p. 111.

119   (1) *Wright v. State*, 473 So. 2d 268 (Fla. 1st DCA 1985); No. 98-3354 (Fla.App. 10/06/1999). At Friedman 1, p. 216, Professor Friedman gives the precedent of *Davis v. State,* 42 Tex. 226 (1875), where the purported victim's mother claimed to have found her child being raped by an adult. The child's body showed nothing more than some redness and swelling, and a physician testified that "a man of [Davis's] dimensions" would have caused greater damage on penetration. An appeal court ruled that this raised a reasonable doubt as to Davis' guilt of the crime charged.

120 (2) *R. v. D.K.*, [2001] Ontario Superior Court of Justice file no. 97-G349.

121 Slaves in Virginia: Friedman II, p. 71.

Searing nostrils: Friedman I, p. 42.

122 *Lady Fulwood's Case* (1637), Cro. Car. 482, 484, 488, 492. For some reason, a court in 1724 seems to have been unaware that *Fulwood* answers the jurisdictional problem. The judges in *Burton v. Morris* (Hob. 182), or at least reporter Hobart, were still wondering how the law worked "if the taking, and the lands, and the marrying or deflowering, were in several countries; for it is felony composed of all those three things, as murder is of the stroke and death."

123 *John Brown's Case* (1684), 1 Ventris 243; 3 Keb. 193 (*sub nom Rex and Brown.*)

124 Subheading: Lord Byron, *Don Juan*.

Justice Maule on consent: Serjeant Robinson, *Bench and Bar* (London, 1889).

Dupuis v. British Columbia (Ministry of Forests), [1993] B.C.C.H.R.D. No. 43.

125 Wealthy women: Friedman II, pp. 215–16, citing *New York Laws* 1848, chap. III.

126 *People v. Walter Clark*, 33 Mich. 112 (1876); and Friedman I, *ibid.*, pp. 218–219.

127 *Ross v. Macleod* (1861), 23 D. (Sess. Cas.) 972; and Megarry I, p. 126.

People v. Gould, 38 N.W. 232 (1888, Mich. S.C.).

128 *Wright v. State*, 20 S.W. 756 (Tex. Crim Ct. Apps., 1892).

129 Bernard Averbuch, in correspondence.

Yallop, David, *The Day the Laughter Stopped* (Hodder and Stoughton, 1976).

130 Spanish fly: Selden, Gary, *Aphrodisia* (Dutton, 1979), p. 170.

Court address by Maurice Garçon, reprinted in Hébert, Jacques, *Obscénité et liberté* (Éditions du Jour, 1970).

R. v. Button (1838), 8 C. & P. 660.

Wedding party: *R. v. Walkden* (1845), 1 Cox C.C. 282.

131 *Commonwealth v. Stratton*, 114 Mass. 303 (1873).

R. v. Wilkins (1861), 169 E.R. 1316.

132 Ford case: Schwarcz, Dr. Joe, *Radar, Hula Hoops and Playful Pigs* (ECW Press: 1999), pp. 141–42.

From Provence to Germany: *Aphrodisia*, as above, note 123.

133 Associated Press, March 5, 1986.

134 *R. v. Collins*, [1973] Q.B. 100.

Intruders in the family bed: See, e.g., *R. v. Young*, (1878), 14 Cox C.C. 114; *R. v. Clarke* (1854), 6 Cox C.C. 412; *R. v. Barrow* (1868), 11 Cox C.C. 199.

Part more private than a foot: Smith, J.C. and Hogan, Brian, *Criminal Law* (Butterworths: 1983, 5th ed.), p. 558, quoting Odgers, [1972] C.L.J. 196.

135 *R. v. Williams*, [1923] 1 K.B. 340.

"Doc": The Rape of the Town of Lovell, Olsen, Jack (Atheneum: 1989).

Quack doctor rapes: See, e.g., *R. v. Case* (1850), 4 Cox C.C. 220; *R. v. Flattery*, [1877] 2 Q.B.D. 410.

136 1878 Irish case: *Hegarty v. Shine*, 14 Cox C.C. 124.

Herpes in Virginia, *Lawyers Weekly*, March 9, 1990, p. 13.

137 *Commonwealth v. Appleby* 402 N.E.2d 1051 (S.C. Mass., 1980).

1934 English caning case: *R. v. Donovan*, [1934] 2 K.B. 498.

138 *D.P.P. v. Morgan*, [1976] A.C. 182.

R. v. Pappajohn (1980), 52 C.C.C. (2d) 481.

139 *R. v. Ladue* (1965), 45 C.R. 287.

140 "There's no harm in asking": Magruder, "Mental and Emotional Disturbance in the Law of Torts," *Harvard Law Review*, May, 1936, 1033 at 1055.

Ishmael Reed kindly responded by letter to my questions about *Reckless Eyeballing*. I was unable to locate the issue of *Ebony* he mentions.

Ogling swimmer: In "Evidence of ogling is clear, board told," Robert MacLeod, *Globe and Mail* (Toronto), September 1, 1989, gives a short summary of the case.

141 *Jessin v. County of Shasta*, 79 Cal. Rptr. 359 (1969).

Disabling the testicles: *Sensobaugh v. State*, 244 S.W. 379 (C.C.A. Tex., 1922).

Involuntary tattooing: *People v. Page*, 163 Cal. Rptr. 839 (Cal. App. Dist. 1 04/15/1980).

Blackstone, IV, 205.

142 My news sources for the Bobbitt story included U.S. wire services and *The Times* (London), Nov. 10, 1993; January 12, 16, 23, 1994; *The Independent* (London), Jan. 22, 1994, p. 1; Sept. 8, 1996.

Copycats: *The Independent*, Feb. 6, 1994, *The Times*, Apr. 14, 1994; Dec. 1, 1996.

143 *The Times* (London), April 19, 1994; *The Independent* (London), Mar. 22, Apr. 19, 1994.

144 *Mackenzie v. Miller Brewing Co.*, No. 97-3542 (Wis.App. 2/22/2000).

145 *Lockley v. Turner*, No. A-1783-99T1 (N.J.Super.App.Div. 8/10/2001).

146 *R. v. Robinson* (2001), 53 O.R. (3d) 448.

R. v. Lamy, [2000] J.Q. No. 2267 (Quicklaw); 2002 SCC 25.

R. v. Barber, [1978] O.J. No. 495 (Quicklaw).

147 Romenesko, James, "The 46 Faces of Sarah," *Milwaukee Magazine*; Smolowe, Jill (with Dolan, Barbara and Sachs, Andrea), "The 21 Faces of Sarah," Time Inc.; stories by Gorney, Cynthia, Nov. 8 and 10, 1990, *Washington Post*; Associated Press, November 8, 1990.

148 *R. v. Fisher* (1837), 8 Carrington and Payne's Reports, 182. Carrington and Payne have Meredith saying, "I suspected you; you are now detected." According to the London *Times*, Dec. 2, 1837, p. 7, he yelled the similarly incredible, "You villain! Have I detected you at last?"

149 *Rogira v. Boget*, 148 N.E. 534 (N.Y.C.A.). The French language authority *Robert* gives a secondary use of *cocotte*, dating from 1789, as "*Fille, femme de moeurs légères*" — "girl or woman of loose morals" and, vulgarly, as a courtesan or *poule* — a "chick" in today's argot.

150 *Califord v. Knight* (1618), Cro. Jac. 514.

Mrs. Miller's pox: *Miller's Case* (1617), 1 Cro. Jac. 430, 15 Jac 1.

Levet's Case (1591), 1 Cro. Eliz. 289.

Marshal v. Chickall (l66l), 1 Sid. 50.

151 Coney Island dancer: *Gates v. New York Recorder Co.*, 155 N.Y. 228.

Snyder v. New York Press Co., 121 N.Y.S. 944 (N.Y.S.C.App.Div., 1910).

Notarmuzzi v. Shevack, 108 N.Y.S. (2d) 172, 1951).

Bastard as endearment: *Marruchi v. Harris*, 1943 O.P.D. 15.

152 Warder increases sentence: The story's origin is barrister and recorder Geoffrey Dorling Roberts.

153 *Eckert v. Van Pelt*, 76 P. 909 (Sup. Ct. Kan. 1904).

154 *Burton v. Crowell Pub. Co.*, 82 F.2d 154 (2nd Cir. 02/10/1936).

Justice Hand at lunch: Brown, Raymond, *The Law of Defamation in Canada* (1994, Carswell), s. 5.9(2), fn. 649, citing Eldredge, *The Law of Defamation* (1977).

155 *Keefe v. Geanakos*, 418 F.2d 359 (1st Cir, 1969).

156 *Thaarup v. Hulton Press Ltd.* (1943), 169 L.T. 309.

157 *Ralston v. Ralston*, [1930], 2 K.B. 238; Megarry 1, 198.

Tinkley v. Tinkley (1909), 25 Times L.R. 264.

158 *Pring v. Penthouse International*, 695 F.2d 438 (10th Cir, 1982).

Spence, Gerry, *Trial by Fire* (Morrow: 1986).

159 *Braun v. Flynt*, 726 F.2d 245 (5th Cir., 1984).

160 *Falwell v. Hustler*, 485 U.S. 46 (1988).

161 *Dworkin v. Hustler Magazine*, 867 F.2d 1188 (9th Cir., 1989).

Ault v. Hustler Magazine, 860 F.2d 877 (9th Cir. 1988).

162 *Leidholdt v. L.F.P. Inc.*, 860 F.2d 890 (9th Cir., 1988).

Guccione v. Hustler Magazine Inc., 800 F.2d 298 (2nd Cir. 08/29/1986).

Joan Collins case: *Lerman v. Flynt Distributing Co.*, 789 F.2d 164 (2nd Cir. 04/29/1986).

163 *Joyner v. Guccione*, U.S. District Court file A-00-CA-799-SS, Dec. 14, 2000.

164 Cows: Canadian Press, October 8, 1999; CBC Radio One.

INDEX

2 Live Crew, 124, 143

Actaeon and Artemis, 82
administering a noxious substance, 201
adoption scam in British Columbia, 25–27
adulterous provocation, 57–60, 227, 229
adultery, xii, 34, 44–59, 61, 250–51
    as defense to murder, 57–60
    artificial insemination and, 51–52
    definitions of, 48–50
    legalese and, 46
    mayhem, and, 58–59
    proof of, by formula, 44–47
    punishment for, xiii, 55
Albritton, Cynthia, 74–75
Aldrich, Judge (U.S.), 241–42
Allen family of Calgary, xiii
Allen, Woody, 44
Altman, Robert, 120
Andrias, Justice Richard, 77
animals, sexual crimes with and of, 69–74
annulment of marriage, 27–32
aphrodisiacs, 200, 203
Arbour, Justice Louise, 224
Arbuckle, Roscoe "Fatty," 197–200
artificial insemination, 51–52
Ashforth, Justice (England), 98
Atici, Zeynep, 217
autoerotic asphyxia, 78–80
Averbuch, Bernard, 198

Balaszy, Charles, 101–03
Barber, Madeline, 224–25

Barenaked Ladies, The, 105
Barry, Joan, 161
"bastard" as non-defamatory, 234–35
bastardy: *see* illegitimacy
battery, 200–02
bawdy house, definition, 179–80
Bazelon, District Appeals Judge, 144
Bedder, Alec, 164–65
Beery, Wallace, 20–21
Benotto, Justice Mary Jane, 54
Berry, Chuck, and *Mann Act*, 161
Best, Patricia, 219–21
bestiality, 69–74, 236
Bible, law in, xii, 107
bigamy, 20, 37–42
bikini theft, 77
Blacharski, Carol, 119
Black, Justice Hugo, 129
Blackburn, Judge W.A., 196
Blackstone, William, 1–2, 22, 42–43, 57–58
Blitz, Estella, 24–25
Bloom, Peter, 72–73
Bobbitt, John and Lorena, xii, xv, 216–18
Boehm, Hilda, 21–22
Boget, Andrew, 232
Bonnett, Greg, 180–81
Bouwhuis Protective Undergarment, 77
Bradley, Justice Ann Walsh, 81
Brady, Matt, 197–98
branding of convicts, 58
Braun, Jeannie, 244–46
breasts, indecency and, xiii, 49–50, 56–57, 90, 105–08

273

Brennan, Justice William, 131, 145–46
Breton, André, 138
Brown, Aldrich, 42
Brown, John, 190–91
Bruce, Lenny, 120
Bryant, Judge David, 218
Buble, Frank and Philip, 73–74
buggery, xiii, 65–68, 134
Buller, Justice, 171
burglary, association with rape, 205–06
Burton, Crawford, 237–38
Burton, Sir Richard, xv
Button, Edward, 201

Califord, Joan, 233
Caminetti, Drew, 159
Campbell, Sir Colin, 45–46
Camplin, Paul, 166
cantharides, 200–03
Caravaglia, Jody, 140
Cardozo, Justice Benjamin, x
Carlin, George, 143–44
Carlin, Justice Frank, 174–75
Carter, Justice Jesse, 21
cartoons as obscene, 139–40
Casey, Justice Paul, 135
Cassels, Justice (England), 239
castration, 215–17
    adultery and, 58–59
    as punishment for crime, 187
    Lorena Bobbitt, 216–17
Cattanach, Justice Angus, 167
cattle, copulation by indecent, 91, 95
Cavallo, Maria, 125
Cavanagh, Justice, 181–82
Cesaroni, Fernando, 125

Chabas, Paul, 116
Chaplin, Charles, and *Mann Act*, 161
Chaplun, Sir John, 43
cheerleaders and voyeurism, 83–84
Chernovsky, Michael, 163
Cherrill, Mary Ann, 93–94
Chic magazine, 244–46
child support of child born out of
    wedlock, 2, 32–37
    retroactive claim for, 53–54
children, sexual abuse of, 65–66,
    227–29
"choirmaster case," 206–07
Cioffari, Philip, 242
Clark, Walter, 193
Clarke, Pauline Mae, 36
clergy, plea of, 57–58
clipper (prostitution), 175–76
Clunis, Judge, 162
Cocteau, Jean, 138
Cohen, Herb, 75
Cohen, Paul, 150
Coke, Lord, 214–15
Coleman, Sonja, 140
Coleridge, Lord Justice, 177–78
Collins, Joan, 251
Collins, Justice S.O. Henn, 25
Collins, Steven, 205–06, 208
Comeau, Johanne, 109–10
Commoys, Margaret and John, 60–61
Comstock, Anthony, xiii, 116–18
condoms, censorship and, 117, 119
consent to sex, xiii, 11, 191
    multiple personality disorder and,
        225–27
    "nature and quality" standard,

205–16
  sado-masochism, xi, 209–10
  venereal disease and, 208–09
consideration (in contracts), 20–22
  forbearance as, 21–22
  sexual favors as, 20–21
contracts for immoral purposes
  car sale, 14
  house payments for cohabitation, 14
  lease of flat for mistress, 14, 170
  prostitutes and, 170–76
  sale of gilt hangings, 115–16
cookies called obscene, 100
Cooper, Alan, 72–73
Cooper, Ann, 2
Cosby, Bill, xii
cosmetic surgery on stripper, ix, x, 15–17
Cox, Margie, 56
Coxe, Sarah, 189
criminal conversation, xiv, 38, 48, 52, 55–56
cruelty, denial of sex as, 32
Crumb, Robert, 139–40
cunnilingus, 67, 248
Cunningham, Imogen, 81
Curll, Edmund, 95–96

Dagg, William and Catherine, 23–24
Dallas Cowboys football club, 152–53
Damen, Lia, 169–70
Dando, Jill, xii, 84
Daniel, Judge C.L, 179
Darling, (Lord) Justice Charles, 14
Dasteghir, Nasira Gulam, 3

de Clérambault, Gaëtan, 84–87
Dead Kennedys, 123–25
Debbie Does Dallas, 152–53
defamation
  "bleached blond bastard," 234–35
  "cocotte," 232, 235
  "dancer at Coney Island," 234
  "eunuch," 236–37
  "French disease," 233
  in cigarette advertizement, 237–38
  "pansy," 239–40
  "pocky whore," 233
  satire and, 242–44
  socialite served subpoena in bath, xiii, 234
  wife's tombstone and, 240
  Wilde case, 68–69
Delmont, Maude, 197, 199
Dershowitz, Alan, 131
de Sade, Marquis, 137–38, 201
De Vries, Peter, 82
Dickens, Hannah, 2
Diggs, Maury, 159
divorce,
  adultery and, 44–52
  grounds for, 32
  religious grounds, 60
  unavailability of, 37–38
Dobbs, Horace, 73
Douglas, Justice William, 83–84
Douglas, Lord Alfred, 68
droit de cuissage, 5
droit du seigneur, 4–5
Dubin, Chief Justice Charles, 111, 113–14
Duff, Chief Justice Lyman, 35

Dupuis, Linda, 191–92
Dussault, Justice René, 109
Dworkin, Andrea, 247–48

ecclesiastical courts, 2
Eckert, T.W., 236–37
Edmund Davies, Lord Justice, 204
Edwards, Carin, 111
Edwards, Colin, 181–82
Egyptian law on marriages in films, 60
Eldridge, Olva, 166–68
Ellenborough, Chief Justice, 94, 170, 172, 174
Eminem, 143n
erotic transference, 3
erotomania, 84–87
"eunuch" as libelous, 236–37
Evans, Anthony, 98–99
evidence of sexual misconduct, xiv
exhibiting a disgusting object, 121–22, 149–50
Exorcist, The (Blatty), 87

Falwell, Rev. Jerry, 246–47, 251
Farnell, Heather, 173
"FCUK" as workplace harassment, 154–55
Federal Communications Commission (U.S.), 142–48
fetishes, 75–84
Fiege, Louis, 21–22
Fisher, Roger, 131
Fisher, William, 228–29
Flynt, Larry, 244–51
Fontaine, Justice T.A., 135
Ford, Arthur, 203

Forget, Justice André, 109
fornication, xiii, 2–4, 6–8, 14–15, 34, 39, 158–61, 170, 192, 194, 241–53
Fortescue Aland, Justice, 65–66
Foster, Chief Justice (England), 97
Foster, Jodie, xi, 84
Frankfurter, Justice Felix, 145n, 151
free expression, 79–82, 113, 119, 130, 141–43, 145–46, 150–02, 209
    oral sex and, 67
    nudity and, 106–07
    pornography and, 79
Free Woman, The, 130
French Connection UK, 154–55
"Fuck"
    alleged etymology of, 1
    as obscene or "fighting word," 149–52, 184–85
    euphemisms for, 130–01
Fulwood, Lady and Roger, 189–90

Gale, Mary, 15–17
Garçon, Maurice, 137
Giger, H.R., 123
Gilgamesh epic, 5
Glass, Geoffrey, 75
Goad, Benjamin, 70
Goddard, Lord Rayner, 239
Godiva, Lady, 82
Goosens, Eugene, 132–33
Gould, William, 194–95
Granger, Thomas, 70
Great Toronto Stork Derby, 32–37
Greco, Judge J.D., 149–51
Greene, Lord Justice, 169
Greenland, Leone, 111

INDEX

Greer, Germaine, 140
grievous bodily harm,
    hot wax on husband's genitals, 218
Griffin-Jones, Mervyn, 136–37
Groves, Kursty, 78
Grutman, Norman, 250–01
Guccione, Muriel, 250
Guccione, Robert, 249–53

Hall, W.R., 12
Hamilton, R.G., 46, 184
Hand, Justice Learned, 237–38
Hanson, Justice, 153–54
Harlan, Justice John, 151
Harrison, Judge James, 185–86
Hawley, Judge Robert, 227
Healy, Maurice, xiv
Hecker, David, 102–03
heiress, law against stealing, 189–91, 193
Hell's Angels, 215
Hendrix, Jimi, 74–75
Henry VII, King of England, 188
Henry VIII, King of England, 15, 37
Herman, Pee Wee, 119–21
Higbee, Justice (Missouri), 13
Hill, Anita, 86–87
hip-hop music, 142
Hogg, Thomas, 70
Holmes, Chief Justice Oliver W., 160
homosexuality, xii, 69, 92–93, 165–66, 209–10, 228–29, 238–40
    as "the love that dare not speak," 69
Hoover, J. Edgar, 105
Hopkins, Daisy, 176–78

Howard, John, 64
Husseini, Safiya, 3–4
Hustler magazine, 246–51
Hutelmyer, Dorothy and Joseph, 56
Huxley, Aldous, 134

Illegitimacy, 36, 39, 43–44, 195, 234–35
impersonating lover motif, 204–06
impotence, 27, 29, 37
incapacity (for sexual intercourse), 27–31, 38–39
indecency, 89–126
    during rock concert, 143n
    farm animals, 91–92, 95
    gingerbread, 100–01
    interfering with dead body, 212
    in Italian courtroom, 125
    on private property, 103–04
    on Sabbath, 89
    performances, xiii, 56–57, 109–14
    "public" aspect, 91–94
Islamic law, xi, 3, 55, 68
"It's A Girl" art installation, 121–22

Jackson, Michael, xii
Jacob, Gwen, 107–08
Jacob, I.E., 98
Jacobs, Elliott, 15–17
Jennings, Anthony, 73
Jolly, Judge E. Grady, 244
Jones, Charles, 76–77
Jones, Judge Atherley, 164
Jones, Judge Edith, 79
Jones, Paula, 251–52
Jones, Sarah, 142, 144
Joyner, David, 252–53

judicial notice
    masturbation and, 49–50
    panties and, 50
Juretic, Nedjelko, 31
jurors as "translators," 231–32
jus primae noctis, see *droit du seigneur*

Keefe, Robert, 145n, 241
Keeton, Kathy, 250–51
Kenny, Lillian, 34
Kenyon, Chief Justice, 94–95
King, Lord Chancellor, 43
Koistinen, Eino, 174–75
Konak, Abdullah Kemal, 217
Kowalke, Tim, 19
Kunstler, William, 120

Lady Chatterley's Lover, xiv, 133–37
Lamy, Éric, 223–25
Lass in Wonderland, A, 136
Lastman, Mayor Mel and family, 53–54
law reports, as mine of instruction, x
Lawrence, D.H., xvii, 133–37
Lennon, John, 105
Leofric of Coventry, 82
lettuce as aphrodisiac, 203
lex talionis, xv
libel, *see* defamation
license plates, indecency and, 121
Liu-liang, Chien, 217
Lockley, Robert, 221–23
"Long Dong Silver," 86
Louie, Grace and family, 53–54
Lynch, John, 99–100

Mackenzie, Jerrold, 219–21

MacKinnon, Justice Frank, 239
Maclennan, Ronald and Margaret, 51–52
Macleod, Donald, 193–94
Macnaghten, (Lord) Justice, 240
Maddy, John, 57–58
Madercine, Angel, 103–04
Mailer, Norman, 130
Mann Act, 158–61
Maples, Marla, 76–77
Marler, Nannie, 11–13
marriage,
    annulment of, 27–32
    contracts, 19, 22–25
    de facto, in Scotland, 51–52
    promise of, 20–21, 192–96
Marshal, Bridget, 233
Martin, Baron, 202
Massachusetts Bay Colony, 55, 158
masturbation, 29–30, 49, 99, 138–39, 211, 238
    as "sodomy," 67
    breasts and, 49–50
    dolphin and, 71–73
    House of Lords and, 139
    Pee Wee Herman and, 119–21
Matheke, Cynthia, 16
Matheson, Norman, 86
Maule, Sir William (Justice), 37
Mavers, Frank, 57
mayhem, 214–18
Mayor of Casterbridge, The, 62
McCardie, Justice, 50–51
McFarlane, Eric, 175–76
McNeil, Eva, 26–27
Medlicott, Monica, 119

Megarry, Sir Robert, xvi, 115
Mercado, Therese, 163
Meredith, Charles, 228
Middleton, Justice William, 35–36
Millar, Charles Vance, 32–37
Monk, Philip, 108
Moore, Harry, 134–35
Moore, Roy, 147
More, Judge Minor, 21
Morey, Alice, 193
Morgan rape case, 210–11
Morrill Act, 39–42
Morrow, Kate, 194–95
Mortimer, John, 138–39
"motherfucker," in classroom, 241–42
multiple personality disorder, 225–27
Murray, Anne, xii, 84
mutilation as punishment for sex crime, 187

National Football League, voyeurism and, 82–84
newlyweds, license fee for sex, 5
Newman, Judge Jon, 250–51
Nigeria, genital theft in, 183–84
Nosanchuk, Judge Saul, 101–02
novelties, contract for illegal, 114–15
nullity of marriage, 27–32
Nuwer, Henry, 244

obscene libel, 97
Obscene Publications Act (1857), 130
obscene words, 117–18, 137, 142–52
obscenity (*see also* pornography), 68, 96–97, 127–57
cartoons and, 139–40
exposing obscene matter to the public view, 149
prosecuting the offensive material, 83
rules of thumb for at U.S. Supreme Court, 131
offering indignity to a corpse, 212
Olsen, Jack, 208
Ono, Yoko, 105
Orchard, James, 92–93
Ormrod, Justice, 32
Osborne, Justice Coulter, 107

Paone, Frederick, 101
Pappjohn, George, 211–12
Paré, Ambroise, 203
Parke, Baron, 202
parody, 46, 242, 246–47, 251
Parsons, Ann and John, 61–62
paternity testing, 21, 161
Pauvert, Jean-Jacques, 137–38
Payne, Judge Joseph, 104
Paynel, William, 60–61
Peeping Tom, 82–84
Penthouse magazine, 242–44, 246
Pepino, Jane, 77
Pepys, Samuel, 97
Perry, George, 140
"person," 98–99, 100–03, 105
Peterson, Mark, 225–26
phallometric testing, 186–87
Pilley, W. Charles, 127
pimps, 207n
Plaster Casters, 74–75
Poirier, A.E., 90
"political correctness," xiii–xv

Polyak, Joseph, 163
polygamy, 39–42
pornography,
 films, 83, 131–33
 incongruities in prosecutions, 138–40
 magazines, *see* obscenity
 Penthouse insufficiently obscene, 242–44
 photographs, 131–32
 poem by high school student, 140
Powell, Judge (Georgia), 91, 95, 97
prenuptial agreements, *see* marriage
Pring, Kimerli, 242–44, 246, 250
promise of marriage, breach of, 20–21, 192–96
prostitution, 157–80
 Cambridge University and, 176–78
 communicating for purposes of, xii, 178–79
 contracts and, 14
 defining, 176–80
 homicide and, 164–65
 living off avails of, 163–64, 166–69, 173–74
 men as prostitutes, 162
 minors as prostitutes, 164
 taxation of, 166–69
Proudfoot, Dawna, 105
Proulx, Justice Michel, 109
provocation, as defense to murder, 57–60, 165–66
punishment for sexual misconduct, 2, 3, 158, 187, 191, 193, 195, 207n, 223

Quebec, *Lady Chatterley's Lover* and, 134–36
Queensbury, Marquis of, 68–69
quiet enjoyment, covenant of in rental agreements, 8–9

Ralston, William, 240
Ramsy, Lucy, 190
Randall, James, 228
rape, 12, 31, 184, 187, 191, 197, 204–13, 225–27, 247
 defenses generally, 184, 212
 defense of honest belief, 211–12
 in Middle Ages, 184
 proof of, 184–85, 191
 punishments for, 184–87
rape-shield laws, 227
Rappe, Virginia, 197–200
Read obscenity case, 97
Reagan, Ronald, xi, 84
reasonable person standard, 165–66
reckless endangerment with knockout pills, 204
Redding, Doreen, 164–65
Redding, Noel, 74–75
Reed, Ishmael, 213–14
Reeves, Peggy and Gerald, 225–27
Regan, Judge John, 107
Rehnquist, Chief Justice William, 247
Rembar, Charles, 130
Reubens, Paul, 119–121
Revere, Paul, and the Raiders, 75
Robertson, Geoffrey, 139
Rogira, Elena, 232
Ross, Jessie, 194
Roth, Samuel, 131
Roux, Mélanie, 109–10
Rowlands, Mayor June, 105

Ruiz, Brenda, 31
Russell, Sir Charles, 45–46
Ryan, Meg, 84

Saarnok, Johannes, 25–27
sado-masochism, 209–10, 214
Sainte-Marie, Genevieve, 253
Santos, Margarita Delos, 204
satire, 242–44
"schmuck" as obscenity, 154
Schumm, Gloria, 20–21
science project on condoms, 119
Scott, F.R., 135–36
Scott, (Lord) Justice, 239–40
Scrutton, Lord Justice, 50–51
seduction, under promise of marriage, 20–22, 192–97
"Seinfeld" (television comedy), 121, 218–19
Seip, Dale, 191–92
Sensobaugh mayhem case, 58–59
September Morn (painting), 116
serjeanty, 6
Seth, Chief Judge, 242
sexual assault (*see also* rape), 184
  with cucumber, 223
  with godemiché, 223–24
sexual harassment, 192
  acronym FCUK as, 154–55
  men as victims of, 221–23
  "reckless eyeballing" as, 213–14
  "Seinfeld" case, 218–21
  Stephanie the cow and, 253
Shakers, marriage and, 32
Shaw, George Bernard, 231
Shaw, Perry and Cecelia, 20

Sidley, Sir Charles, 97–98
Sladek, Diane and Michael, 218
slander, *see* defamation
Smith, F.E. (Lord Birkenhead), 47–48
Smith, Marie, 178
Snyder, Emilie, xiii, 234
sodomy, 68–69
  cunnilingus and masturbation as, 67, 190n
  in 19th-century Ohio, 66–67
Spanish fly, 200–05
spanking, 210
Sparks, Judge Sam, 252–53
Spence, Gerry, 243
St. Claire, Lindi, 168–69
statutory rape, 11
"stealing" heiresses, 188–90
Steiner, George, xi
Stern, Howard, 146–47
Stevens, Judge Lillian, 75
Stevens, Justice John Paul, 144–45
Stewart, Justice Potter, 127, 131–32
Stewart, Timothy, 149
stoning as punishment for sexual crime, 3–4, 55, 68
"street walking," 178–79
strippers, negligence and, 180–82
Stuart, Chief Justice (Yukon), 102–03
Sundquist, Derrick, 67
"suppositious" birth or heir, 42–44
Swift, Lloyd, 179

Taliban (Afghanistan), 3, 68, 158
Tamm, District Appeals Judge, 144
Tauro, District Judge, 141

taxation
   of prostitution, 166–69
   of strippers, 169–70
Taylor, Agnes, 2
tenures in medieval times, 6–7
testicles, disabling, 215
Texas *Penal Code*, 58, 196
Thaarup, Aage, 239–40
Thallman, George, 104
theft of sexual organs, 183–84
Then, Justice Edward, 224
Thomas, Justice Clarence, 86–87
Thompson, Associate Justice, 153–54
Thurtle, James, 92–93
Tinarwo, Shanangurai, 217
Tooker, John, 61
Topfree Ten, 106–07
toplessness and women, 106–08
torts
   husband's against wife, 240–01
   in strip clubs, 180–02
Town Police Causes Act, 99
trademark, 153
transvestism, 69
Tripp, Linda, 81
Turner, Ronda, 221–23

Uhse, Beate, 118
Ulysses (James Joyce), xi
underwear
   as personal protection device, 77–78
   theft of, 77–78
undue influence on elderly man, 26

Vagrancy Act, 98
van den Heever, Justice, 235
Van Graafeiland, Judge, 152–53
Van Pelt, W.W., 236–37
vasectomies not mayhem, 214–16
Venus of Urbino, 81
Vincent, Justice Walter, 114–15
voyeurism, 80–82

Waite, Chief Justice, 41
Walker, Judge W.S.C., 12
Wallis, Rev. Frederic, 176–78
Warren, Chief Justice Earl, 131
weapons, and sexual assault, 223–25
Webb, James, 93
Weekes, Justice Robert, 186–87
Wefing, Justice, 222n
Weiler, Justice Karen, 108
whipping as punishment for sexual crimes, 2, 3, 158
White House, illicit sex in, xi
White, Justice Byron, 131
White-slave trade Act, see *Mann Act*
"whore" as defamatory, 232–33
wife, giving away of by deed, 61, 63–64
wife-selling, 60–63
Wilcox, Judge J., 81
Wilde, Oscar, 68–69
Williams, Owen, 206–07
Williams, Peter, 85–86
wills, encouraging promiscuity and illegitimacy in, 33
Wilson, Adele, 85–86
Winchell, Walter, 235

Wisconsin law on sex with mentally
    ill, 225
Wiseman buggery case, 65–66
Woolsey, Judge John, xi
workers' compensation and the sex
    trade, 173–75
workplace, sexual activity in, 10–11
Wright, James, 100
Wright, John Ted, 184–86
Wright, Justice (Bodmin Assizes), 236
Wright, W.C., 196–97
writ *de ventre inscipiendo*, 42–44

Young, Benny, 67
Young, Judge, 163

Zaffarano, Michael, 152
Zappa, Frank, 74–75